Windows 98 Answers!

Certified Tech Support, Third Edition

About the Authors

Martin Matthews and Carole Boggs Matthews are the best-selling authors of more than 50 computer books covering topics as diverse as Windows, FrontPage, Outlook, Excel, PageMaker, CorelDRAW, networking, and Paradox. They have been working with software for more than 25 years and are experts in Windows, Office, graphic design, and desktop publishing.

For Saving Time

To Do This	Do This
Change the date and time	Double-click the time in the taskbar
Open Windows Explorer	Press SHIFT while double-clicking My Computer
View the desktop icons when open windows cover them	Click the Show Desktop icon on the Quick Launch toolbar
Make your favorite programs immediately available	Drag them to the Quick Launch toolbar
Jump from one dialog box to another open application	Press ALT-ESC
Automate the scheduling of periodic tasks such as scanning for errors and defragmenting a hard disk	Run the Maintenance Wizard from Start | Programs | Accessories | System Tools

For Using the Internet

To Do This	Do This
Get to your favorite Web sites fast	Drag their icons from the Address toolbar to the desktop
Search for a Web site	Open Start | Find | On The Internet
Return to a site you visited last week	Click History in the Internet Explorer toolbar, click last week's icon, and click the site
Make sure you find all the information you are searching for	Use several different search engines by clicking Search in the Internet Explorer toolbar and then click Choose A Search Engine in the Search Explorer bar
Recover the taskbar in full-screen view	Move the mouse pointer off the bottom edge of the screen
Make a Web page or image your desktop wallpaper	Right-click the desktop and choose Active Desktop | View As Web Page. Then right-click the desktop again, select Properties, click Browse on the Background tab, and select any Web page (.htm file) or image (.gif or .jpg file)
Attach a file to an e-mail message in Outlook Express	Compose the message and drag the file from either the desktop or any folder to the open message

For Managing Your Files

To Do This	Do This
Save a "scrap" of selected text for future use	Drag the scrap to the desktop. It is automatically saved as a document scrap
Permanently delete files without placing them in the Recycle Bin	Hold down SHIFT while pressing DELETE
Copy, move, or delete a file, or send it to a floppy disk or to a fax	Right-click a file on the desktop, in the right pane of the Windows Explorer, in My Computer, or in any folder window
Undo the last ten copy, move, or rename operations	Repeatedly click the Undo command in the Edit menu or the Undo button in the toolbar
Transfer files between two different folders and/or drives	Open two separate instances of Windows Explorer
Copy files between drives on your computer or on a network	Click the left mouse button and drag the file, or press SHIFT while dragging to move the file

For Navigating Windows 98

To Do This	Select This	Or Click This	Or Press This
Close active window	System | Close	☒	ALT-F4
Connect to a network drive	Tools | Map Network Drive	🖿	. . . .
Copy a file while dragging	. . . .	. . . .	CTRL
Copy objects to Clipboard	Edit | Copy	🗐	CTRL-C
Cut objects to Clipboard	Edit | Cut	✂	CTRL-X
Discontinue connection to a network drive	Tools | Disconnect Network Drive	⬚	. . . .
Find files	Start | Find Files	. . . .	F3
Maximize current menu	System | Maximize	☐	. . . .
Minimize all windows when the taskbar is selected	Context menu | Minimize All Windows	🗹	ALT-M
Minimize current window	System | Minimize	▬	. . . .
Move objects to Recycle Bin	File | Delete	☒	DELETE
Open context menu	. . . .	Right-click	SHIFT-F10
Open parent folder	. . . .	⬆	BACKSPACE
Open Start menu	. . . .	🏁 Start	CTRL-ESC
Open Windows 98 Help	Start | Help	. . . .	F1
Paste Clipboard contents	Edit | Paste	🗐	CTRL-V
Permanently delete objects	. . . .	. . . .	SHIFT-DELETE
Refresh current window	View | Refresh	. . . .	F5
Rename object	Context menu | Rename	. . . .	F2
Return window to its previous size	System | Restore	🗗	. . . .
Select all objects	Edit | Select All	. . . .	CTRL-A
Selected object properties	File | Properties	🗎	ALT-ENTER
Start a program	Start | Program	Double-click	. . . .
Switch tasks	. . . .	Taskbar	ALT-ESC
Switch running programs	. . . .	. . . .	ALT-TAB
Switch tabs	. . . .	Tab	CTRL-TAB
Undo last operation	Edit | Undo	↩	CTRL-Z

Windows 98 Answers!

Certified Tech Support,
Third Edition

Martin S. Matthews
Carole Boggs Matthews

Osborne/**McGraw-Hill**

Berkeley • New York • St. Louis • San Francisco
Auckland • Bogotá • Hamburg • London
Madrid • Mexico City • Milan • Montreal
New Delhi • Panama City • Paris • São Paulo
Singapore • Sydney • Tokyo • Toronto

Osborne/**McGraw-Hill**
2600 Tenth Street
Berkeley, California 94710
U.S.A.

For information on translations or book distributors outside the U.S.A., or to arrange bulk purchase discounts for sales promotions, premiums, or fund-raisers, please contact Osborne/**McGraw-Hill** at the above address.

Windows 98 Answers! Certified Tech Support, Third Edition

234567890 AGM AGM 901987654321098

ISBN 0-07-882455-9

Publisher	**Copy Editor**
Brandon A. Nordin	Claire Splan
Editor-in-Chief	**Proofreader**
Scott Rogers	Stefany Otis
Acquisitions Editor	**Indexer**
Joanne Cuthbertson	David Heiret
Project Editor	**Computer Designer**
Jody McKenzie	Michelle Galicia
Editorial Assistant	**Illustrator**
Stephane Thomas	Lance Ravella
Technical Editor	**Series Design**
John Cronan	Michelle Galicia

Contents @ a Glance

Contents

Acknowledgments

Stream International spent considerable time and effort collecting many of the questions and drafting their answers, thus providing the core of this book. For this we are very appreciative. Special thanks to Betty Johnsky.

John Cronan technically reviewed all three editions of this book and has done much of the revision for Windows 98. John, who is an author in his own right, thoroughly tested everything the book says and gave us lots of feedback on the results. John made a significant contribution to this book and for that we are very grateful. **Thanks, John!**

Patricia Shepard did much of the work turning the material in the first edition into the second edition. Pat, who is also an author in her own right, did this with much dedication and attention to detail, for which we are very appreciative. **Thanks, Pat!**

The crew at Osborne was ably led by **Joanne Cuthbertson** in acquisitions and **Jody McKenzie** in editorial, with support from **Claire Splan**, copy editor, and **Stephane Thomas,** editorial assistant. As always, this team made the project as easy as possible and, in many instances, even fun. **Thanks, Joanne, Jody, Claire, and Stephane!**

Carole and Marty Matthews
July 1998

Introduction

Windows 98 represents a major change in the way you use your computer and includes many new facilities and features that were not there in the past. It is therefore natural that you'll have a great many questions about how to use what is there as well as how to handle the situations when things don't go quite right. With literally hours waiting on a toll phone line to get tech support from Microsoft, almost nonexistent documentation, and online help that never quite answers the question you are asking, there is a great disparity between the questions being asked and the answers that are available. The purpose of the book is to fill that void.

The more than 400 questions that are answered in this book have as their core the questions Stream International has been asked in its role of providing tech support to Windows 95 and 98 users. To these real-world questions, we have added our experience of more than a year of using Memphis (the original code name for Windows 98) and Windows 98 itself in both beta and released versions. We have delved into every nook and cranny of the product and experienced a great many of the problems first-hand. As a result, we have located practically every source of answers and have referenced many of them here.

The book then brings together the "on the firing line" experience of a Windows 98 tech support company with the authors' experience in researching and using the product— about as much as a person can have and not be one of the programmers writing Windows 98 (and we have spent a lot of time talking to those people, too).

Windows 98 Answers! is divided into 13 chapters, each of which focuses on a major subject. Within each chapter the questions and answers are further divided into topics, grouping similar questions. To find a particular answer, use the table of contents to identify the chapter and section in which it's located. You can then look for the central topic of your question. Around your question, you'll find others that

relate to it and will add to the original answer. You can also go right to a chapter, and then look at the Answer Topics headings and @ a Glance summary at the beginning of the chapter. Finally, you can use the index to alphabetically locate a topic that doesn't pop out at you from either the table of contents or the Answer Topics at the beginning of each chapter.

Besides the questions and answers, there are many **tips, notes**, and **sidebars** throughout the book that give you insight, which only considerable experience would otherwise bring, into how best to do something. In addition to the tips, notes and sidebars, there are a number of **warnings** that point out areas that can cause considerable problems if they are not avoided. All chapters have a section at their beginning called **@ a Glance**. These sections give you an introduction to the chapter's subject and how to address or accomplish the issues related to it. Reading all of the @ a Glance sections will give you a broad understanding of Windows 98 and answer many of your questions before you ask them.

Conventions Used in This Book

Windows 98 Answers uses several conventions designed to make the book easier for you to follow.

- **Bold type** is used for text that you are to type from the keyboard. Bold type is also used for web addresses, as in **http://www.osborne.com**.

- *Italic type* is used to call attention to important terms or to words and phrases that deserve special emphasis.

- SMALL CAPITAL LETTERS are used for keys on the keyboard such as ENTER and SHIFT.

- When you are expected to enter a command, you are told to *press* the key(s). If you are to enter text or numbers, you are told to *type* them.

And now let's get to your questions ....

Chapter 1

Top Ten FAQs

Answer Topics!

Top Ten FAQs @ a Glance

Whenever you install a new piece of software, questions arise simply because of its unfamiliarity. When the software is an operating system, those questions take on an even greater significance, because the operating system is so basic to everything that is done on your computer. Among the Windows 98 questions collected by Stream International, the following ten questions were those asked most often by callers. Here are the answers.

 ## 1. I like some features of the Active Desktop, but how do I select just the ones I want?

Active Desktop gives the Windows 98 desktop its Webcentricity. Active Desktop covers a wide range of features in Windows 98 that include the Channel bar, single-click ability, a stock ticker across the bottom of your screen, and the ability to use a Web page as wallpaper (or a background image). Here are some things that you can do to control the Active Desktop:

- **Turn Active Desktop on or off** by right-clicking a blank area of the desktop to open the context menu, and choosing Active Desktop | View as Web Page. Repeat the same steps to reverse the process. With View as Web Page turned off, Web-related objects such as the Channel bar and Web-page wallpaper are removed, but Web features such as single-clicking, if enabled, are not.

- **Customize desktop content** by right-clicking a blank area of the desktop to open the context menu, and choosing Active Desktop | Customize My Desktop. This opens the Web tab of the Display Properties dialog box shown in Figure 1-1. Here you can turn off just the Channel bar or add other objects such as a stock ticker (shown next) by clicking Add and visiting online

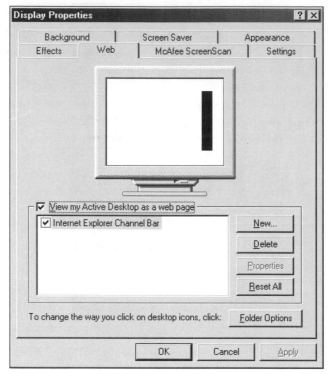

Figure 1-1 Customize desktop content from the Web tab of the Display
Properties dialog box

Microsoft's Active Desktop Gallery to preview and install
these objects.

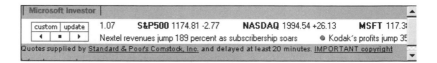

● **Customize desktop settings** by right-clicking a blank
area of the desktop, choosing Active Desktop | Customize
My Desktop, clicking Folder Options, and clicking Yes,
which both closes Display Properties and opens Folder
Options. The Folder Options dialog box's General tab
allows you to choose a Custom style for your desktop

Custom Settings [?] [X]

┌─ Active Desktop ──────────────────────────────────┐
│ ⦿ <u>E</u>nable all web-related content on my desktop: [<u>C</u>ustomize] │
│ ○ <u>U</u>se Windows classic desktop │
└───┘

┌─ Browse folders as follows ───────────────────────┐
│ ⦿ Open each folder in the sa<u>m</u>e window │
│ ○ Open each folder in its own <u>w</u>indow │
└───┘

┌─ View Web content in folders ─────────────────────┐
│ ⦿ <u>F</u>or all folders with HTML content │
│ ○ <u>O</u>nly for folders where I select "as Web Page" (View menu) │
└───┘

┌─ Click items as follows ──────────────────────────┐
│ ○ <u>S</u>ingle-click to open an item (point to select) │
│   ⦿ Underline icon titles consistent with my <u>b</u>rowser settings │
│   ○ Underline icon titles only when I <u>p</u>oint at them │
│ ⦿ <u>D</u>ouble-click to open an item (single-click to select) │
└───┘

                            [OK   ]   [Cancel]

Figure 1-2   Customize desktop and folder settings from the Custom Settings dialog box

between the full Web style and the Classic style. By first choosing Custom and then clicking Settings, you open the Custom Settings dialog box shown in Figure 1-2 where you can determine which of the Web-related features you want to use.

● **Add a Web page as wallpaper** by browsing to the page of your choice in the Internet Explorer. Then open the File menu, choose Save As, select the \Windows\Web\Wallpaper folder, enter a name, and click Save. Next, right-click a blank area of the desktop, choose Active Desktop | Customize My Desktop, click the Background tab | Browse, open the \Windows\Web\Wallpaper folder, double-click your Web page, and click OK.

 ## 2. How do I convert a drive to the FAT32 file system?

FAT32 is a system that uses a file allocation table (FAT) for storing information on disks. The original FAT used in DOS and Windows up through the initial releases of Windows 95 was a 16-bit system referred to just as "FAT." In the OSR2 (OEM Service Release 2) release of Windows 95 a 32-bit version was introduced called "FAT32." This is now available in Windows 98. FAT32 increases the largest disk partition from 2GB to 2TB (terabytes or 1,024GB) and substantially improves the efficiency of the file system. On the down side, you cannot dual-boot FAT32, and most older utilities no longer work with it.

To convert a disk to FAT32, open the Start menu and choose Programs | Accessories | System Tools | Drive Converter (FAT32). Use the wizard that appears to step through the conversion process.

 ## 3. How do I find my files and programs?

To find any file, whether a program or a data file, you can take three independent paths through Windows 98 by using My Computer, Windows Explorer, or Find.

To use My Computer, follow these instructions:

1. Double-click the My Computer icon on the desktop. The My Computer window will open, as shown in Figure 1-3.

2. Double-click the drive that you want to search and then the folders that you believe contain the files you're looking for. Each folder that you double-click either opens a new *folder window,* or replaces the contents of the previous folder window, as shown in Figure 1-4.

3. When you find the file and the file is either a program or a data file associated with a program (it will have the program's icon), you can start the program and open the data file by double-clicking the file.

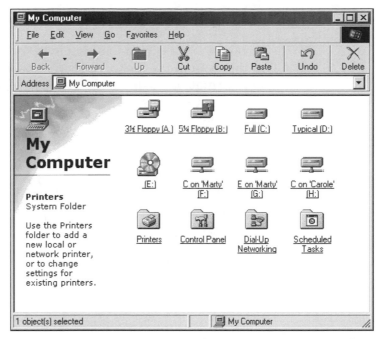

Figure 1-3   My Computer window offers a high-level view of the drives and system folders available to you

Figure 1-4   By clicking successive folders you will reach a folder window with the file you want

To use Windows Explorer, follow these steps:

Explorer

1. Hold-down SHIFT and double-click My Computer or open the Start menu and choose Programs | Windows Explorer. Figure 1-5 shows the open Explorer window.

2. Click the drive and folder you want to open in the left pane (or *Explorer* bar), and then double-click the file you want to start or open in the right pane.

 Tip: *Right-clicking a file in the right pane of the Explorer window or in a folder window opens a context menu, shown next, that allows you to copy, move, delete, or send a file to a floppy disk or to a fax.*

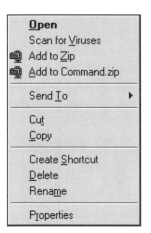

The next set of steps shows you how to use Find:

1. Click Start and choose Find | Files Or Folders. The Find dialog box opens as shown in Figure 1-6.

2. Enter the file or folder name, text contained in the file, last modification date, or other criteria to search for.

3. Select the drives (and folders, if desired) you want to search in and click Find Now. When the search is complete, the files will be listed at the bottom of the Find dialog box. You can do anything with those listings (open, start, copy, move, and delete them) that you can do in either Windows Explorer or My Computer.

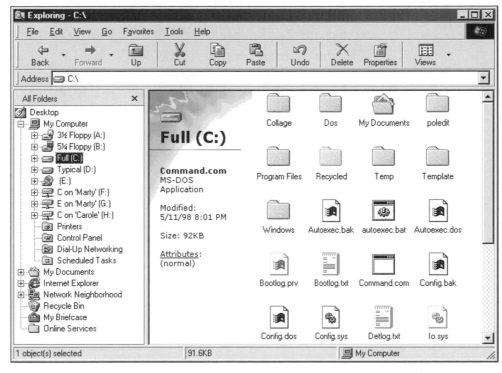

Figure 1-5   Windows Explorer offers greater versatility in opening folders and finding files

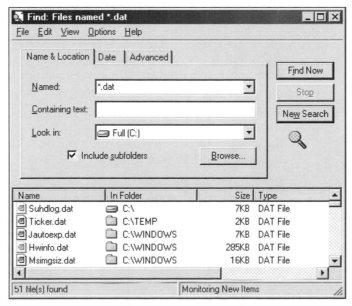

Figure 1-6   Find can quickly locate a group of widely separated files

 Note: *The files displayed in the Find dialog box are not copies, but the* original *files and anything you do to those found files are done to the originals.*

 ## 4. Do I have to reinstall my applications after installing Windows 98 on the system that had Windows before?

If you install Windows 98 over your existing Windows 3.1x or Windows 95 directory or folder, then you do not need to reinstall your applications. If you install Windows 98 into a new folder, then you will have to reinstall all your Windows applications. Copying files from your Windows 3.1x or Windows 95 folder to Windows 98 is not sufficient.

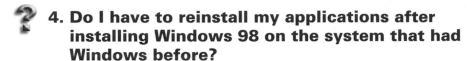 *Tip:* *There is almost no need to keep Windows 3.1x or Windows 95 on your computer (virtually all programs run as well or better under Windows 98), so Windows 98 should be installed over your existing Windows.*

5. I installed Windows 98 on a newly formatted disk and now I can't find the fax program. How can I get it back?

Windows 98 does not include Microsoft Fax or Microsoft Exchange, which were available in Windows 95. If you upgraded from Windows 95 to 98 and had Microsoft Fax and Exchange installed on the system when you upgraded, you can continue to use those versions. Also, the Windows 95 versions of those programs are on the Windows 98 CD, although well hidden. You can find them in the \Tools\Oldwin95\Message\US folder for U.S. versions of the programs and in the \Tools\Oldwin95\Message\Intl folder for international versions.

To install Microsoft Fax, double-click Awfax.exe. To install Microsoft Exchange (called Windows Messaging Service here), double-click Wms.exe. Before doing either installation, double-click to open and then read the text file Wms-fax.txt. The Windows Messaging Service includes the Microsoft Mail Post Office.

 6. Ever since I installed Windows 98, some applications have had problems with certain .DLL files. Do I have to reinstall my applications?

Probably not. During setup Windows 98 replaces many .DLL or driver files with the Windows 98 version of those files, even if the Windows 98 version is older. Windows 98 does keep a backup of all files that have been replaced. You can restore the original copy of the driver file with the Version Conflict Manager. To do that, open the System Information utility by opening the Start menu and choosing Programs | Accessories | System Tools | System Information. In the System Information window, open the Tools menu and choose Version Conflict Manager. (You can also open Start, choose Run, type **vcmui**, and then click OK.) In the Version Conflict manager, which is shown in Figure 1-7, select the driver(s) that you want restored and click Restore Selected Files.

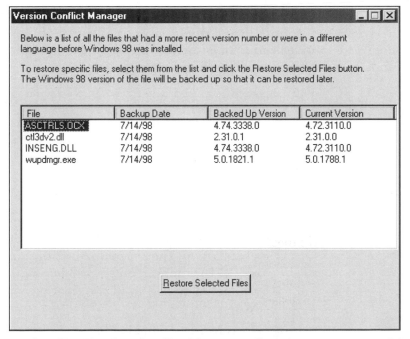

Figure 1-7   The Version Conflict Manager allows you to restore driver files that have been replaced by Windows

 ### 7. What do I do if an application I am running stops responding?

Press CTRL-ALT-DEL to end an application that is no longer responding to the system. When you press these three keys at the same time, the Close Program dialog box will open, listing all active applications. Select your application and click the End Task button. Windows 98 will allow you to continue working in the other applications that are running without having to reboot the whole system.

! ***Warning:*** *Do not press CTRL-ALT-DEL a second time, unless you want to reboot your computer and lose any information that has not been saved.*

 ### 8. How do I do a clean boot with Windows 98?

When troubleshooting Windows 98 or a specific application, you sometimes have to run the system in the simplest possible configuration to single out the source of the problem or a conflict. In previous operating systems, you had to create a separate boot disk and boot off this floppy. Windows 98 gives you an easier way of creating a clean environment. Use these steps for that purpose:

1. Restart your computer.
2. When you see the list of the processor, memory, and ports in your computer, immediately press F8 or CTRL. You will see a menu of the following options:

   - **Normal** This starts regular Windows 98 without changes.

   - **Logged** This starts regular Windows 98, and also creates a file in your root directory called Bootlog.txt that lists all the steps during startup. This is very useful in tracking down problems during Windows 98 startup. You can read the Bootlog.txt file with Notepad.

   - **Safe Mode** This is a special diagnostic mode in which Windows 98 is started with the most generic default settings: VGA display driver, no network,

Microsoft mouse driver, and the minimum device drivers necessary to start Windows. No CD-ROM drives, printers, or other peripheral devices are used. Config.sys and Autoexec.bat are ignored. You can also get this by pressing F5 instead of and at the time you would have pressed F8 or CTRL.

- **Step-By-Step Confirmation**   This is also called *interactive start*. It starts Windows 98, but asks if you want to execute each line in your Config.sys and Autoexec.bat files (or the Windows 98 default if you don't have these files). Type **Y** if you want to process the line; type **N** if you don't. You will receive an error message if one of the command lines fails (an indicator of where the system fails). It will process the Registry and load all Windows drivers.

- **Command Prompt Only**   This starts only the DOS part of Windows 98. All drivers are loaded and all command files processed, but the graphical user interface (GUI) is not started. You are left at the C:\ prompt. You can type **win** to load the GUI. You can also get the Windows 98 DOS command prompt by pressing ALT-F5 after the system and memory check.

- **Safe Mode Command Prompt Only**   This is the same as the Safe Mode option, but stops at the C:\ prompt without loading the GUI. Type **win** to load the GUI. You can also get this by pressing SHIFT-F5 after the system and memory check.

- **Previous Version Of MS-DOS**   (This is only available if you have dual-boot MS-DOS/Windows 98 set up on your system.) This starts your computer in the previous version of MS-DOS that was on your computer when you installed Windows 98. You can also get this by pressing F4 after the system and memory check.

 Note: *With FAT32 you can no longer dual-boot with Windows 3.1x/DOS.*

 9. How do I recover from a power failure or unintentional rebooting during the Windows 98 installation process?

The Windows 98 installation program includes a Safe Recovery option. Depending on where the installation was interrupted, you may be able to turn your computer off and then on (don't just press CTRL-ALT-DEL), run Setup again, and choose the Safe Recovery option when you are prompted. If this doesn't work the first time, try doing it a second time.

 10. I'm trying to save my Internet logon password so I don't have to enter it each time, but I'm having trouble (Save Password is dim and not usable). Why can't I save it?

The reason this is happening is probably because you have not installed the Client for Microsoft Networks, which allows you to store passwords. If you are not connected to a network this makes sense because nothing tells you that you need to do it. Here's how to install the Client for Microsoft Networks, which you can do even if you are not connected to a network:

1. Open Start, choose Settings | Control Panel, and double-click Network.

2. Click Add, choose Client, and click Add again.

3. Click Microsoft under Manufacturers, and then double-click Client for Microsoft Networks under Network Clients.

4. Click OK, insert your Windows 98 CD if requested, and reboot your computer when asked if you want to.

The next time you sign on to the Internet you will need to enter your paswsword one last time, but you will also be able to click Save Password. Then the next time you sign on you will lnot have to re-enter it.

Chapter 2

Installing Windows 98

Answer Topics!

Installing Windows 98 @ a Glance

Given that Windows 98 replaces MS-DOS and Windows 3.1 or Windows 95, you might expect that it would have a fairly complex and lengthy installation. In fact, just the opposite is the case. If you use the Typical installation and have a fairly standard system, the Windows 98 installation is simplicity itself. You have to answer less than half a dozen questions—that's it! Windows 98 even reboots for you once you start copying files. It takes only a few minutes of your time, although it will take between 30 and 60 minutes of your computer's time.

Of course, there are always hitches, and that is what this book is for. The questions and answers grouped under the following topics will help you understand what to do before, during, and after installation:

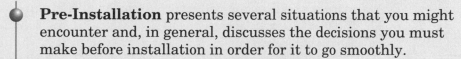

Pre-Installation presents several situations that you might encounter and, in general, discusses the decisions you must make before installation in order for it to go smoothly.

Equipment Considerations discusses equipment resources needed and specific equipment compatibility.

 Operating Systems Considerations relates to operating system compatibility, addressing both installing from other operating systems, and installing other operating systems to run with Windows 98.

 Problems During Installation presents several situations that could occur during installation and how to handle them.

Post-Installation offers alternatives to decisions you made during a previous installation, solutions to new needs you have, and ways to use more of Windows 98 after it has been installed.

PRE-INSTALLATION

 I have just bought the Windows 98 upgrade. I have completely erased all information from my hard disk and formatted it, so that it is empty, clean, and ready for Windows 98 Setup. Am I ready to begin installing Windows 98?

It depends on whether you have a Windows 98 Startup disk. The Startup floppy disk you create during a Windows 98 installation (or after, from the Add/Remove Programs control panel) provides drivers for standard IDE and SCSI CD-ROM drives. The obvious question is, how do you create a disk from an operating system you're trying to install? The answer is you find a friend or co-worker who already has Windows 98 installed on his or her computer and have that person make you a Startup disk. Assuming your CD-ROM is recognized by drivers on the disk, you can run Setup.exe. However, if it is not recognized, you have to have system files and drivers available either on a Startup floppy or already installed on the computer to access your CD-ROM and start Windows 98 Setup. Also, since this is a Windows upgrade, you must have available an original Disk 1 installation floppy disk for MS-DOS 5.0 or later, Windows 3.1 or later, or a floppy or CD for Windows 95 (although the program does not need to be installed). You'll be asked to insert your prior operating system's first installation disk or CD if Setup can't find it on your hard disk.

Warning: As the answer to this question implies, *reformatting your hard disk to install Windows 98 is not something to take lightly. Although it will ultimately provide you with the "cleanest" of installations, there may be some bumps in the road along the way.*

Must I make a lot of decisions during the setup of Windows 98?

The installation procedure for Windows 98 is more automated and user friendly than in all previous operating systems. One of the advantages of the installation is that it can be done entirely from within Windows. If Windows has never been installed on the system, the setup procedure will install a small subset of Windows just to run the installation process. During the setup, the Setup Wizard walks you through making minimal choices and selecting options, as you can see in Figure 2-1. You always have the option to return to the previous screen(s) if you decide that you made a wrong choice.

Windows 98 Setup autodetects the hardware components that are installed on your computer and automatically loads necessary drivers, configures them, and writes all the information into the *Registry*—the database that stores all configuration information for the system.

During setup, every operation is recorded in the setup log. If the setup fails at some point, Windows 98 will recover from just before the action that caused the setup to fail, and the user will be presented with an option to make necessary adjustments in the setup choices.

Can I install Windows 98 without user input?

Windows 98 allows system administrators to create batch setup scripts so that no or minimal input will be required from the users. The administrators can create an automated mandatory installation routine for the users on the network.

This feature involves creating custom batch scripts with the Microsoft Batch 98 program on the Windows 98 CD in the Tools\Reskit\Batch folder and storing scripts in the Msbatch.inf file. Finally, the system administrator runs the

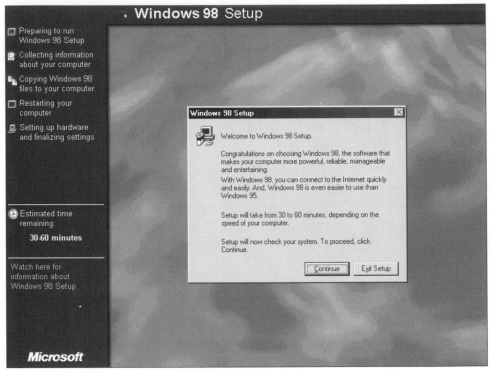

Figure 2-1 Windows 98 Setup controls most installation details without your intervention

workstation setups, using the MS SMS (System Management Services) network login or any other network software management system to perform the mandatory setup. See Help within the Batch 98 program for information on using batch setup.

 Tip: *Install Microsoft Batch 98 by opening the \Tools\ Reskit\Batch folder on the Windows 98 CD and double-clicking Setup.exe.*

What are the differences among different types of setup?

There are four options presented to you during setup: Typical, Portable, Compact, and Custom. The four choices allow you to choose the components that will be installed with Windows 98, depending on your disk space and whether you have a portable computer. The components that are installed by each option are listed in Appendix A. Briefly, the four choices are as follows:

● **Typical setup** resembles the Express setup in Windows 3.*x*. This type of setup will run through most of the setup routine without requiring user input. The only choices that the user will have to make are the location of the Windows 98 folder and country location, as shown in Figure 2-2.

● **Portable setup** will install the files necessary to run Windows 98 on a laptop or notebook PC, including such components as power management; My Briefcase, a tool for file synchronization; and the system files necessary to establish a cable link between two computers for file exchange.

● **Compact setup** will install the bare minimum files necessary to run Windows 98.

● **Custom setup** will allow users to make their own choices on what components to install.

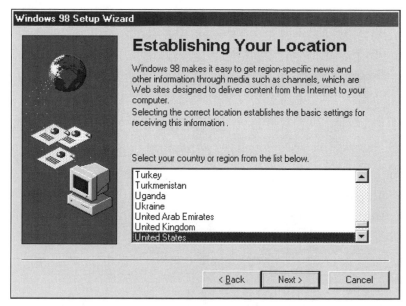

Figure 2-2 You only have to provide minimal information to set up Windows 98

Pre-Installation Considerations

To prepare for the installation of Windows 98, run through the following steps. This will ensure that you and your computer are in the best possible shape for the installation.

- **Compare your hardware** with the minimum and recommended hardware needed for Windows 98, as shown in Table 2-1, and consider upgrading your hardware before upgrading to Windows 98.

- **Clean up your hard disk** by removing all unused files. Windows 98 requires a lot of disk space (for example, 120 to 295MB for an upgrade from Windows 95). Use the installation of Windows 98 as an excuse to do the disk cleaning you always intended to do. Uninstall or remove the programs you aren't using, and delete the data and miscellaneous files that are no longer of value.

  While it is a drastic step and you should consider it carefully, the very best way to clean up your hard disk is to back up all important files and to reformat it (which erases everything on your hard disk). After installing Windows 98, re-install just the application and data files you need. You'll be amazed at how much more space you have. See the question that begins "I have just bought the Windows 98 upgrade" earlier in this chapter for some additional planning ideas.

- **Back up important files on your hard disk**. While the installation of Windows 98 will probably go without a hitch, there is nothing like the comfort of having a backup of *all* your important files in case the worst should happen. You need to back up all the data files you don't want to lose (these include word processing, spreadsheet, database, and drawing files). Back up your Config.sys and Autoexec.bat files from your root (\) directory or folder, and back up your .INI, .DAT, and .PWL files from your Windows folder. You may also have network and/or communications configuration and script files that need to be backed up. You don't need to back up your applications, since you already have them on their distribution disks.

- **Create a bootable floppy** from your current operating system. If you're upgrading from Windows 3.1*x*, use your current version of DOS using the **format a:/s** command and a new disk, or one that

can be written on in your drive A. If you're upgrading from Windows 95, click Start and choose Settings | Control Panel and double-click Add/Remove Programs, click the Startup Disk tab, and, finally, click Create Disk. This allows you to recover if something happens to your hard disk that prevents you from booting from it.

- **Optimize your hard disk** by running ScanDisk (Thorough option), and Defrag *before* you run Windows 98 Setup. ScanDisk checks your disk for both physical and software errors, and in many instances corrects them for you. Disk Defragmenter defragments your disk by putting related file segments together in the same area of the disk. Use the version of ScanDisk in the \Win98 folder on the Windows 98 CD. You can't easily get to the Windows 98 version of Disk Defragmenter before installation, so use the DOS 6.*x* version if you have it, the Windows 95 version, or a recent version of Norton Speed Disk that is part of the Norton Utilities from Symantec.

- Review the four primary decisions that you will have to make during installation:

  - **Install from Windows or from DOS?** If you are currently running Windows 3.1, 3.11, Windows for Workgroups, or Windows 95, it is recommended that you start Windows 98 Setup from Windows. In all other circumstances you need to start Setup from DOS.

  - **Install into the current Windows directory?** When you install Windows 98 into your current Windows directory or folder, you'll replace your current version of Windows, and it will no longer be available. This is the recommended approach. If you want to keep your current version of Windows 3.1x available to you in a "dual boot" situation, you need to install Windows 98 into a new folder.

Note: *You cannot "dual boot" between Windows 95 and Windows 98. Also, you cannot dual boot between Windows 3.1x and Windows 98 if your hard disk uses FAT32 (file allocation table) in either operating system. The later release of Windows 95 or the OSR 2 version that came installed on new computers was FAT32, and Windows 98 can be converted from FAT (or FAT16) that was used in the original release of Windows 95 and Windows 3.1x to FAT32.*

Remember that if you install Windows 98 into a new folder, you'll have to re-install any Windows applications you want to use with Windows 98.

● **Save your current DOS and Windows files?**   If you choose to install Windows 98 in the same directory as your old Windows, you will then be given this choice. While it takes up to 50MB of your local hard disk (it can't be on a network drive or a floppy), it allows you to completely and cleanly uninstall Windows 98 and re-install your previous DOS and Windows.

If, after Windows 98 is running for a while, you want to remove your old Windows and DOS files, you can do so by clicking Old Windows... and then clicking Remove in the Install/Uninstall tab of the Add/Remove Programs control panel reached from the Start | Settings | Control Panel option. Alternatively, you can run Uninstal.exe from the \Windows\Command folder.

● **Use Typical, Portable, Compact, or Custom installation?** If you have a portable (laptop or notebook) computer, or if you have a computer with very limited disk space, you should use either the Portable or Compact installation. If you know you want to install components not installed in a Typical installation, then use the Custom installation. In most circumstances, a Typical installation is the easiest and preferred type. See the discussion later in this chapter on the differences among the types of installation. Also see Appendix A for a list of components that are installed in the various types.

Tip: *If you are installing over Windows 95, Setup will detect your previous installation type and install components accordingly; you won't have to (or be able to) choose.*

By using the Add/Remove Programs control panel's Windows Setup tab in the Windows 98 Control Panel (opened from Start | Settings), you can easily add or remove Windows 98 components after installing Windows 98 and without rerunning Setup.

Element	Minimum	Recommendation
Processor	486DX-66MHz	Pentium 200MHz
Memory	16MB	32MB
Free disk space	200MB	400MB
Display	VGA (640×480, 256 colors)	SVGA (800×600, Hi Color 16-bit)
Mouse	Yes	Microsoft-compatible device
CD-ROM	2X	12X CD-ROM
Modem	None	33.6Kbps fax/modem
Sound board	None	16-bit

Table 2-1   What You Need to Install Windows 98

 My company is planning to install Windows 98. What are the resources available to help me with this migration?

Microsoft Press has published the Windows 98 Resource Kit, which has a wealth of technical information on how to implement Windows 98. It contains the following:

- A planning guide
- Technical information on installing, configuring, and networking
- Software utilities
- An e-mail alias for Windows 98 Resource Kit-related issues and comments: rkinput@microsoft.com

 Note: *The Windows 98 Resource Kit Tools Sampler on the Windows 98 CD (\Tools\Reskit\Setup.exe) only provides what its name implies—a sample of the tools and information available from the full kit, as shown in Figure 2-3. If you want the entire text of the Resource Kit and all of its tools, you will need to purchase the retail book and its accompanying CD.*

Third-party support is available through companies such as Stream International, which offers consulting services to

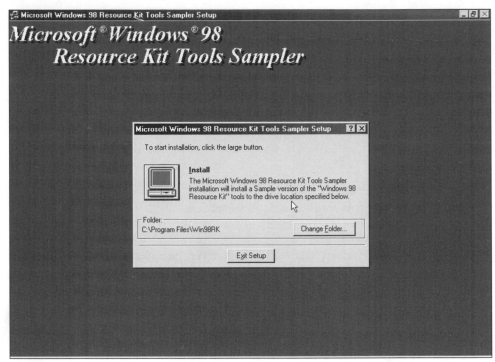

Figure 2-3 The Windows 98 Resource Kit Tools Sampler is only that—a sample of the full kit

help your company plan and implement enterprisewide migration to Windows 98.

 Tip: *For additional information on installing Windows 98, connect to the Microsoft Windows 98 Web site (**http://www .microsoft.com/windows98/**). There is a link for tips on a "smooth installation."*

EQUIPMENT CONSIDERATIONS

 Can I set up Windows 98 if I have compressed my hard disk with Stacker?

Depends. Windows 98 Setup is incompatible with Stacker version 4.1 or earlier. Before you start Setup, verify that there is at least 1.5MB of free hard disk space on the host

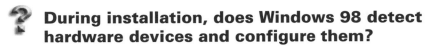

drive, or 8MB if you use a permanent swap file. If there is not enough free space on the host drive, you must run the compression software to increase this amount.

 Note: *Windows 98 Setup may not find your boot drive if you have compressed it with Stacker. If you get a message to that effect, you will need to decompress your hard drive, remove Stacker, and then rerun Windows 98 Setup.*

 Tip: *DriveSpace 3 is included with Windows 98 and it's recommended that you upgrade earlier Microsoft compression utilities such as DoubleSpace or uninstall non-Microsoft compression utilities and run DriveSpace 3.*

During installation, does Windows 98 detect hardware devices and configure them?

Yes. During installation, Windows 98 analyzes your computer to identify the hardware resources that are available. To the extent possible, it configures the appropriate drivers and stores the hardware information in the Registry.

Can I install Windows 98 correctly on a hard disk partitioned with OnTrack Disk Manager?

Yes. Windows 98 is compatible with all versions of Disk Manager. It also provides a protected-mode driver for Disk Manager versions 6.03 and later. If you use this version, Windows 98 automatically uses its protected-mode driver, which will give you faster 32-bit disk access.

Tip: *If you are using OnTrack on a FAT32 drive, you may experience long delays during startup. With OnTrack version 7.0x you can use the /L:=0 switch to work around the delay.*

How much hard disk space do I need for Windows 98?

The installation requirement for hard disk space varies depending on the options you choose. For the basic components of the operating system in both a Typical and

Compact installation, you will need the disk space shown in Table 2-2. If you choose to install some of the features not included in a Typical install, you can as much as double the amount of disk space required. For example, if you install WebTV, it will add approximately 50MB to the basic components shown in Table 2-2. Additionally, when you are done with the installation, you should have at least 10 to 20MB left for temporary files.

 Tip: *A good rule of thumb is that you might need 300MB for a Windows 3.1x or Windows 95 upgrade, 360MB for a clean installation using FAT, and 260MB for a clean installation using FAT32.*

 ## How much RAM do I need to run Windows 98?

The absolute minimum is 16MB. Despite what you may have heard, Windows 98 will run fine with only 16MB. It is just that most people also want to run one or more applications. While that's possible with 16MB, it is recommended you have at least 24MB, and you will notice a major boost in performance with 32MB of RAM. The primary considerations are what applications you will be running and how many of them at one time. If you are running Microsoft Word or Excel alone, 24MB is fine. You can even run them together in that space, although you can switch back and forth much faster

Installation Option	Additional Disk Space Required	
	Compact	Typical
New installation (FAT)	165MB	255MB
New installation (FAT32)	140MB	175MB
Windows/Windows for Workgroups 3.1x upgrade	120MB	195MB
Windows 95 upgrade	120MB	195MB

Table 2-2 Disk Space Required for Basic Windows 98

with 32MB. If you are running CorelDRAW, you will be happier with 64MB.

Will Windows 98 run on my 486 33MHz machine?

No. You will need a 486DX 66MHz-based or higher computer to run Windows 98.

Can I install Windows 98 on my PowerPC?

No. Windows 98 is designed to run only on Intel-based computers. This means that you cannot install it on computers using PowerPC or DEC Alpha chips.

OPERATING SYSTEMS CONSIDERATIONS

Can I have more than one operating system installed on my PC at one time?

Yes. You can install Windows 98 in its own folder and retain your old DOS and Windows 3.1 in a dual boot situation. If you boot and do nothing, you will get Windows 98. If you boot and press F4, you'll get your old DOS, from which you can run your old Windows. Or you can partition your drive and use a third-party utility such as PowerQuest's PartitionMagic to select the applicable operating system. Using separate partitions and a newer utility provides a greater degree of safety as each partition is segregated from the other. This is the only way you can install both Windows 95 and Windows 98.

Warning: *If you install Windows 98 into its own folder, you'll have to re-install the applications you want to run under Windows 98.*

Note: *You can only dual boot Windows 3.1x and Windows 98 on a partition formatted with FAT, not FAT32.*

 If Windows 98 is the operating system upgrade, what operating systems can I upgrade over?

You can install the Windows 98 upgrade over the following:

- MS-DOS version 5.0 or higher (equivalent versions of DR DOS or PC DOS have not been tested by Microsoft)
- Windows 3.1 or higher
- Windows for Workgroups 3.1 or higher
- Windows 95 in either a FAT or FAT32 partition

You can also install Windows 98 on the same computer with the following operating systems:

- Dual boot OS/2 with MS-DOS installed on the FAT partition
- Dual boot Windows NT with MS-DOS installed on the FAT partition

 Can I dual boot between Windows 95 and Windows 98?

No, not unless you install each into a separate partition and use a third-party partitioning application such as PowerQuest's PartitionMagic. You can also use Fdisk to create partitions, but the utility programs offer many tools and ease-of-use features that make using different operating systems on the same computer much easier, especially when the systems use different file structures such as FAT and FAT32.

 Can I install Windows 98 on a computer that has OS/2 and Windows and still dual boot?

Yes, you can. Be aware that Windows 98 cannot access the HPFS partitions used in OS/2, so you have to have a FAT partition with enough disk space to install Windows 98. Don't install Windows 98 on top of your existing Windows if you also want to keep it.

To install Windows 98, boot into DOS and start Windows 98 Setup. Setup disables the OS/2 Boot Manager because during the setup process Windows 98 Setup has to have full control over the system. You can re-enable OS/2 Boot Manager after the setup is complete.

To do this:

1. Start Windows 98.

2. Click Start, choose Run, and type **fdisk**.

3. Choose Set Active Partition, as shown in Figure 2-4. Enter the number of the Boot Manager Partition. This partition is the 1MB Non-DOS partition.

4. Close Fdisk and restart the computer. You can now use the Boot Manager.

Warning: *If you boot into MS-DOS from a floppy disk and run Windows 98 Setup, you won't be able to start OS/2. You need to delete the Autoexec.bat and Config.sys that OS/2 uses* before *running Windows 98 Setup.*

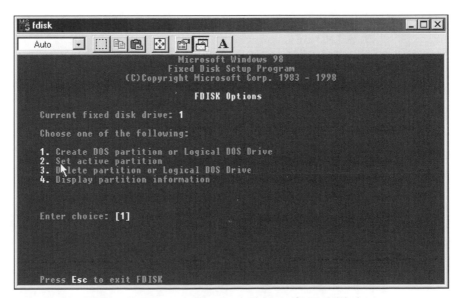

Figure 2-4   Fdisk allows you to set partitions for multiple operating systems

 If I am not ready to make the changeover, can I set up Windows 98 and Windows 3.1 as a dual boot, and still have access to all of my files on the hard disk using either version?

You can. When you install Windows 98, the Setup prompts you for the folder to install to. The default is your existing Windows folder. Select a different folder to install Windows 98 into, and you'll be able to access your old Windows 3.1*x* through dual boot.

Once installed, Windows 98 will not recognize your installed applications. To correct that, start Windows 98 and re-install your applications into their existing folders. The result is that Windows 98 will register the applications, and you can still use them in your old Windows without having to make two copies of each program, one for each operating system. If you install new applications, make sure to do two installs—one under Windows 3.*x* and one under Windows 98.

 Note: *You cannot dual boot to Windows 3.1 if you install Windows 98 in a FAT32 partition.*

 Which is better to start Setup from, Windows or MS-DOS?

Starting Windows 98 Setup from Windows is the preferred option. However, you should start the setup from MS-DOS in the following cases:

- You don't have Windows installed.
- You have Windows 3.1 installed.
- You have OS/2 installed either by itself or as dual boot.
- You have Windows NT installed either by itself or as dual boot.

What versions of MS-DOS and Windows do I need to upgrade to Windows 98?

You need Windows version 3.1 or higher, Windows for Workgroups version 3.1 or higher, Windows 95, or MS-DOS version 5.0 or higher.

 Note: *Windows NT cannot access FAT32 partitions.*

 How can I install Windows 98 on my PC that has Windows NT 4.0 installed?

You can install Windows 98 on a Windows NT machine only if you dual boot between Windows NT and MS-DOS. There are a few restrictions:

- Windows 98 must be set up in a separate partition or hard disk from Windows NT.

- The Windows 98 partition must be FAT, not FAT32, with enough disk space (see the question earlier in the chapter on disk space required for various installs).

To Install Windows 98

Run Windows 98 Setup from the Windows NT Boot Loader Operating System Selection menu's Windows 95 option. (If Windows 95 is not an option, choose MS-DOS.)

After you complete the setup, Windows 98 will become an option on your Startup menu, along with Windows NT and MS-DOS.

PROBLEMS DURING INSTALLATION

 I received the error message "Cannot open file" while running Setup. What does this mean?

You may need to free up memory by disabling (typing **REM** in front of) or removing the Smartdrv.exe statement in your

Autoexec.bat, or by closing any applications that may be running in Windows. Windows 98 does not use SMARTDrive, so it is not necessary to have it in your Autoexec.bat.

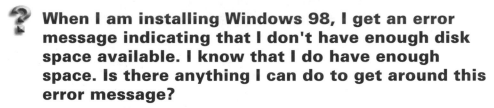

When I am installing Windows 98, I get an error message indicating that I don't have enough disk space available. I know that I do have enough space. Is there anything I can do to get around this error message?

You can have Setup ignore the checking for available disk space by using the /id switch with the Setup.exe command (at the DOS prompt or in a Run command, type **setup /id**).

What does it mean when I get the error message "Standard Mode: Fault in MS-DOS Extender" when running Setup from DOS?

There may be a conflict in the upper memory area. Upper memory blocks (UMBs) are the unused part of upper memory from 640K to 1MB. If an EMM386 statement appears in your Config.sys file (use Windows Notepad or DOS Edit to view it), it is enabling upper memory blocks. Disable this statement by typing **REM** in front of it, save your altered Config.sys, reboot, and then rerun Setup.

When running Setup, why do I get an error message that my path is invalid?

The drive you are trying to install Windows 98 on has zero bytes available (such as a CD-ROM would have), or the drive is not ready or not mounted with a removable hard drive. Install Windows 98 to a different drive or make the removable hard disk drive ready.

If more than zero bytes of hard disk space are available, but not enough for Windows to be installed, you will receive an error message such as: "Insufficient disk space" or "Not enough disk space."

I am using a Logitech mouse on my computer. When I run Windows 98 Setup, the mouse does not work until I restart the computer to boot into Windows 98. How come?

If you have a Logitech Series C mouse, you have to start the Setup program with the following command: **setup /il**. This will make your mouse available during the initial stages of setup.

 I terminated the installation of Windows 98 after it requested the folder name to contain the Windows 98 files. On my second install, I was waiting for the prompt for the folder name but never got it. Windows 98 remembered my first try and automatically created the folder name originally entered. How do I remove Windows 98 and start the installation over?

Windows 98 installation creates a file called Setuplog.txt to keep track of each step of Setup. If the setup fails at some point, Windows 98 Setup refers to this file to determine the last successful step. To restart Setup from scratch, delete this file (it is in the root folder). You might also want to delete the Detlog.txt and Detcrash.log files if you have them.

How do I restart Setup after an earlier attempt has failed?

Use the following steps to restart:

1. Turn off your computer (do *not* press CTRL-ALT-DEL), and wait ten seconds. Then turn it back on.

2. Start Setup again. Setup will prompt you to use Safe Recovery to recover the failed installation.

3. Choose the Use Safe Recovery option, shown in Figure 2-5, and click Next. Hardware detection will skip the part that caused the initial failure.

Figure 2-5 Use Safe Recovery to restart Windows 98 Setup from an incomplete installation

4. If the computer stops again during the detection process, restart Setup and repeat the process until the hardware detection process is finished.

5. After Setup is complete and Windows is running, you can use the information in Setuplog.txt and Detlog.txt to check for the devices that caused the problems.

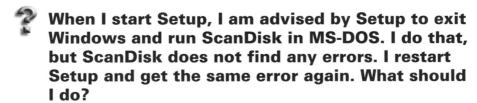

When I start Setup, I am advised by Setup to exit Windows and run ScanDisk in MS-DOS. I do that, but ScanDisk does not find any errors. I restart Setup and get the same error again. What should I do?

You can force Setup to run without running ScanDisk by adding the /is switch to the Setup.exe command line. (At a DOS prompt or in a Run command, type *d:\setup /is,* where *d* is the drive with Setup on it.)

Setup fails to start. What should I do?

You can do any of the following:

1. Check for sufficient conventional memory. Windows 98 requires 432K. If this is not available, remove any unnecessary drivers from your Config.sys file or terminate-and-stay-resident (TSR) programs that are started in your Autoexec.bat file. As a general rule, to install Windows you need drivers only for your hard disk and maybe your CD-ROM, and you normally do not need any TSR programs. Use either Windows Notepad or DOS Edit to clean out all unnecessary commands in your Config.sys and Autoexec.bat files.

2. Check the RAM configuration in Config.sys.

    ● Using MS-DOS 5.x or later, the commands should include

        Device=Himem.sys
        Device=EMM386.exe NOEMS
        DOS=High,UMB

    ● Check for adequate extended or XMS memory; the requirement is at least 3MB of XMS. If you are using MS-DOS 6.x, when you first see the MS-DOS message, press F8 and choose Step-By-Step Confirmation to verify that Himem.sys is loading. If it is not, verify that the file exists in your DOS or Windows directory and that your Config.sys file has the Device=Himem.sys statement.

    ● At the DOS prompt or in a Run command, type **mem/c/p** to check for free conventional and XMS memory.

How can I set up Windows 98 into a folder separate from my current Windows folder?

During setup you are prompted to enter a directory or folder in which to install Windows 98, and your current Windows folder is suggested as a default.

To install Windows 98 into a new folder:

1. Click Other Folder.

2. Click Next and enter the new folder name. If the folder does not exist, the setup routine will create it for you.

I was running Setup and it stopped during hardware detection. What should I do?

Use the following steps:

1. Turn the computer off, wait ten seconds, and turn it back on. (Do *not* press CTRL-ALT-DEL if Setup hangs!)

2. When the PC is back online, restart Setup using Safe Recovery (you'll be prompted to do this). This will bypass the portion of hardware-testing detection that caused the problem. If your system stops again, it will be in a different detection module. Perform these steps as many times as necessary to allow your system to complete detection.

 What switches can I use with Setup.exe?

The Setup switches allow you to alter the Setup in a specific way. You type the switches at the time you enter a Setup command, as shown here:

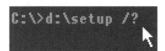

Following is a list of the command-line switches you may use with Setup when you start it in either the Run command or at the DOS prompt:

/?   Provides help on the possible switches of the Setup.exe.

batchfile   Tells Windows 98 Setup to use the file and path *batchfile* to get the script containing the Setup options.

/c   Prevents Windows 98 Setup from loading the SMARTDrive disk cache.

/d   Prevents Windows 98 Setup from using the existing version of Windows for the first stage of Setup. Instead, it will load a brand new, small subset of Windows. This option is useful if the existing version of Windows is experiencing some problems.

/f	Prevents Windows 98 Setup from looking in the local cache for filenames, saving a little memory, but running Setup slower.
/ic	Tells Windows 98 Setup to do a clean boot without drivers. Drivers are "REMed" out in the Autoexec.bat and Config.sys files.
/id	Prevents Windows 98 Setup from checking for the necessary disk space. This option can be used if the setup reports less space than you know you have.
/ie	Prevents Windows 98 Setup from displaying the Startup Disk screen.
/ih	Tells Windows 98 Setup to run ScanDisk so you can see its results. Useful if you receive an error.
/il	Tells Windows 98 to load the Logitech Series C mouse driver. This option is needed if you have a Logitech Series C mouse.
/im	Prevents Windows 98 Setup from checking for the necessary memory space.
/in	Prevents Windows 98 Setup from running the Network Setup module.
/iq	Prevents Windows 98 Setup from running ScanDisk at the beginning of setup from MS-DOS. This option is useful if you are using non-Microsoft disk-compression software.
/ir	Prevents Windows 98 Setup from updating the Master Boot Record (MBR).
/is	Prevents Windows 98 Setup from running ScanDisk at the beginning of setup from Windows. This option is useful if you are using non-Microsoft disk-compression software.
/iv	Prevents Windows 98 Setup from displaying informational billboards.
/iw	Prevents Windows 98 Setup from displaying the License Agreement screen.
/ix	Prevents Windows 98 Setup from doing a character set check.
/nostart	Copies the minimal DLLs required by Windows 98 Setup and then exits without installing Windows 98.

/na#	Prevents Windows 98 Setup from telling you other applications are running, where #=1 won't display the message, #=2 won't display the message for MS-DOS applications, and #=3 won't display either message (same result if you use the switch without a number).
/nf	Prevents Windows 98 Setup from prompting to remove the floppy disk in drive A after copying files. Useful when installing from a bootable CD.
/nr	Prevents Windows 98 Setup from checking the Registry.
/pi	Tells Windows 98 Setup to keep forced hardware settings instead of using default settings as required by some BIOS.
/pj	Tells Windows 98 Setup to load by default Advanced Configuration and Power Interface (ACPI).
/s *filename*	Tells Windows 98 Setup to load a specific Setup.inf file.
/srcdir	Tells Windows 98 Setup where the source files directory is.
/T:*tmpdir*	Tells Windows 98 Setup to use the path and folder named *tmpdir* to store all its temporary files.

 I am installing Windows 98 from the CD-ROM. The system went dead after the first reboot late in the process. Why did this happen and what can I do about it?

You might have both real-mode and protected-mode drivers installed for the CD-ROM, and they are in conflict. Remove the CD-ROM real-mode drivers from your Config.sys and Autoexec.bat files (that is, all mention of your CD-ROM). If the problem persists, boot into Windows in Safe mode by pressing F8 before Windows 98 loads and choosing Safe Mode from the Startup menu. If Windows will not start even in Safe mode, re-install it. If you can get into Safe mode, reboot, press F8 again, and choose Logged (\Bootlog.txt) to see where the system fails.

Look for the Detcrash.log file. If it is present, the problem is with hardware detection. Check Ios.ini in your Windows folder, and remark out the drivers that are loading in Config.sys (by putting **rem** and a space at the beginning of lines that load any drivers found on the unsafe list in the Ios.ini file) in case there is a problem with these protected-mode drivers. From the Start menu, select Settings | Control Panel and then double-click System. Then check the Device Manager for any conflicts. Change the display driver to standard VGA.

Try the Step-By-Step Confirmation boot after pressing F8 just before Windows 98 starts and observe what is being loaded. Rename Autoexec.bat and Config.sys so they don't load on the next boot.

POST-INSTALLATION

 I installed Windows 98 on a system with two CD-ROM drives. One CD-ROM drive was not detected. Why?

This happens if Windows 98 loads protected-mode drivers for the primary CD-ROM drive, but the secondary CD-ROM drive is running with real-mode drivers loaded by the Config.sys and Autoexec.bat files. Windows 98 assumes that both drivers reference the same device, so it assigns the same drive letter for both, making them appear as one drive.

Assign the CD-ROM drive that is running to a different drive letter with these steps:

1. Click Start and choose Settings | Control Panel.

2. Double-click System, and then click the Device Manager tab.

3. Select the CD-ROM you want to change, click Properties, and click the Settings tab, shown in Figure 2-6.

4. In the Reserved Drive Letters section, set Start Drive Letter and End Drive Letter to the drive letter you want the CD-ROM to use. Click OK.

5. Click Start and click Shut Down.

6. Then click the Restart option.

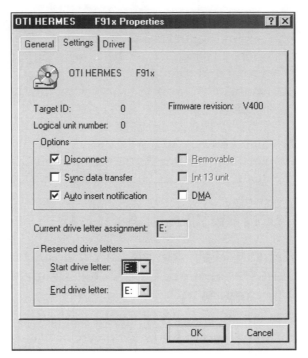

Figure 2-6   You can change a CD-ROM's drive letter in the drive's Properties dialog box

How do I know that Windows 98 Setup installed the components that I want?

Windows 98 Setup creates the following log files during the setup: Setuplog.txt, Detlog.txt, and Bootlog.txt. If the setup fails, another file is created called Detcrash.log. All of these files are in the root (\) directory or folder. You can view these files (but do not change them) by using Notepad, as shown in Figure 2-7.

● **Setuplog.txt** is the file that keeps track of each step of setup. If the setup fails at the stage before hardware detection, Windows 98 Setup refers to this file to determine the last successful step. Setuplog.txt ensures that the setup does not fail twice due to the same cause. It

```
Setuplog.txt - Notepad                                    _ □ ×
File   Edit   Search   Help
[OptionalComponents]

[System]

[NameAndOrg]

[Destination]

[]

fsCmosAVCheck: Attempting CMOS Anti Virus Test
fsCmosAVCheck: CMOS Anti Virus Test SUCCEEDED
Drive=:A:, Host=::, Flags=:0x107:
Drive=:C:, Host=::, Flags=:0xd:
Drive=:D:, Host=::, Flags=:0xd:
Drive=:E:, Host=::, Flags=:0x205:
Drive=:F:, Host=::, Flags=:0x1:
Drive=:G:, Host=::, Flags=:0x1:
vfs.boot=:C:, vfs.boothost=::
FSLog: BIOS Heads=:128:, BootPart Heads=:128:
batch settings:
[Setup]
InstallType=1
```

Figure 2-7   You can view Setup log files using Notepad

will make the correction in the failed step and continue the setup.

- **Detcrash.log** is created if the setup fails during hardware detection. This file stores information on what hardware component caused the failure and what resources the setup routine was accessing just before the crash. After such a crash, if you rerun Setup, it will automatically go into Safe mode and will continue the recovery process, skipping the module that failed. If setup is successful, Detcrash.log is deleted upon completion of setup.

- **Detlog.txt** contains a list of detected hardware components and the parameters for each detected device.

- **Bootlog.txt** is the file that describes what takes place during the system startup processes.

 ### How do I install a feature of Windows 98 that I did not originally install?

To add or remove a Windows 98 component outside of Setup, use the following steps:

1. Click Start and choose Settings | Control Panel.
2. Double-click Add/Remove Programs.
3. Click the Windows Setup tab, as shown in Figure 2-8, and select/deselect the items you want to add or remove. Click OK when you are done.

 Tip: *You should have the Windows 98 CD, source files location, or disks handy in case you need them.*

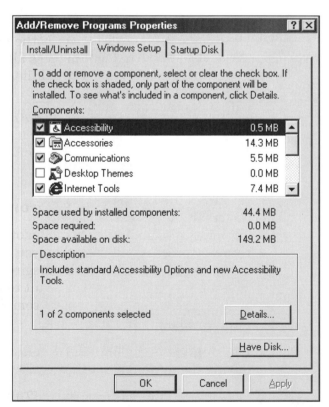

Figure 2-8 The Add/Remove Programs Properties dialog box allows you to install programs you did not install during Setup

 When I look at the Windows 98 CD in the \Win98 folder using Windows Explorer, I mainly see .CAB files. How can I get a list of the files that are in the .CAB files?

Follow these steps to list all files in the .CAB source files on the CD:

1. Insert the Windows 98 CD into its drive.

2. In Windows Explorer, right-click the .CAB file and click View from the context menu.

Alternatively, open an MS-DOS window, and for the Windows 98 CD or a folder location of the source files, type the following to create a master list:

```
extract /a /d d:\win98\win98_02.cab > win98.txt
```

where *d:\Win98\Win98_02.cab* is the path and filename of the first .CAB file. This will process all the .CAB files in sequence and generate a list of all files in the file Win98.txt.

 Note: *There are several sets of .CAB files. You need to run each set separately to get a complete list of files. For example, change "\Win98_02.cab" to "\Driver11.cab" to add the driver files to Win98.txt.*

 How do I remove Windows 98 from my computer?

If during setup you chose the option of saving your system files, shown in Figure 2-9, so that you could uninstall Windows 98 (as described at the beginning of this chapter), and then after installation you want to remove Windows 98, you can use the following steps to completely restore your previous operating system:

1. Open the Start menu and choose Settings | Control Panel.

2. Double-click Add/Remove Programs and, if necessary, click the Install/Uninstall tab.

3. Select Windows 98 and click Remove.

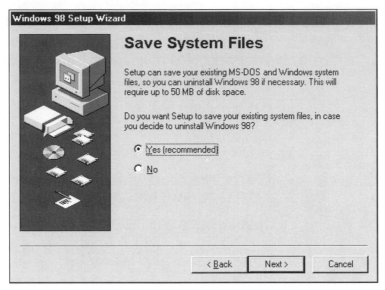

Figure 2-9 Windows 98 Setup Wizard recommends saving previous operating system files in case you want to remove Windows 98

 Warning: *The previous procedure will not work if you compressed the disk on which Windows 98 is located after it was installed.*

 Note: *If you are having problems starting Windows 98 and want to remove it, boot it into DOS by pressing F8 just before Windows 98 starts, choose Command Prompt Only, and type **uninstal** at the DOS prompt.*

If you did not choose the option of saving your system files so you could uninstall Windows 98, use the following steps to remove Windows 98 and re-install your previous system:

1. Reboot your computer using a DOS disk that contains the SYS.COM command.

2. At the DOS prompt, type **sys c:**. Remove the disk and reboot your computer.

3. Re-install your previous version of DOS.

4. Delete the folders that contain Windows 98 files, and re-install your previous version of Windows and all your Windows applications.

Note: *Windows versions prior to the OSR 2 release of Windows 95 do not support FAT32 partitions. If you converted Windows 98 to FAT32 and you want to remove Windows 98 and re-install Windows 3.1x, you will need to run Fdisk and reformat your disk to FAT.*

Chapter 3

What's New in Windows 98

Answer Topics!

What's New in Windows 98 @ a Glance

One of the first impressions you'll have of Windows 98 is that it isn't much different than Windows 95—and at first look you won't be wrong, especially if you have been using the OSR 2 release with the Active Desktop of Internet Explorer 4. As you shouldn't judge a book by its cover, nor should you judge an operating system by its opening screen. If nothing else, you can look at Windows 98 as representing the accumulation of almost three years of bug fixes, driver updates, hardware improvements, system performance tools, and Internet technology innovations added to the initial release of Windows 95. And as quickly as computing technology is changing, three years worth of upgrades is a lot. Windows 98 represents a major step forward in functionality on desktop and portable PC platforms by providing a system that is even easier, faster, and more powerful to use. In addition, it is designed to maintain compatibility with the existing Windows and MS-DOS applications and hardware in which you have invested.

This chapter covers the following:

 What About the Name? gives an explanation of what the new Windows name means.

 New Features and Enhancements includes information about plug-and-play, the Registry, multitasking, and the Recycle Bin.

Internet Features discusses the myriad of improved and new ways you can use the Internet and its underlying technology to make computing more interesting and fun.

 Enhancements to Windows 3.x is for users who skipped Windows 95 and covers changes such as using the Clipboard,

performing drag-and-drop between applications, handling games that require exclusive access to the system, improvements to system resources, handling memory, security features, and using Paintbrush.

● **Help** includes a discussion of learning Windows 98 basics, using shortcut keys, and online help.

● **Hardware Considerations** covers hardware requirements and capabilities.

WHAT ABOUT THE NAME?

 What does the name "Windows 98" really mean? Does the numbering system mean that Microsoft will release a new version of Windows every three years?

"Windows 98" is a version number that gives users a sense for the "model year" of their software, in the same way that customers have a sense of the model year of their cars today. Whether Microsoft will release a new version in 2001, and what shape that operating system will take, is anyone's guess.

Note: *More as a matter of interest than importance, if you open the System control panel's General tab in Windows 98 you'll see it referred to as 4.10.1998. In Windows 95 this was 4.00.95. This seems to say Windows 95 is Windows 4.0 and Windows 98 is Windows 4.1.*

What is Windows 98? And what was Memphis?

"Windows 98" is the official product name of this new major version of Microsoft Windows. It replaces Windows 3.*x*, Windows for Workgroups 3.*x*, and Windows 95. "Memphis" was the code name for the development project that produced the successor to these earlier products. Memphis was used as the name until the official product name, Windows 98, was announced. Since the first beta release of Windows 98 there have been several interim builds, service releases, and CDs sent to thousands of beta testers. If you are using a beta version of Windows 98 you do not have the full package and are in jeopardy of the "beta bomb" going off and making your computer non-functional. Spend the $90 and get the real McCoy.

NEW FEATURES AND ENHANCEMENTS

 Note: *Some of the questions in this section address features that were first introduced in Windows 95. They're not technically "new" in Windows 98, but they are included here because they're new to Windows 3.1x upgraders.*

 ### How is Windows 98 different from earlier Windows versions?

Windows 98 is faster and is user-friendlier than earlier versions. It also includes tools that make managing your files easier, as well as provide access to the Internet and to e-mail. See the sidebar "Some Important New Features of Windows 98" for a list of these features.

Some Important New Features of Windows 98

Windows 98 may not impress many at first glance, but give it an opportunity to demonstrate what it can offer you. There are several new features and enhancements to earlier tools and applications, including the following:

● **Backward compatibility** ensures that most of the programs and hardware with which you ran Windows 3.*x* and MS-DOS, or Windows 95 will run with Windows 98. There may be some glitches, but they are few.

● **Enhanced taskbar and Start menu** are the focal points of a graphic interface that provides an intuitive way to find the functions and programs you want. You simply click Start and a menu of your

computer's contents makes it very easy for you to navigate the new operating system. Or you can launch programs by clicking their icons from toolbars placed on the taskbar, such as the new Quick Launch toolbar, located next to Start.

● **Active Desktop, Windows 98 Explorer, and Internet Explorer 4** provide an integrated means of using your computer as one tool to do desktop computing in concert with the Internet and intranets, all with standardized navigation tools and user interface functionality. You can easily subscribe to Web sites and have site updates "pushed" to your desktop or use channels to download entire sites for offline viewing.

● **Advanced plug-and-play** allows you to "plug in your new hardware and play it." Windows 98 figures out what hardware you have or are installing, and handles the configuration setup and management for you (for the most part!).

● **Multimedia** accessories offer the future of using the computer as both a workstation and entertainment center. These accessories include some enhanced standbys such as CD Player, Media Player, and Sound Recorder, and support for new technologies such as DVD, streaming audio and video from the Internet or intranets, and WebTV.

● **Multiple display support** allows you to combine two or more monitors to spread your desktop over a large area. When multitasking functions such as word processing and numeric calculations, you could have Microsoft Word running full screen on one monitor, Microsoft Excel on another, and drag and drop data between the two.

● **Internet connection** is now easier than ever using the Internet Connection Wizard to set up a new or existing Internet account, and access your online accounts such as e-mail and newsgroups. The Connect To The Internet icon starts the wizard and gets you online and connected in short order.

Connect to the Internet

- **Outlook Express** provides an e-mail client with the latest features to access multiple e-mail accounts, send personalized stationery, filter unwanted messages, and conveniently perform the basic functions of sending, forwarding, and replying to e-mail. The Outlook Express icon is always close at hand, located both on your desktop and on the taskbar's Quick Launch toolbar.

- **FrontPage Express, Personal Web Server, and Web Publishing Wizard** offer the tools you need to modify and create Web pages, host a Web site, and copy Web content from your local system to an Internet service provider (ISP).

- **Advanced power management** lets you set up power schemes for various computing situations and individually control the time it takes to power down your monitors and hard disks.

- **Year 2000 support** is available at the operating system level (including MS-DOS) to provide applications the underlying means to understand the new date transition as it relates to the new millennium.

- **Enhanced system information and maintenance** is provided by automatic scheduled programs such as the Maintenance Wizard and Scheduled Tasks, which can run system utilities during times the computer is not being used. The System Information utility provides detailed information on your system and acts as a gateway to several high-level system utilities.

- **FAT32 Converter** lets you easily convert your hard disk partitions to a newer FAT allocation table capable of supporting the newest and largest hard disks. Cluster size is also reduced to minimize wasted disk space.

- **New accessibility options** include a wizard that assists you in selecting features that best suit your needs and a magnifier that lets you selectively increase the size of the area under your mouse pointer.

Can I access my home computer from the computer at my work?

Yes, by using a feature called the Dial-Up Server in conjunction with a dial-up connection from a remote

computer, such as the one at your office. Once a connection is made you can view and access all the resources that are available on the computer set up as the server, including other computers on a local area network. The Dial-Up Server feature is not installed as part of a Typical installation. Set it up with these steps:

1. Click Start, choose Settings | Control Panel, and double-click Add/Remove Programs.

2. Click the Windows Setup tab and then double-click the Communications component. Select Dial-Up Server and click OK twice to start loading the additional software.

3. Open Windows Explorer by clicking Start and choosing Programs | Windows Explorer.

4. Click the Dial-Up Networking folder in the All Folders bar, open the Connections menu, and then click Dial-Up Server. The dialog box of the same name opens as shown in Figure 3-1.

5. Click Allow Caller Access, click Change Password, type a new password, confirm it, and then click OK.

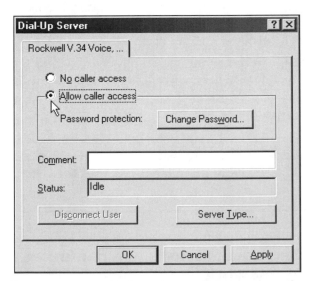

Figure 3-1 Set up a computer to act as a dial-up server for remote access to its resources

Tip: *Always password-protect remote access to your computer resources.*

After you set up a dial-up connection to your home computer, you can map a drive on that computer using the Windows Explorer Tools menu's Map Network Computer option with the convention *computername**drive*. Your home computer drive will appear as an additional drive in the All Folders list and you can access it as you would any other drive on your remote computer.

Do I have to reboot every time I want to change my screen resolution from 800×600 pixels to 1024×768 pixels?

No, you should not have to reboot. If your video card and Windows 98 are comfortable with one another you should only see a momentary pause while the new resolution takes effect. Change this setting with these steps:

1. Right-click an empty area of your desktop and choose Properties from the context menu.

2. Click the Settings tab and select the screen area setting you want by moving the slider.

3. Click Apply, and then click OK to close the Display Properties dialog box.

Tip: *If you change colors in the Settings tab you will be given the option of rebooting your computer before applying the new setting. First try the default option of applying the change without restarting; if you experience any problems you should plan on restarting for any future changes.*

How do I make my desktop an extension of the Internet?

By reading the questions in the section "Internet Features" later in this chapter.

 ## Are there special keyboard shortcuts for the Microsoft Natural keyboard?

Yes. Here is a list of the shortcut keys for the Microsoft Natural keyboard:

WINDOWS-R	Display the Run dialog box
WINDOWS-M	Minimize all
WINDOWS-SHIFT-M	Undo minimize all
WINDOWS-F1	Open Help
WINDOWS-E	Open Windows Explorer
WINDOWS-F	Find files or folders
WINDOWS-CTRL-F	Find computer
WINDOWS-TAB	Cycle through taskbar buttons
WINDOWS-BREAK	Display the System Properties dialog box

 ## What are multitasking and multithreading, which I hear so much about?

Multitasking enables you to run several programs at one time. *Multithreading* is a technique used to ensure that tasks run in the most efficient way possible without one program degrading the system by taking all the resources.

Windows 98 handles the scheduling of processes to allow multiple applications to run at the same time—in other words, multitasking. There are two types of multitasking: *cooperative* and *preemptive.* Under cooperative multitasking (implemented in Windows 3.*x*), the system required applications to check the system message queue and to give up control of the system to other running applications. Windows 98 supports cooperative multitasking for 16-bit Windows applications. For 32-bit applications, however, Windows 98 implements preemptive multitasking. In this environment, Windows 98 assigns system time to running applications, preventing a single resource-intensive application from monopolizing the system resources. With multithreading in Windows 98, the applications do not have to yield to other applications to share resources. Each 32-bit application can have multiple *threads,* distinct units of code that can receive a time slice from the system. A complex application can have several threads processed by the system

at the same time through preemptive multitasking. This gives the application more stability and robustness.

 ## What is advanced plug-and-play?

Plug-and-play makes it easier for you to add new hardware to your computer. It is a term for the PC architecture standard developed jointly by leading hardware and software vendors. Hardware labeled "plug-and-play" has been built according to these standards. When you add or remove plug-and-play hardware components and peripheral devices, such as modems, printers, video cards, and so on, the computer automatically recognizes the device (or its absence) and adapts to the new configuration. This eliminates some of the tedious procedures required to install hardware under the MS-DOS and Windows 3.*x* operating systems. Often you were required to manually change jumpers on the device to configure, for example, the IRQ (interrupt request), and then to spend hours troubleshooting hardware conflicts.

Full plug-and-play depends on having the following components:

- A plug-and-play operating system, such as Windows 98
- A plug-and-play BIOS (basic input/output system) on the computer's motherboard
- Plug-and-play hardware devices (when you buy hardware, ask if it is plug-and-play compliant; most newer hardware is)

With Windows 98 you can still get some of the benefits of plug-and-play without the computer and other hardware being plug-and-play compliant, but as you buy new equipment, consider plug-and-play.

Windows 95 was the first PC operating system that supported plug-and-play; Windows 98 has advanced the idea to where it's a practical reality. Information about the installed hardware devices is stored and maintained in the Registry database. When a new device is added to the system, Windows 98 will check the Registry for available resources, such as IRQs, I/O (input/output) addresses, and DMA (direct memory access) channels, and dynamically assign them to the new device, avoiding the possibility of hardware conflicts.

 ## Where is configuration data maintained? What is the Registry?

The *Registry* is the database Windows 98 uses to store and retrieve information about user settings, hardware configurations, installed applications, application file types, and other system information. While there is no single file entitled "Registry," there are two files, System.dat and User.dat, that contain the Registry information. You can access much of the information in the Registry by clicking the Start button and selecting Settings | Control Panel. The Control Panel window, shown in Figure 3-2, is displayed. Each category of information contains its own icon, such as Keyboard, Mouse, Passwords, Add New Hardware, Multimedia, or Network. Double-click the icon representing the data you want to change or add to. Because Registry information can be changed in several categories, there is no single Registry icon.

Windows 98 and Windows 98 applications use the Registry to store configuration and file association

Figure 3-2 The Control Panel, which provides access to the Registry

information. Whenever a new 32-bit application is installed, its information is stored in the Registry. Whenever a new hardware component is added or removed, or a user makes changes to the desktop, the information goes into the Registry.

Tip: *In Windows 3.x, this information was stored in multiple .INI files (System.ini, Win.ini, and Progman.ini) plus the application-specific files (Winword.ini, Excel.ini, 123r4.ini, and so on), while the information for OLE was stored in the Reg.dat file. For compatibility purposes, Windows 98 will still maintain the .INI file settings for use by older applications.*

The two Registry files, System.dat and User.dat, can be directly edited by use of the Regedit.exe program in the Windows folder. It is strongly recommended that this *not* be done, because there is nothing to tell you what you are doing, and you can cause major changes in the behavior of Windows 98. See Chapter 13 for questions that deal directly with the Registry.

What tools and utilities for my system are included with Windows 98?

Windows 98 has the following utilities for system maintenance, most of which are found on the Start | Programs | Accessories | System Tools menu:

- **Backup/Restore** backs up or restores files to tape, floppy disk, and network drives.

- **Compression Agent** works in conjunction with drives compressed with DriveSpace 3 (see below) to allow you to change the level of compression.

- **Disk Cleanup** lists several categories of files that can be safely deleted to free disk space.

- **Disk Defragmenter** optimizes and speeds up your hard disk.

- **Drive Converter (FAT32)** changes the file allocation table of a disk from the previous standard, FAT (or FAT16), to a format that provides several enhancements, including recognition of larger disk sizes and smaller cluster sizes, which decrease the amount of unusable space.

- **DriveSpace 3** compresses hard and floppy disks, and configures disk drives that you have already compressed using DoubleSpace or earlier versions of DriveSpace.

- **Maintenance Wizard** sets up a schedule for running ScanDisk, Disk Defragmenter, and Disk Cleanup to keep your system at optimal levels.

- **Net Watcher** monitors network resource usage on your computer.

- **ScanDisk** checks for and repairs logical and physical errors on your hard drives.

- **Scheduled Tasks** allows you to schedule the running of any program, in addition to those set up in the Maintenance Wizard.

- **System Information** provides in-depth information about your computer, and through its Tools menu, provides access to several advanced system utilities.

- **System Monitor** checks system resources, threads, processor usage, and other system usages.

 Tip: *Not all utilities are installed during a Typical setup. You may have to add them through the Add/Remove Programs control panel. To do this, click the Start button, choose Settings | Control Panel, and double-click Add/Remove Programs.*

INTERNET FEATURES

 Note: *Chapter 6 is devoted to questions that pertain to the Web integration features of Windows 98 and Chapter 11 contains a section that describes the Internet-related multimedia features.*

What are the new features that allow you to create and distribute HTML content?

There are three tools in Windows 98 that cover the creation and distribution of HTML content:

- **FrontPage Express** allows you to create HTML pages either for your local intranet or the Internet. FrontPage Express provides most of the HTML editing functionality of its big brother, Microsoft FrontPage, allowing you to modify existing HTML content, such as the Web page appearance of folder windows, and create your own Web pages.

- **Web Publishing Wizard** allows you to transfer Web content from your computer to an Internet service provider (ISP) server where it is easily accessible by anyone. Web Publishing Wizard provides a simplified means to copy Web content you've created in FrontPage Express (or any other HTML editor) to a hosting Web server.

- **Personal Web Server** allows you to use your computer as a Web or FTP (file transfer protocol) server for limited Internet access or your own intranet. Personal Web Server is a much expanded version of earlier software that allows you to host Web and FTP content on the Internet or a local intranet, and manage their respective environments.

These tools are found by clicking Start | Programs | Internet Explorer. Depending on your installation (see Chapter 2 and Appendix A for Setup options) you might have to install one or more of them from the Add/Remove Programs control panel for them to be available.

 ## What new Internet features are available in Windows Explorer?

One Internet-integration feature you can find in Windows 98 and in the Windows 95 Plus! Internet Explorer 4 combination is the transformation of Windows Explorer into a Web browser. With an Internet connection and a few mouse clicks you can be surfing the Web from this familiar interface, as shown in Figure 3-3. Open Windows Explorer (click Start and choose Programs | Windows Explorer), and then double-click on Internet Explorer in the All Folders bar (left pane) to see these Web features:

● **Browser in right pane** displays Web pages as you would see in a standalone browser window.

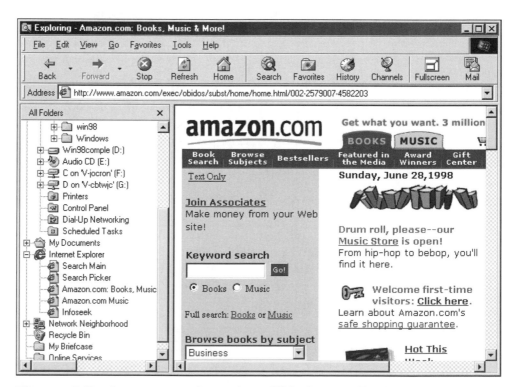

Figure 3-3 Internet transformation of Windows 98 Explorer

● **Explorer Bar** offers several different "looks" to the left pane including the file, folder, and drive hierarchy inherited from Program Manager; a search bar that provides easy access to one or more search engines; a Favorites bar of channel and links that you often use; a History bar of two weeks of Internet travels, organized by day; and a Channel bar that makes subscription "push" content available for offline viewing. The Explorer Bar options are on the View menu.

Note: *The Search, Favorites, History, and Channel bars are also available from other Internet access areas of Windows 98 such as Internet Explorer and the Active Desktop; however, the All Folders bar that displays the resources on your local and networked drives is only found in Windows Explorer.*

● **Dynamic toolbar** changes its button selection depending on whether you are in a Web function or are browsing local or networked drives.

● **Address bar** provides a keyboard entry means to type URL (Uniform Resource Locator) or UNC (Universal Naming Convention) addresses. For example, you can type **http://www.usatoday.com** to find *USA Today*'s Web site or c:\My Documents to locate your own data files.

● **Find option** on the Tools menu mimics the option of the same name on the Start menu that gives you links to Internet search engines and "white pages" for finding people who are on e-mail.

How can I make my desktop look and behave more like I'm surfing the Web than using standard Windows functionality?

Windows 98 provides several features for you to merge how you use the Internet and your desktop. From any folder window, My Computer, or Windows Explorer you can choose a complete Web makeover, an appearance and usage almost identical to Windows 95, or you can create a customized blend

between the two extremes. See what options are available to you with these steps:

1. Double-click My Computer on your desktop, open the View menu, and click Folder Options.

2. In the Folder Options dialog box, choose Custom, and then click Settings. The Custom Settings dialog box displays, as shown in Figure 3-4, several Web-like features you can use or not, including the ability to single-click items to open or launch them.

Is there anything new to assist in getting connected to the Internet?

Internet Explorer

Windows 98 makes setting up and connecting to an online service or ISP easier than ever. With a "clean" install (as opposed to an upgrade from a previous version of Windows) you will see the Connect To The Internet icon on your desktop. Double-click this icon to start the Internet Connection Wizard, which will take you through the steps of establishing an Internet (and creating a new account if you don't already have one), mail, newsgroup, and white pages connection. After you complete the wizard, the Connect To The Internet icon will be replaced by the Internet Explorer icon.

Tip: *You can rerun the Internet Connection Wizard by clicking Start | Programs | Internet Explorer | Connection Wizard.*

How can I "squeeze" more bandwidth out of my existing hardware to gain faster Internet access?

Probably the most innovative way to get the most use out of existing components is to multilink two or more analog modems and achieve their combined bandwidth. By setting up Dial-Up Networking connections for each modem on a separate phone line you can connect to a server that supports multilink and essentially get the sum of the speeds of your modems. For example, by dusting off your 14.4Kbps modem and installing it alongside your 33.6Kbps modem, you should be able to get data transfer rates in the neighborhood of

Custom Settings [?] [X]

Active Desktop

  ○ Enable all web-related content on my desktop: [Customize]

  ⦿ Use Windows classic desktop

Browse folders as follows

  ○ Open each folder in the same window

  ⦿ Open each folder in its own window

View Web content in folders

  ○ For all folders with HTML content

  ⦿ Only for folders where I select "as Web Page" (View menu)

Click items as follows

  ○ Single-click to open an item (point to select)

    ○ Underline icon titles consistent with my browser settings

    ⦿ Underline icon titles only when I point at them

  ⦿ Double-click to open an item (single-click to select)

[OK]   [Cancel]

Figure 3-4 Choose from several Internet-like features you can use on your computer

48Kbps. You can even combine analog modems with ISDN (Integrated Service Digital Network) adapters. Set up your modems with the following steps:

1. Install and set up your modems or adapters. (See Chapter 10 for modem installation questions.)

2. Create a Dial-Up Networking connection for one modem, if not already done, by opening the Dial-Up Networking folder in Windows Explorer and running the Make New Connection Wizard.

3. After completing the wizard, right-click the connection icon in the Dial-Up Networking folder and choose Properties.

4. Click the Multilink tab and add additional modems or ISDN adapters to the connection. When you connect to

your ISP, Windows 98 will use your combined bandwidth to transfer data.

 Note: *Data transfer across the Internet is affected by several factors to ensure we never achieve theoretical limits. Much as 56Kbps modems never provide their full rate, don't be surprised if your multilink rate is not the exact arithmetic sum of your modem speeds.*

ENHANCEMENTS TO WINDOWS 3.*x*

 In Windows 3.*x*, I could only keep one piece of data on the Clipboard. This is a serious limitation when I need to manipulate multiple portions of documents. Do I still have the same limitation on Clipboard contents in Windows 98?

Yes and no. You still can retain only one item when you do Copy or Cut. However, Windows 98 provides a mechanism for temporarily storing "document scraps" on the desktop. These are selected segments of a document that become a separate file when you drag it to the desktop.

To create a document scrap, open the original document and select the text or graphic that you want to copy, and then drag it to the desktop. This will create a *document scrap* on the desktop—a file with the copied piece of data. The item will have a title that includes the words "Document scrap..." and then the first several words of the copied piece, as seen here:

You can now drag this scrap to other documents or programs. You can create as many scraps as you want, and you can have not only text scraps, but pictures as well. You can only use this feature if the program used to create the document supports OLE2 drag-and-drop functions. For example, it will work with WordPad and Paint, but not Notepad.

I understand Windows 98 allows drag-and-drop between applications. Does this mean a new version of OLE is being used, and will "normal" Windows 3.1 applications lose their OLE functionality?

The 16-bit applications will not lose their existing OLE functionality, because Windows 98 still runs the 16-bit applications in the same manner that Windows 3.1 did. But 32-bit applications will have additional OLE2 functionality that 16-bit applications don't have, such as the ability to create scraps on the desktop.

Will Windows 98 be able to handle games that require exclusive access to the system?

Most MS-DOS applications can run concurrently with other MS-DOS, Windows 16-bit, and Win32-based applications. There are some MS-DOS applications (mostly games) that require exclusive access to the system. Such applications can be run in MS-DOS mode, which is still Windows 98. It is created by the Virtual Memory Manager as an exclusive operating environment. This mode does not allow multitasking and directs all resources to the MS-DOS application. To run in MS-DOS mode, choose Shut Down from the Start menu and select Restart In MS-DOS Mode.

In Windows 3.*x*, I was constantly running out of system resources. What improvements have been made to this limitation of the system resources?

While the system resources are still there, much of what was using them up is now handled in other ways. Specifically, much of the code has been moved from 16-bit into 32-bit code, which does not suffer from the 64K limitation. It is very unlikely that you will run out of system resources in Windows 98.

 ## Is there a macro recorder like Windows 3.*x* used to have?

Not anymore. In its place is the Windows Scripting Host (WSH) that allows you to run scripts you have written in either Visual Basic Script (VBScript) or JavaScript (Jscript). See Chapter 13 for a number of questions on the WSH. You can also create scripts to expedite connecting to your Internet service provider or online service, if they require it. You can install the WSH and use scripting in dial-up connections with these steps:

1. Make sure scripting is installed by clicking Start, choosing Settings | Control Panel, and double-clicking Add/Remove Programs. Click the Windows Setup tab, double-click the Accessories component, and verify there is a check mark next to Windows Scripting Host. If not, click the component and click OK twice.

2. In WordPad, open the file Script.doc, located in your Windows folder and read through the instructions on how to use the script language.

3. Open Notepad, type in the necessary commands (you might need to contact your ISP or online service to obtain the specific instructions), and save the script file in your \Windows\Start Menu\Programs\Accessories folder with a .SCP extension.

4. In Windows Explorer, open the Dial-Up Networking folder, right-click the Internet connection you want the script to be used with, click Properties, and then click the Scripting tab.

5. Browse to the file, set options as necessary, and click OK.

 ## How does Windows 98 handle memory?

Memory allocation is provided through the Memory Pager and is based on the *demand-paged virtual memory system.* Windows 98 is treating the memory as a flat, linear address space that can be accessed through 32-bit addressing. Each process is allocated a virtual address space of 4 gigabytes (GB). This virtual memory space is divided into pages. A certain amount of information is stored in memory, and the rest is written back to the temporary storage space on the hard drive, called a *page file* (*swap file* in Windows 3.*x*). When the application needs the information that is stored in this space, the information is paged back to memory. This process is called *demand paging*. Each process is only aware of its own memory, so it cannot accidentally overwrite information paged out by another process. This makes the whole system much more stable. Obviously, the more memory you have, the less disk activity you have for this purpose. Windows 98, therefore, can make good use of lots of memory.

What network security features are implemented in Windows 98?

Windows 98 has several security features implemented directly in the system. These features are listed here:

● *Logon security* can prevent a user from getting access to Windows 98 in two ways. In a standalone system or peer-to-peer network, you can set the Primary Network Logon by opening the Control Panel, double-clicking Network, and choosing the Configuration tab. In addition, in a client-server network, you can get server validation of the user logging on by opening Poledit.exe, the System Policy Editor (found on the Windows 98 CD under \Tools\Reskit\Netadmin\Poledit), and choosing Require Validation By Network For Windows Access. This is an improvement over Windows 3.*x,* where a user could still access Windows even if the server validation failed; he or she was only prevented from accessing the network resources.

Note: See the question "How do I remove the Network Neighborhood icon on a PC that is not networked?" in Chapter 4 for procedures to use the System Policy Editor.

● In Windows 98, a user or administrator can enable *user-level security*. This security level can allow or prevent individual users or groups access to drives on that computer. A list of valid users and passwords is stored on a Windows NT or Novell NetWare server, and the access level for local resources is specified on the actual Windows 98 computer. This feature is accessed through the Access Control tab of the Network control panel.

● *Share-level security* allows or restricts access to specific resources, such as printers, disks, folders, and CD-ROMs on a computer. The password is assigned when sharing a resource through the Control Panel or Start menu (for printers), and My Computer or Explorer for disks and folders. This feature is available only in the peer-to-peer environment under Windows 98 or other Microsoft networks, but not under Novell NetWare. This feature is accessed through the Access Control tab of the Network control panel.

● In Windows 98, a system administrator can define user profiles through the System Policy Editor. In doing so, individual users can be prevented from accessing specific resources on the network or the workstation, and they can be restricted from modifying the system configuration or installing new hardware and software.

What happened to Paintbrush?

Paintbrush was replaced by Paint, a 32-bit application. Paint is an OLE server, which allows the creation of OLE object information that can be embedded or linked into other documents. It is also MAPI enabled, so it is easily integrated with mail clients such as Outlook Express for sending images as e-mail.

I keep hearing rumors that Microsoft is working on a portable version of Windows 98 (one that works on multiple processors). Is this true?

No. Microsoft is not working on a portable version of Windows 98. Windows NT is a portable operating system, and it's available for high-end Intel and Alpha machines.

Windows 98 is optimized for Intel processors, and much of its internal code is Intel Assembler, which puts Windows 98 at the heart of today's mainstream line (but dedicates it to the Intel line).

How are the system resources handled by Windows 98?

In Windows 98, system resources are handled by Virtual Machine Manager, which replaced Win386.exe in Windows 3.1.

Virtual Machine Manager creates an environment in memory called the *virtual machine*. Each application sees this virtual machine as a separate computer that is running only this one application and dedicating all its resources to it. This allows each application to access all the resources it needs. Each Windows-based application, both 16-bit and 32-bit, runs in a single virtual machine called *System VM*. Each MS-DOS-based application runs in its own *DOS VM*.

HELP

How can I learn the basics of Windows 98?

Use Welcome to Windows to learn the basics. If it doesn't appear when you start Windows 98 you can open the window by clicking the Start button and choosing Programs | Accessories | System Tools | Welcome To Windows. You will find an online tour of new features, as well as a launching point to register and connect to the Internet, as shown in Figure 3-5.

How can I get more information about Windows 98?

For more information about Microsoft Windows 98, there are a number of Internet sites that are useful. Of primary importance is Microsoft at **http://www.microsoft.com/ windows98**. For other Web sites, open the Internet Explorer, click Search in the toolbar and enter **"windows 98"** including the quotation marks.

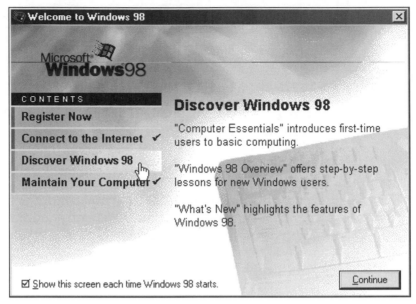

Figure 3-5   Discover Windows 98 provides new users and upgraders with valuable tips

❓ What keyboard shortcuts are used in Windows 98?

The command card inserted in the front of this book contains the shortcut keys used in Windows 98.

❓ How do I use the online help in Windows 98?

In Windows 98, online help is not just context sensitive, it's also interactive. You can still press F1 and get the help that is appropriate for the situation you are in, but the Help in Windows 98 goes a step further. In many Help windows, you will find a link that will walk you through the necessary steps to complete the task and take you to the necessary location.

You can resolve a lot of your problems and issues by going into Help, selecting the Index tab, and typing **troubleshooting**. This will take you to a menu with different troubleshooting scenarios. For example, if you are having problems printing, you can select "Troubleshooting, Printers..." and it will present you with an interactive printing troubleshooting guide (as you can see in Figure 3-6),

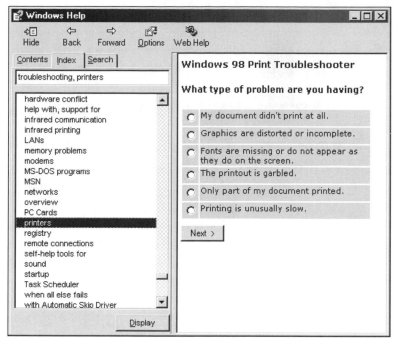

Figure 3-6   Windows 98's Help window provides troubleshooting
assistance

which will take you through different troubleshooting steps.
You will be able to quickly resolve the majority of common
problems without having to call technical support or your
friendly computer guru.

You can also do a keyword search of the entire Help topic
inventory by clicking the Search tab, typing a word or phrase,
and clicking List Topics. Any topic that has an instance of
your typed words will be listed. You can then open each topic
and see if its context is what you're looking for.

How can I make sure my drivers are the most recent available?

Microsoft provides a Web site that you can connect to that
maintains an inventory of the latest drivers for the most
popular software and hardware. Your system is analyzed and
any drivers on your system that are older than those in the
database will be identified. You can choose to replace files or

not. To connect to the Windows Update Web site, click Start
and choose Windows Update in the upper part of the Start
menu. Click the Product Updates link, as shown in Figure
3-7, and let the Web site search your system.

HARDWARE CONSIDERATIONS

 ### What is the cluster size on a disk under Windows 98?

It depends on whether your disk is FAT16 or FAT32. If
FAT16, the cluster size for storing data on a disk is the same
as for MS-DOS 6.*x* and Windows 3.*x,* which can be up to 32K,
depending on the size of the logical partition. The sectors are
512 bytes. If FAT32, the cluster sizes are smaller for the

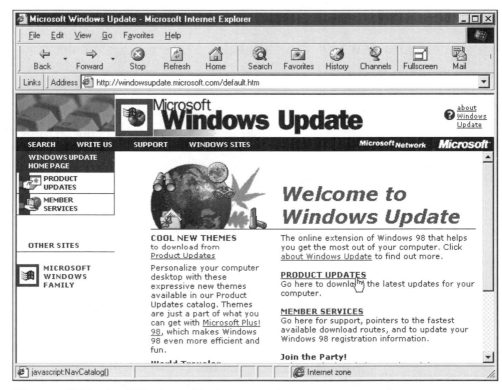

Figure 3-7   Let Windows Update search your computer for
outdated drivers

same disk size, allowing better use of disk space. Table 3-1 shows some differences between the two file allocation tables.

 I have a lot of serial devices that I used to run with my DOS sessions. Are there any limits on the number of ports supported by Windows 98?

In Windows 98 there are actually more ports supported than in the previous versions of Windows. The actual number of ports with which Windows 98 can communicate is 128 serial and 128 parallel. An additional 127 devices are available if your computer and devices support the USB (universal serial bus) standard that allows you to connect to USB devices through a daisy chain or USB hubs.

 Can I have a RAM disk in Windows 98? How do I use it?

Sure you can. Edit your Config.sys file to create a RAM drive by adding the line

Device=c:\Windows\Ramdrive.sys

This will create a 64K RAM drive and assign the next available drive letter to it. If you have enough memory available, you can specify a bigger size, for example:

Device=c:\Windows\Ramdrive.sys 256

This is still a very small area to serve as a temporary disk—2MB are needed in many instances to be effective.

Partition Size	Cluster Size (FAT16)	Cluster Size (FAT32)
512MB	16KB	4KB
2GB	32KB	4KB
8-16GB	Not available	8KB
16-32GB	Not available	16KB
32GB and greater	Not available	32KB

Table 3-1 Cluster Sizes

 Tip: *The purpose of a RAM drive is to give you a very fast disk by using RAM as temporary disk storage. However, this takes away from the memory you have available and can slow your programs, depending on the memory you have. So use it with caution.*

You can create a RAM drive in expanded memory by using the /E switch, like this:

Device=c:\Windows\Ramdrive.sys /E

After rebooting your computer, you will see the new drive in My Computer or Windows Explorer.

 ### After all the great things I've heard about Windows 98, I heard that these improvements will be available only if I am running 32-bit applications. Is this true?

It is true that 32-bit protected-mode applications will utilize the robustness of Windows 98 to the full extent. However, Windows 98 has made important changes in the way that 16-bit applications are handled. Although 16-bit applications are still run very similarly to the way Windows 3.1 ran them (in the same memory space so they can see each other, or their OLE functionality would no longer exist), Windows 98 has improved cleaning up after the 16-bit applications. That is, while any 16-bit application is running, Windows 98 cannot track what resources are being used; once all 16-bit applications are closed, Windows 98 will go in, clean up the memory, and release any system resources the 16-bit applications may not have released. But during the execution of any 16-bit application, Windows 98 cannot clean up these resources, and the 16-bit applications will continue to use and not release the resources.

Chapter 4

Setting Up, Customizing, and Optimizing Windows 98

Answer Topics!

Setting Up, Customizing, and Optimizing @ a Glance

Different people like different things. That is as true with computers as with anything else. Windows 98 accommodates this facet of our nature better than any previous operating system. Almost everything that you find in the Control Panel represents a way that you can set up, customize, or optimize Windows 98. The control panel options enable you to set up your mail system, modem, network, and printer; customize how your keyboard, mouse, and display behave; as well as optimize how you use your file system and memory. In the Display control panel alone, you can change not only the color of the screen and the type of wallpaper displayed, but also the size, color, and font used in windows and their components like title bars, scroll bars, and message boxes. (See Table 4-1.)

This chapter discusses ways to set up and change various Windows 98 features as well as to work more efficiently with Windows 98:

- **Changing Your Display** discusses animated cursors, as well as how to change the way information on the desktop is displayed by customizing the colors, backgrounds, and screen savers. This section also covers changing icons, creating shortcuts that enable you to quickly start programs, and modifying the way various procedures are performed, such as changing wait times or logoff screens.

- **Taskbar** shows you how you can work more efficiently by customizing the taskbar. Options can be added to the Start menu, the location and size of the taskbar can be changed, and the options in the taskbar can be removed or added to.

- **Customizing the Way You Use Windows 98** discusses how you can modify the Windows startup logo, how to drag windows with their contents displayed, and how to use some of the old Windows 3.1 features, such as displaying the file extensions. This section also covers how to use your Windows 3.1 Program Manager.

- **Working with Programs** includes information about using Windows 98 more effectively, such as adding command-line switches to shortcuts, changing the sort order for folders, starting a program automatically, creating program groups, and assigning hot keys to start an application.

● **Video Settings** provides information about changing display and video drivers.

● **Disk Drives** covers changing the drive letter for the CD-ROM, changing the location of the swap file, and changing and modifying partitions on the hard drive.

● **Mouse** gives information about changing mouse characteristics.

● **Windows Explorer** discusses ways you can change the display of drives and folders to meet your specific needs.

● **Accessibility Options and Tools** shows how to activate and adjust the various accessibility features.

● **Optimizing Windows** covers procedures for making Windows 98 functions more efficient.

For a quick view of some of Windows 98's more important features, see Table 4-1.

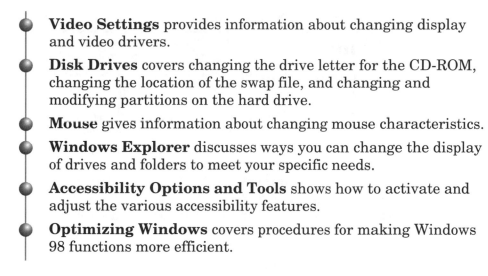

Icon	Name	Function
Accessibility Options	Accessibility Options	Allows you to customize the keyboard, mouse, display, and use of sound to compensate for various disabilities
Add New Hardware	Add New Hardware	Leads you through the configuration of your system to accommodate adding and removing hardware
Add/Remove Programs	Add/Remove Programs	Provides the means to install or uninstall application programs, to add or remove Windows 98 components, and to create a Windows 98 Startup disk
Date/Time	Date/Time	Allows you to set the current date and time being maintained in your computer and to identify your time zone

Table 4-1   Some Important Features in Windows 98

Icon	Name	Function
Display	Display	Enables the selection of patterns and wallpaper to be used on your desktop; the screen saver you want to use; the appearance of your screen, including colors, sizes, and fonts; the appearance of your desktop icons; whether and how you view your Active Desktop as a Web page; and the resolution and number of colors that are used in your display
Fonts	Fonts	Displays the fonts currently installed on your computer and provides the means to add and remove fonts
Game Controllers	Game Controllers	Allows you to configure and test one or more joy sticks or game controllers
Internet	Internet	Displays Internet Explorer's Properties dialog box where you can customize how your browser displays content, selectively chooses content, connects to the Internet, and basically performs to your needs
Keyboard	Keyboard	Allows the changing of the sensitivity, the language that is implemented, and the type of keyboard that Windows 98 thinks you are using
Mail and Fax	Mail and Fax	Provides the means to configure messaging services such as Internet Mail, Microsoft Mail, and address books (not in a Typical "clean" installation; however, it will carry over from previous versions of Windows when upgrading)
Modems	Modems	Leads you through the configuration of your modem(s)
Mouse	Mouse	Provides the means to determine the use of the mouse buttons, the speed of double-clicking, the type of mouse pointers, the motion of the mouse pointer on the screen, and the type of mouse you are using
Multimedia	Multimedia	Allows the selection and configuration of audio, video, MIDI (Musical Instrument Digital Interface), CD, and other multimedia devices

Table 4-1 Some Important Features in Windows 98 (*continued*)

Icon	Name	Function
Network	Network	Allows for the configuration of your network components, the identification of your workstation, and the type of access you want to allow to your files
Passwords	Passwords	Allows you to change your logon password and the passwords used in other services, to enable the remote administration of your computer, and to determine if everyone using your computer will use the same preferences
Power Management	Power Management	Allows you to control when Windows 98 powers down your monitor and hard disks
Printers	Printers	Leads you through setting up and sharing a new printer, as well as providing for the management of the work waiting to be printed
Regional Settings	Regional Settings	Provides for the setting of your preferences for number, currency, date, and time formatting
Sounds	Sounds	Enables the association of sounds with events, such as the receipt of mail and exiting Windows
System	System	Allows you to manage and optimize your hardware resources
Telephony	Telephony	Allows you to establish settings for different dialing locations and add drivers that support other telephony schemes
Users	Users	Lets you manage the profiles of a computer's multiple users

Table 4-1   Some Important Features in Windows 98 (*continued*)

CHANGING YOUR DISPLAY

 I have seen animated cursors in NT. How can I get this for Windows 98?

Windows 98 provides an animated hourglass that drops the sands of time and rotates when the system is in a waiting period. To display an animated hourglass:

1. Click Start, and choose Settings | Control Panel.

2. Double-click the Mouse control panel and click Pointers to display that tab.

3. Open the Scheme drop-down list box and select Animated Hourglasses.

4. Select the Busy mouse pointer from the list box to see the animated effects in the preview box, as shown here:

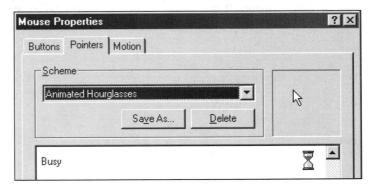

 How can I change the fonts used on my desktop?

Use the following steps to change the fonts used in Windows:

1. Right-click the desktop and choose Properties to open the Display Properties dialog box. Then click the Appearance tab, which is shown in Figure 4-1.

2. In the Item list, choose the desktop element that you want to change the font for (Icon, Title Bar, and so on); in the Font list, choose the font you want.

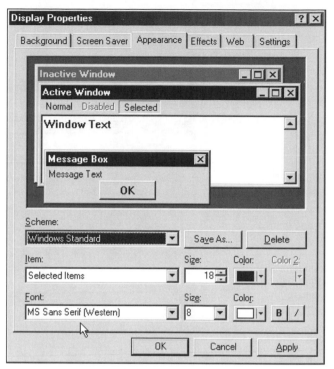

Figure 4-1   Change your desktop fonts in the Display Properties
dialog box

   Tip: *You can also change the size, color, and style (whether
it's bold or italic) of each font used on the desktop.*

 ## How can I change the icons for the folders I have placed on my desktop?

If you drag the original folder or file to the desktop, you
cannot change its icon. To work around this, create a shortcut
for the folder or file, pick the icon you want for it, and place
the shortcut on the desktop, rather than the original folder
itself. To change an icon for a shortcut:

1. Right-click the icon and choose Properties.

2. Click the Shortcut tab and then click Change Icon.

3. Enter or browse for the filename in which you want to search for an icon, and then select an icon, as you see here:

4. Click OK twice.

✚ *Tip:* *You can find Windows 98 default icons in \Windows\ System\Shell32.dll, in \Windows\System\Iconlib.dll, and in \Windows\Moricons.dll. You need to turn on Show All Files in the Folder Options dialog box View tab to see these files in Windows Explorer.*

 I want to change the name of the My Computer icon. How can I rename the icons on my desktop?

To rename desktop items, do the following:

1. Click the item you want to rename (for example, My Computer).

2. Do one of the following:

   ● Press F2 and type a new name (for example, **Bob's Computer**).

● Click the icon title, and it will become selected, allowing you to type a new name.

Tip: *Using the preceding steps, you can rename My Computer, Network Neighborhood, My Documents, Internet Explorer, Online Services, and Outlook Express desktop icons. You cannot rename the Recycle Bin.*

How can I easily change screen resolution in Windows 98?

Screen resolution is the result of the number of pixels used to cover your screen and the number of colors that can be displayed. Standard VGA, the minimum for Windows 98, is 640×480 pixels and 16 or 256 colors (8-bit color). A higher resolution, sometimes called Super VGA, is 800×600 pixels and 16- or 24-bit color. You can change screen resolution in the Display Properties dialog box with these steps:

1. Right-click the desktop for the context menu, and choose Properties to open the Display Properties dialog box.

2. Click the Settings tab. Then change the pixel density (Screen Area) and the number of colors (Colors) to get the resolution you want, as shown in Figure 4-2.

How do I change the wait time before my screen saver kicks in?

To change the characteristics of your screen saver, do the following:

1. Right-click the desktop, select Properties, and click the Screen Saver tab.

2. In the Screen Saver list, choose the screen saver you want.

3. If the screen saver offers it, click Settings and complete the options for configuring that type of screen saver.

4. In the Wait spinner, pick the time you want the system to wait before the screen saver appears.

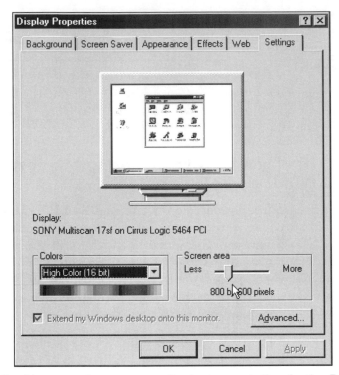

Figure 4-2 You can change your display's resolution in the Display Properties dialog box

5. If you want to protect access to the computer by using a password to turn off the screen saver, make sure the Password Protected box is checked and click Change to specify the password.

6. Click Preview to test the screen saver, and click OK when done.

How do I change the way the date and time are displayed in Windows 98?

Use the following steps to do this:

1. Click Start, then select Settings I Control Panel.

2. Double-click the Regional Settings control panel.

3. Select the Date tab or the Time tab to make the changes you want.

Tip: *You can also change Regional, Number, and Currency settings here.*

4. Click OK when done.

Tip: *To actually change the date and time, double-click the time in the taskbar.*

How can I create my own background (wallpaper)?

You can create your own Windows wallpaper with your company's logo or any graphics that you want by saving images as wallpaper in the Paint program or in Internet Explorer by following these instructions.

Saving Wallpaper in Paint

1. Click Start and choose Programs | Accessories.
2. Click Paint and create an image, or open an existing bitmap (files ending with .BMP, .PCX, and .TIF, among others), .JPG, or .GIF image for the background that you want.
3. Choose File | Save As, select 24-bit Bitmap (for non-.BMP files), and give a name to your new background.
4. Choose File, select either Set As Wallpaper (Centered) or Set As Wallpaper (Tiled), and it will replace your current background with your new one.

Saving Wallpaper in Internet Explorer

In the Internet Explorer you can save images you have gotten off the Internet as wallpaper by right-clicking an image that you want, and choosing Set As Wallpaper from the context menu. It will replace your current background.

 Warning: *Graphics on the Internet are protected by the same copyright laws as other printed and electronic material. Make sure you have the originator's permission to use his or her work, especially for commercial purposes.*

 **What is an easy way for me to customize my desktop—change colors, wallpaper, icons, and screen savers?**

All are easily changed. Right-click an empty spot on the desktop and choose Properties. This will open the Display Properties dialog box. In the Background tab you can set the pattern or wallpaper that you want to use. In the Appearance tab that you saw in Figure 4-1 earlier, you can change the color of your desktop. In the Effects tab you can change icons, and in the Screen Saver tab you can choose which screen saver you want to use.

How can I get files and folders on my desktop?

Very simply—drag them there from either My Computer or Windows Explorer. Use these two steps:

1. Open My Computer or Windows Explorer, and locate the file or folder you want to move.

2. Drag the file or folder to an empty spot on the desktop.

 Tip: *When you drag a file or folder to the desktop, unless the file is a program, you will physically move the file or folder from its original folder to the desktop ("folder"). If what you really want is a copy on the desktop, then press and hold CTRL while dragging the object. You should also consider a third alternative—placing a shortcut on the desktop that points to a file or folder.*

I have chosen 800×600 small fonts, yet my fonts and icons are not as small as I expect them to be. What could be causing this, and how can I change it?

Most probably, one of the Accessibility options, High Contrast, has been enabled. To turn off this feature:

1. Click Start, choose Settings | Control Panel, and double-click Accessibility Options.

2. Select the Display tab, as shown in the following illustration, and click to remove the check mark in the Use High Contrast check box.

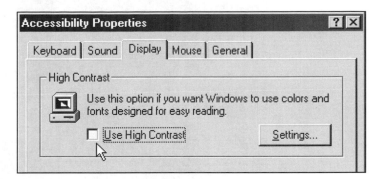

Can I modify the Windows 98 logoff screens?

There are two bitmap files in the Windows folder that are used during logoff. Logow.sys is the "Windows is shutting down..." screen, and Logos.sys is the "You may now safely turn..." screen. Both are normal bitmaps. Back them up (right-click them, choose Copy, right-click white space in the Windows folder, and choose Paste), and modify them with Paint, opened from the Start menu under Programs | Accessories. Figure 4-3 shows Logos.sys being modified. Be sure to save the modified files under their original names. Windows will then use them when shutting down.

How do I remove the Network Neighborhood icon on a PC that is not networked?

It is not simple to get rid of the Network Neighborhood. You cannot just delete the icon from the desktop or drag it to your Recycle Bin. You can turn it off using the System Policy Editor, which you can find on the Windows 98 CD. Use the following steps:

1. Double-click \Tools\Reskit\Netadmin\Poledit\ Poledit.exe on the Windows 98 CD, and click OK. When told the template cannot be found, click OK, and then click Cancel in the Open Template File dialog box.

Figure 4-3 Paint can modify the Windows 98 logoff screens

2. In the System Policy Editor window, open the Options menu and click Policy Template.

3. Click Add and then double-click Windows.adm. Click OK.

4. From the File menu, choose Open Registry, and then double-click Local User.

5. Click the plus sign opposite Windows 98 System to open it, and then open Shell and Restrictions.

6. Click Hide Network Neighborhood to enable this restriction, as shown in Figure 4-4. Click OK and then close the System Policy Editor. You'll need to reboot for the icon to go away.

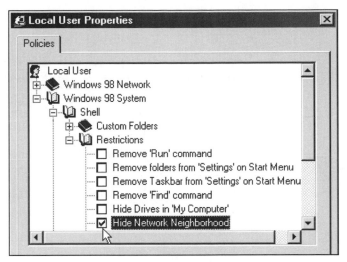

Figure 4-4 The System Policy Editor can be used to customize some elements of your desktop

 What is a shortcut and how do I use it to start programs from the desktop?

A *shortcut* is a very small file that represents or points to a usually much larger file or a folder in another location. A shortcut is useful because you can use it to remotely start a program, open a data file, or open a folder. For example, if you have an application that you use often, you can place a shortcut to that application on the desktop and start the application by double-clicking the shortcut, all the while leaving the application program file in its original folder.

To create a shortcut on the desktop, use one of the following techniques:

● If you want a shortcut of a program file (one with an .EXE or .COM extension), all you have to do is drag the program file to the desktop or wherever you want the shortcut, and

one will automatically be created for you. The original program file will remain where it was originally.

● Press and hold *both* CTRL and SHIFT while dragging any file or folder to the desktop, and select Create Shortcut(s) Here from the context menu. Make sure you release CTRL-SHIFT before you release the mouse button.

● Right-drag the file or folder to the desktop and select Create Shortcut(s) Here from the context menu that appears.

● Right-click the file or folder, select Create Shortcut(s) Here from the context menu, and drag the shortcut to the desktop.

I want my printer shortcut on the right side of the screen. I drag the icon there, but it snaps back to its position on the left. What can I do?

The icons are being automatically rearranged by Windows 98. Right-click the desktop, choose Arrange Icons from the context menu, and then click AutoArrange to turn the check mark off. Without AutoArrange, the icons will remain wherever you drag them.

Can I use my favorite screen saver, Pipes, from Windows NT in Windows 98?

Sure, support for OpenGL is shipped with Microsoft Windows 98, but Windows 98 also includes 3D Pipes as a screen saver you can use with a Typical installation. To select it:

1. Right-click the desktop, select Properties, and click the Screen Saver tab.

2. Open the Screen Saver drop-down list, choose 3D Pipes, and click OK.

My wife and I both share our home computer. Can we customize how the desktop appears for each of us?

Yes, you can by creating separate user profiles for each person who uses a computer. Create user profiles with these steps:

1. Click Start and choose Settings | Control Panel, and then double-click Users.

2. Read the opening Enable Multi-User Settings Wizard box and then click Next.

3. Type a name for the new user and then click Next.

4. Type a password, if wanted, and then click Next.

5. Select the display and other options you want to be individualized, and whether to make copies of existing items or create new ones. Click Next and then Finish.

The next time someone logs on to Windows, his or her user name and password (if set up) will open a desktop that can be personalized.

 Tip: *You can quickly switch between users by clicking Log Off on the Start menu.*

 How can I make sure I am using protected-mode disk drivers?

You can determine if you are using protected-mode disk drivers with these steps:

1. From the Start menu choose Settings | Control Panel, and then double-click System.

2. Open the Performance tab, click File System, and choose the Troubleshooting tab, as shown in Figure 4-5.

3. If you have *not* checked Disable All 32-Bit Protected-Mode Disk Drivers you are using protected-mode drivers.

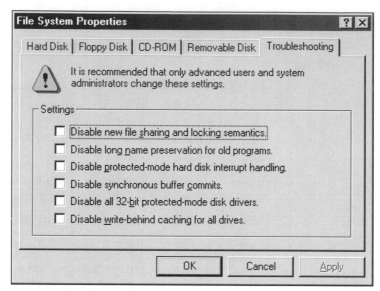

Figure 4-5   You are using protected-mode disk drivers if Disable All
32-Bit Protected-Mode Disk Drivers is not checked

TASKBAR

 How can I add options to my Start menu?

You can place options at the top part of the Start menu to
start applications and/or open folders, as shown in Figure 4-6.
There are three ways to do this:

● Drag files and/or folders from My Computer or Windows
Explorer to Start on the taskbar. This will automatically
create a shortcut, place the shortcut in the \Windows\
Start Menu folder, and place an option named after the
shortcut on the Start menu.

● Right-click a vacant area of the taskbar, choose Properties,
and open the Start Menu Programs tab. Click Add,
browse for the program file of the program you want on
the Start menu, click Open, click Next, click Start Menu,
and click Next again. Type the name you want to use on
the Start menu, click Finish, and then click OK to close
the Taskbar Properties dialog box.

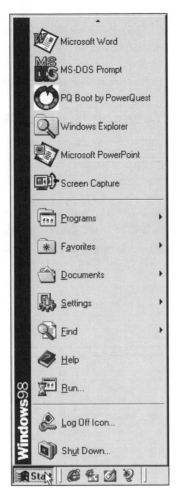

Figure 4-6   The Start menu can contain options to start your applications

● Open Windows Explorer and locate the file or folder in
  the right pane that you want to add to the Start menu.
  In the left pane (or All Folders Explorer bar) of Windows
  Explorer, click the plus sign opposite the Windows folder.
  Then scroll the list of folders until you can see the Start
  Menu folder. If the option you want to add is a program,
  simply drag it to the Start Menu folder. A shortcut will be
  created in the Start Menu folder. For other types of files,
  press and hold CTRL-SHIFT while dragging the file to the
  Start Menu folder. Then choose Create Shortcut(s) Here
  from the context menu.

 Tip: *If you place more shortcuts on the Start menu than will fit in one screen length, arrows will appear at the top and/or bottom of the Start menu. Click these arrows to view shortcuts and options that are hidden.*

How do I change the location and size of the taskbar?

You can drag the taskbar to any of the four sides of the screen, and you can drag an edge of the taskbar to size it. Use these steps:

● Point the cursor to a blank area of the taskbar, hold down the left mouse button, and drag the taskbar to another edge of the screen. For example, Figure 4-7 shows the taskbar on the right edge of the screen.

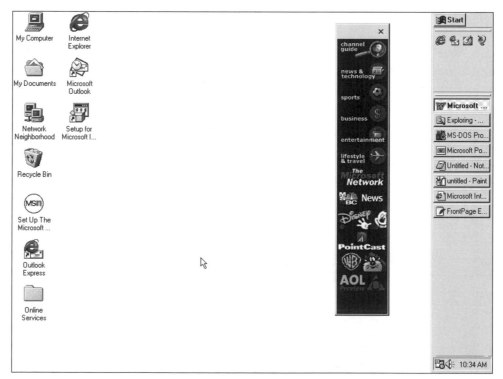

Figure 4-7 The taskbar can be dragged to any edge of the screen

● Resize the taskbar by moving the mouse pointer to the inside edge of the taskbar. When the pointer becomes a double arrow, drag the mouse pointer in or out to size the taskbar as you desire. You can see a multiple row taskbar in Figure 4-8.

What are those icons that appear to the right of Start, and can I change them?

The four default icons (shown in Table 4-2) that appear to the right of the Start menu make up the Quick Launch toolbar.

You can easily set up the Quick Launch toolbar to display the programs you use most often. To remove an icon, you can drag it from its location to someplace else (for example, the desktop) or you can right-click the icon and select Delete from

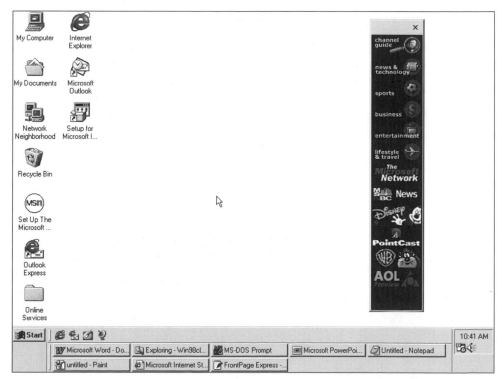

Figure 4-8 You can size the taskbar by dragging its inside edge

Icon	Name	Description
![Internet Explorer icon]	Internet Explorer	Opens Internet Explorer, the browser that is included with Windows 98
![Outlook Express icon]	Outlook Express	Opens Outlook Express, the e-mail and messaging client included with Windows 98
![Show Desktop icon]	Show Desktop	Closes all open windows to minimize tasks so you can quickly display your desktop; clicking a second time restores all windows to their original configuration
![View Channels icon]	View Channels	Opens a full-screen Internet Explorer where you can open and view channels listed in the Channel bar or those you have subscribed to

Table 4-2   Quick Launch Toolbar Default Icons

the context menu. You can also drag any icon from the desktop, Windows Explorer, My Computer, or any other window to have it appear on the toolbar. Follow these steps to add Windows Explorer:

1. Right-click Start and click Open.

2. Double-click the Programs icon to open the folder of the same name.

3. Drag the Windows Explorer icon to the position on the Quick Launch toolbar where you want it. An I-beam will appear to let you know where the icon will appear, as you can see here:

 ### Can I add other toolbars to the taskbar besides the Quick Launch toolbar?

Sure. There are four standard toolbars (the Quick Launch toolbar is displayed by default) that you can place on the taskbar and you also have the option of copying any folder on your computer to the taskbar. The four standard toolbars are described in Table 4-3.

Toolbars	Description
Address	Displays an address bar where you can quickly open objects on your local computer as well as across your network or the Internet. See Chapter 6 for more information on using the new Internet integration features of Windows 98.
Links	Displays the Links toolbar in Internet Explorer which provides access to your favorite Web pages. See Chapter 6 for more information on using the new Internet integration features of Windows 98.
Desktop	Displays the icons that normally appear on your desktop.
Quick Launch	Displays a "starter kit" of useful icons that you can modify to your needs.

Table 4-3 Standard Toolbars

Here's how to add toolbars to or remove them from the taskbar:

1. Right-click an empty area of the toolbar to display its context menu.

2. Click Toolbars and select any of the four standard toolbars to add or remove them from the taskbar.

3. Right-click the taskbar again, click Toolbars, and this time click New Toolbar to open the New Toolbar dialog box shown in Figure 4-9.

4. Locate the folder you want to appear as a toolbar on the taskbar and click OK.

 Tip: *You can size the toolbars within the taskbar by dragging the vertical bar on their leftmost end. Programs or folders are added to toolbars by dragging their icons to the toolbar; remove them by dragging them elsewhere or by right-clicking and selecting Delete from their context menu.*

 Besides adding toolbars, what other customization can I do to the taskbar?

You can customize the taskbar by right-clicking an empty area of the taskbar and choosing Properties. The Taskbar Properties dialog box will open as shown in Figure 4-10.

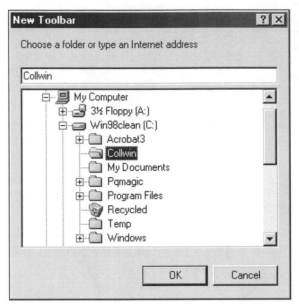

Figure 4-9 Display any folder on your computer as a toolbar on the taskbar

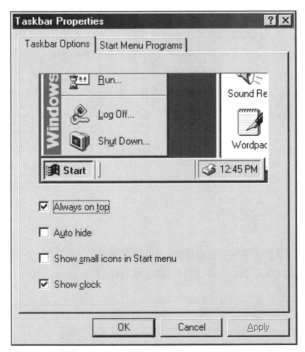

Figure 4-10 The taskbar can be customized in the Taskbar Properties dialog box

On the Taskbar Options tab you can control four attributes of the taskbar, as follows:

● **Always On Top** prevents the taskbar from being covered by other windows. If this is turned off, then maximizing a window would cover the taskbar.

● **Auto Hide** will hide the taskbar until you move the mouse pointer to the edge of the screen containing the taskbar, and then it will appear.

Tip: *Always On Top must be enabled for Auto Hide to work with maximized windows.*

● **Show Small Icons In Start Menu** allows you to contain more options in the Start menu.

● **Show Clock** turns the display of the clock in the taskbar on and off.

In addition to these customizing options in the Taskbar Properties dialog box, you can customize the position and size of the taskbar and add toolbars, as you saw earlier.

How can I turn off the clock on my taskbar?

The clock is controlled in the Taskbar Properties dialog box. Use these steps to turn it off:

1. Right-click an empty spot on the taskbar and choose Properties.

2. Click the Taskbar Options tab, and clear the Show Clock check box to disable it. Choose OK.

Tip: *You can set the clock (system time, date, and time zone) by double-clicking the clock in the taskbar. If you hold the mouse pointer over the taskbar clock, you can see the date, as shown here:*

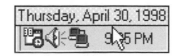

CUSTOMIZING THE WAY YOU USE WINDOWS 98

 Can I bypass the Windows 98 startup logo?

Yes. You can turn off the logo by adding an entry to a file named Msdos.sys in your root folder. Msdos.sys, though, is a hidden, read-only file, so you must go through some extra steps to access it. Do so with these instructions:

1. In Windows Explorer, open the View menu and choose Folder Options. In the View tab, choose Show All Files.

2. Also in Windows Explorer, locate and right-click the file Msdos.sys (*not* Msdos.dos) in the root folder of your boot drive, and choose Properties to open the Msdos.sys Properties dialog box.

3. Click the Read-Only and Hidden check boxes to turn them off, and then click OK.

4. Make a copy of Msdos.sys to serve as a backup by right-clicking Msdos.sys and choosing Copy. Right-click an open area of the right pane of the Windows Explorer window in the root folder, and choose Paste. You can either leave the name "Copy of Msdos.sys" or change it to some other name like **Msdos0.sys**.

5. Right-click the original Msdos.sys, choose Open With, scroll the list of programs, and double-click Notepad, which you will use to edit the file.

6. Locate the section entitled "[Options]" and add the line **Logo=0**, like the one shown in Figure 4-11.

7. Choose Save from Notepad's File menu. Close Notepad, reset the Read-Only and Hidden attributes, and reboot your computer. You will no longer see the Windows 98 logo.

 Tip: *If you change your mind, changing the line to read* **Logo=1** *or removing it altogether will enable the logo again. You can also go back to the original file by deleting the new Msdos.sys and renaming Copy of Msdos.sys or Msdos0.sys to just Msdos.sys.*

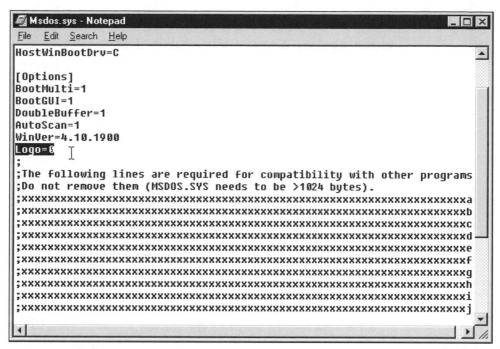

```
Msdos.sys - Notepad                                      _ □ ✕
File   Edit   Search   Help
HostWinBootDrv=C

[Options]
BootMulti=1
BootGUI=1
DoubleBuffer=1
AutoScan=1
WinVer=4.10.1900
Logo=0    I
;
;The following lines are required for compatibility with other programs
;Do not remove them (MSDOS.SYS needs to be >1024 bytes).
;xxxxxxxxxxxxxxxxxxxxxxxxxxxxxxxxxxxxxxxxxxxxxxxxxxxxxxxxxxxxxxa
;xxxxxxxxxxxxxxxxxxxxxxxxxxxxxxxxxxxxxxxxxxxxxxxxxxxxxxxxxxxxxxb
;xxxxxxxxxxxxxxxxxxxxxxxxxxxxxxxxxxxxxxxxxxxxxxxxxxxxxxxxxxxxxxc
;xxxxxxxxxxxxxxxxxxxxxxxxxxxxxxxxxxxxxxxxxxxxxxxxxxxxxxxxxxxxxxd
;xxxxxxxxxxxxxxxxxxxxxxxxxxxxxxxxxxxxxxxxxxxxxxxxxxxxxxxxxxxxxxe
;xxxxxxxxxxxxxxxxxxxxxxxxxxxxxxxxxxxxxxxxxxxxxxxxxxxxxxxxxxxxxxf
;xxxxxxxxxxxxxxxxxxxxxxxxxxxxxxxxxxxxxxxxxxxxxxxxxxxxxxxxxxxxxxg
;xxxxxxxxxxxxxxxxxxxxxxxxxxxxxxxxxxxxxxxxxxxxxxxxxxxxxxxxxxxxxxh
;xxxxxxxxxxxxxxxxxxxxxxxxxxxxxxxxxxxxxxxxxxxxxxxxxxxxxxxxxxxxxxi
;xxxxxxxxxxxxxxxxxxxxxxxxxxxxxxxxxxxxxxxxxxxxxxxxxxxxxxxxxxxxxxj
◀                                                              ▶
```

Figure 4-11   The file Msdos.sys provides some startup parameters to Windows 98

How can I drag a window and still see the contents of the window? I don't want just the window border.

This is one of several visual enhancement features that Windows 98 incorporated from Windows 95 Plus!.

1. Right-click an empty area of the desktop and choose Properties from the context menu.

2. From the Display Properties dialog box, click Effects, and then select the last check box, Show Window Contents While Dragging. (The Display Properties dialog box is the same dialog box you get when you open the Display control panel.)

3. Click OK.

Tip: *You can also change this effect and other visual enhancements from the View tab of the Folder Options dialog box, under Visual Settings.*

 I need to exclude a certain area in upper memory. How do I do this in Windows 98?

Upper memory is the area between 640K and 1MB. It is used for many purposes, including your ROM BIOS and video memory. Some of it can and should be used for the storage of Windows 98 itself, but you may want to prevent Windows 98 from loading into a certain area so you can use it for some other purpose. To do that, use the following steps:

1. Right-click My Computer and choose Properties. The System Properties dialog box will open. (This is the same dialog box you get when you open the System control panel.)

2. Click the Device Manager tab, and then double-click Computer. The Computer Properties dialog box will open.

3. Click the Reserve Resources tab and select Memory.

4. Click Add and type your exclude range. Click OK three times to close the various dialog boxes you opened.

 How can I get my file extensions back? Seeing just the files and icons confuses me.

Use the following steps to show file extensions:

1. Open Windows Explorer's or My Computer's View menu and choose Folder Options.

2. In the View tab, uncheck the box Hide File Extensions For Known File Types and under Hidden Files, select Show All Files.

3. Click OK.

 How do I remove the list of files under the Documents menu on the Start menu?

To clear the files in the Documents menu, do the following:

1. Right-click a blank area of the taskbar and choose Properties.

2. Click the Start Menu Programs tab.

3. Click Clear in the Documents Menu section of the dialog box.

How can I get my old Windows 3.1x Program Manager to be easily available?

To get easy access to the Windows 3.1 Program Manager, do the following:

1. Click Start and choose Settings | Taskbar & Start Menu.

2. Click the Start Menu Programs tab and click Add.

3. Click Browse and double-click the Windows folder.

4. In the Windows folder, scroll past the folders to the program files, select Progman.exe, click Open, and click Next.

5. Click Start Menu to select it as the folder where you want to place the Progman shortcut and then click Next.

6. Type the full name **Program Manager**, click Finish, and then click OK. Now when you click Start, the Program Manager option will be available at the top of the Start menu.

Warning: *The Program Manager is a 16-bit application; by using it, you give up many of the features of Windows 98—most importantly, long filenames. You'll notice that the Rename option is gone from the File menu for this reason, and you can't click twice on a name in the Program Manager to change it. You also can't drag a file from the Program Manager to the desktop, My Computer, or Windows Explorer.*

I feel like getting "under the hood" with Windows 98 more than the Control Panel offers, but I'm not quite ready to get involved with the Registry. Is there a middle ground for customizing how to use Windows 98?

Yes there is. Included on the Windows 98 CD is a utility called Tweak UI, which provides a dialog box–approach for setting a number of user interface items that are either scattered about Windows or aren't readily accessible.

Install Tweak UI with these steps:

1. On the Windows 98 CD, open Tools | Reskit | Powertoy and right-click Tweakui.inf.

2. Click Install, and then close the Help window that will appear to continue the installation.

3. Click the Start button and choose Settings | Control Panel and double-click the new Tweak UI control panel.

WORKING WITH PROGRAMS

 How do I add command-line switches to shortcuts for applications that are on my desktop?

Use the following steps to add command-line switches to a shortcut:

1. Open the shortcut's Properties dialog box by right-clicking the shortcut and choosing Properties.

2. Click the Shortcut tab.

3. In the Target box, you should see the command line that is run when the icon is opened. Add the switches to this line.

For example, to run Microsoft Word 97 with the /n switch so that it doesn't automatically open up a new document, you would put the following entry in the "Target:" line: **C:\Program Files\Microsoft Office\ Office\Winword.exe /n**.

How do I assign a hot key to quickly launch an application?

You can assign a hot key to any shortcut. Use these steps to do this:

1. Right-click the shortcut icon and choose Properties.

2. Click the Shortcut tab, click in the Shortcut Key box, and press a function key or key combination you want to use for the shortcut key.

3. Click OK to complete the operation.

Tip: *To immediately start a screen saver (as when your boss walks in while you're playing Solitaire) create a shortcut to the screen saver file (search the Windows folder for *.scr files), and then assign it a shortcut key.*

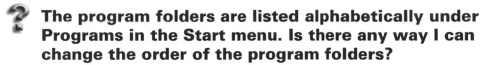

The program folders are listed alphabetically under Programs in the Start menu. Is there any way I can change the order of the program folders?

Yes, there are two ways. First, you can simply drag the folders where you want them on the list. A black line will appear where the file will go. Second, you can rename the folders with a number on the left of the name. With such a number, the folders will be sorted by number rather than alphabetically.

Use the following steps to rearrange folders:

1. Right-click Start and choose Open.

2. Double-click Programs. Every folder in this group appears under Start | Programs.

3. Click the folder you want to appear at the top of the list.

4. Press F2 to rename and type **1.** in front of the name.

5. Repeat this for the rest of the folders by adding a number in front of the folder name in the order in which you would like them to appear. For example, if you want the Microsoft Office folder to appear first, click it once, press F2, and type **1.** in front of the "Microsoft Office" label. If you want the Windows Explorer to appear second, click it once, press F2, and type **2.** in front of the "Windows Explorer" label, and so on.

I installed Windows 98 in a folder other than Windows 3.1. Can I convert my Windows 3.1 program groups to the Windows 98 folders?

Yes. Do the following:

1. Click Start and choose Run.

2. Type **grpconv /m** and click OK.

3. Select the group you want to convert.

4. Click Open and then click Yes in the Program Manager Group Converter dialog box. Close the Select A Group To Convert dialog box when you are done.

You can also convert the group by double-clicking the group name.

 ## How do I create a file association in Windows 98?

A file association relates a data file to a program that can open it, so that you can double-click the file in My Computer or Windows Explorer and it will launch the application, which in turn will load the file. To create a file association, use these steps:

1. Open My Computer, open the View menu, and choose Folder Options.
2. Click the File Types tab and click New Type. The Add New File Type dialog box will open.
3. Enter the description and extension, and click New under Actions.
4. Type **open** for the Action, and then click Browse to find the application to associate with the file type. Click Open, click OK, and then click Close to complete the process.

 ## Can I disassociate a file from its type so that it will not open with its associated program?

Yes. To do this use the following steps:

1. Open My Computer or Windows Explorer.
2. Choose Folder Options from the View menu.
3. Click the File Types tab. In the list of file types, select the one you want to change. The settings for that file type are shown in the File Type Details box as shown in Figure 4-12.
4. Click Remove and then click Yes in the confirmation message box that displays. The selected file will no longer be associated with that program.
5. Click Close when done.

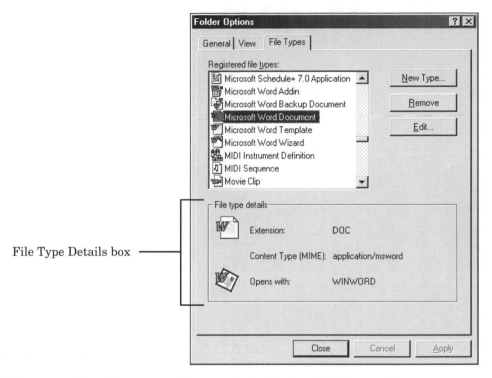

Figure 4-12 Remove a file association in the File Types tab

 How do I create a program group in Windows 98?

In Windows 98, a program group is nothing more than a folder in the \Windows\Start Menu\Programs folder. To create a new group, use the following steps:

1. Right-click Start and choose Open.

2. Double-click the Programs folder. Here are all your program groups.

3. Right-click inside the folder, choose New, and click Folder. This creates a new folder, as shown in Figure 4-13. You can rename it what you want and drag to it the shortcuts you want to include in it.

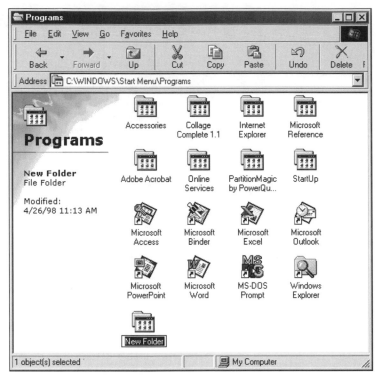

Figure 4-13   A folder in the \Windows\Start Menu\Programs folder is a program group

❓ How can I load a program automatically when I start Windows 98?

Use the following steps to load a program automatically when Windows 98 starts:

1. Click Start and choose Settings | Taskbar & Start Menu.
2. Click the Start Menu Programs tab, and then click Add.
3. If you don't know the exact filename of the application, click Browse, select the item you need, and click Open.
4. In the Create Shortcut window, click Next.
5. In the Select Program Folder window, select the \Start Menu\Programs\StartUp folder. Then click Next.
6. In the Select A Title For The Program window, type a name for the shortcut, and click Finish.

7. Click OK to complete the task. The program will automatically start the next time you start Windows.

 I want to run a program minimized in the background at all times, without manually minimizing it. How can I load and minimize a program automatically when I start Windows 98?

First, you must place a program in the StartUp folder, as discussed in the previous question about how to load a program automatically when Windows 98 boots. Then follow these instructions to have it minimized:

1. After placing a program in the StartUp folder, click Start and choose Settings | Taskbar & Start Menu.

2. Click the Start Menu Programs tab and click Advanced.

3. Click the plus sign opposite the Programs folder and open the StartUp folder.

4. Right-click the program you need and choose Properties.

5. Click the Shortcut tab and select Minimized in the Run drop-down list.

6. Click OK. The program will now start up minimized the next time you start Windows 98.

How do I load a program every time Windows starts without putting it in the StartUp folder?

Add a run command within the Win.ini file. To do this:

1. Click Start and choose Run. Open the System Configuration Editor by typing **sysedit** in the Run dialog box, click OK, and then click the Win.ini window.

2. Edit the Win.ini file by adding a Run command in the [windows] section—for example, **run=c:\progra~1\ winzip\winzip32.exe**, as shown in Figure 4-14.

Tip: *You have to use the DOS 8.3 filename and extension format (which limits filenames to a maximum of eight characters to the left of the period and three characters, usually the file type, to the right of the period), because Win.ini is a rollover from 16-bit Win 3.x.*

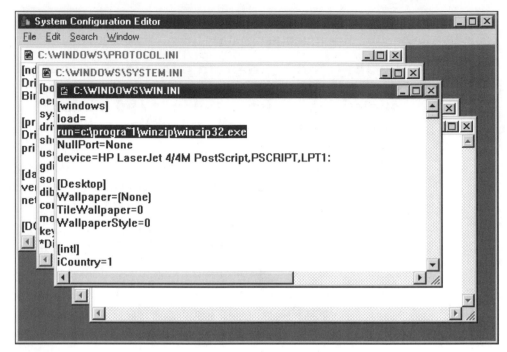

Figure 4-14   A Run command in the Win.ini file

3. Close System Configuration Editor and save the changes.

The next time you restart Windows 98 the program you entered in the Run command will open as well.

How do I remove an item from the Start menu on a local computer?

To edit the Start menu, do the following:

1. Click Start and choose Settings | Taskbar & Start Menu.

2. Click the Start Menu Programs tab and click Remove. A list of shortcuts and folders in the Start menu will be displayed.

3. Select the shortcut or folder you want to remove and then click Remove.

How can I specify a working folder for a program?

You cannot change the working folder for the original file in Windows 98—it must be done from within the program itself. However, you can create a shortcut to the original file and specify the working folder in the shortcut's Properties window. See the discussion earlier in this chapter on how to create a shortcut. Use the following steps to specify the working folder for a shortcut:

1. Right-click the shortcut and choose Properties from the context menu.

2. Click the Shortcut tab.

3. Enter the working folder in the Start In text box.

 Tip: *Many applications that have the capability within them to specify a working folder, such as Microsoft Word 97, will override the specification in the shortcut.*

What are the techniques I can use to start my programs?

You can use several techniques to start your programs, depending on how frequently you use them. Some of the most common options are to place shortcuts (or in some cases, icons, such as the taskbar toolbars) to your programs in the following locations (see the earlier discussion on creating shortcuts in the question "What is a shortcut and how do I use it to start programs from the desktop?" earlier in this chapter):

● **Directly on the desktop** by dragging the shortcut there. The shortcuts will remain where you drag them until you move or delete them unless AutoArrange is turned on.

● **To a taskbar toolbar such as the Quick Launch toolbar** by dragging a shortcut or program icon to it. (See the discussion on this earlier in this chapter.)

● **On the Start menu** by dragging the program files there. Several programs can be placed on the Start menu itself.

(See the discussion on this in the question "How can I add options to my Start menu?" earlier in this chapter.)

 In the Favorites folder, which appears on the Start menu, in folder windows, and in windows that support Internet Explorer integration. You can copy shortcuts to the \Windows\Favorites folder or choose Add To Favorites from a window that offers a Favorites menu. See Chapter 6 for more information on using the new Internet integration features of Windows 98.

 In a folder on the desktop by creating a new folder there and dragging shortcuts to it. If you leave the folder open, the shortcuts will be available at all times and you can ALT-TAB to the folder from any other program.

 In the Programs menu by dragging shortcuts in Windows Explorer to the \Windows\Start Menu\ Programs folder, either directly or to a new or an existing subfolder to group the programs. When you group them, you get to them by clicking Start, selecting Programs, and then the group.

 In the StartUp folder by dragging shortcuts in Windows Explorer to the \Windows\Start Menu\Programs\ StartUp folder. Programs in the StartUp folder are automatically started when Windows 98 is started.

Tip: *Objects on the desktop get covered by open windows, and you cannot use ALT-TAB to reach them. You can click the Show Desktop icon on the Quick Launch toolbar to see your desktop, and then click the icon again to restore any previously opened windows.*

 ## Can I uninstall a program?

If you installed a 32-bit application you can probably uninstall it using the Add/Remove Programs control panel.

This will remove the application and all its files. Try that with these steps:

1. Click Start and select Settings | Control Panel; then double-click the Add/Remove Programs icon.

2. Select the Install/Uninstall tab.

3. Select the program to be uninstalled, as shown in Figure 4-15, and click Add/Remove.

4. Click OK.

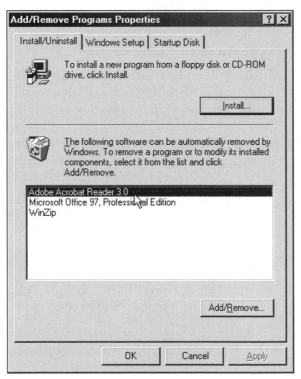

Figure 4-15 Windows 98-compliant applications can be uninstalled in the Add/Remove Programs control panel

VIDEO SETTINGS

 When I change my display settings in Windows 98, do I have to restart my computer to have the change take effect?

No, you can change both resolution and the number of colors displayed with only a short pause before they take effect. To change either of these display attributes, do the following:

1. Right-click an empty area of the desktop, choose Properties from the context menu, and click the Settings tab.

2. Choose the Colors and Screen Area settings you want and click OK.

3. Click OK in the message box that appears. Your screen should refresh in a few seconds; if not, Windows 98 will restore your original configuration.

 How can I change my video driver?

To change your video driver, use the following steps:

1. Click Start and choose Settings | Control Panel.

2. Double-click the Display icon, and then click the Settings tab.

3. Click Advanced.

4. Click Change in the Adapter tab, which starts the Update Device Driver Wizard. Click Next.

5. In the second wizard dialog box, leave the default option selected to allow Windows to search for an updated version of the correct driver. Click Next.

6. Specify a location besides your hard disk, if applicable, where Windows will search for an updated driver. The Microsoft Windows Update choice will attempt to connect you to a Microsoft Web site that maintains

updated drivers for most manufacturers. (You must register your copy of Windows 98 before you can use this feature.) Click Next.

7. Follow the remaining wizard prompts to keep your current driver or install a new one.

DISK DRIVES

I have bought a second hard drive, and I want it to be drive D, but D is my CD-ROM. How can I change the drive letter that is assigned to my CD-ROM?

Use the following steps to change a drive letter:

1. Click Start and choose Settings | Control Panel.

2. Double-click the System icon.

3. Click the Device Manager tab.

4. Click the plus sign next to CD-ROM and select your CD-ROM, click Properties, and click the Settings tab.

5. In the Reserved Drive Letters section, you can set Start Drive Letter and End Drive Letter to be the drive letter you want the CD-ROM to use, as you can see in Figure 4-16. Set it the way you want, and then click OK.

6. Reboot the computer. The CD-ROM will have the new letter. Remember, however, if you had some applications already installed from the CD-ROM using the old drive letter, you might have to redirect their requests for information from a CD.

I want to have my swap file on drive D. How do I change the location of the swap file?

To change the location, do the following:

1. Right-click My Computer and choose Properties.

2. Click the Performance tab and click Virtual Memory.

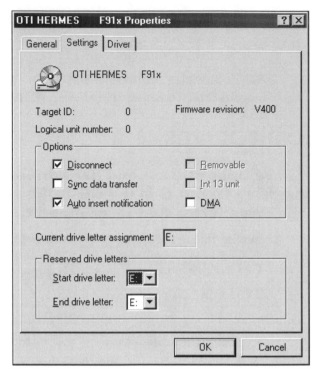

Figure 4-16 Change a CD-ROM's drive letter in its system Properties dialog box

3. Select Let Me Specify My Own Virtual Memory Settings. Then, opposite Hard Disk, select the drive you want to use, as shown in Figure 4-17. Change the Minimum and Maximum spinners to reflect how much free hard drive space you want to make available for your swap file.

Warning: *Under most circumstances, Windows 98 can do a better job of real-time management of your swap file than you can. So you should not need to take over that function.*

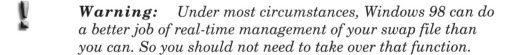

How do I change the partitions on the hard drive?

The functionality for this did not change from DOS and Windows 3.*x*. Unlike in Windows NT, you cannot adjust the partitions or create volume sets in Windows 98. You still have to use Fdisk to create partitions. See discussions in Chapter 2 on the use of Fdisk.

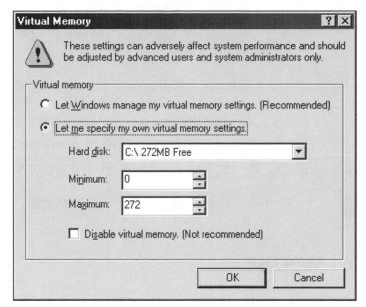

Figure 4-17   The Virtual Memory dialog box lets you specify the drive and amount of space to be dedicated to a swap file or virtual memory

My hard drive space is compressed with a third-party compression package. I wanted to partition using Fdisk to create an extra logical drive, but Fdisk shows only half of the disk space I can see using the DIR command. How can I modify partitions?

If you installed a disk compression program from Microsoft or another vendor, Fdisk displays only the uncompressed, not the compressed, size of the drives. In some instances, Fdisk cannot delete partitions created by third-party applications. You will have to use that application to delete or modify that partition.

Can I convert a removable hard drive to FAT32 in order to gain more space and decrease the cluster size?

Yes, but be aware that if you transfer the drive to a computer that does not support FAT32 (such as one with an early, or "original retail," version of Windows 95, or Windows 3.x) it cannot be read. To convert a drive or removable disk to FAT32, follow these steps:

1. Click Start and choose Programs | Accessories | System Tools | Drive Converter (FAT32). The Drive Converter (FAT32) Wizard starts. Click Next.

2. Choose the drive you want converted and click Next.

3. Follow the remaining wizard prompts to convert the drive.

Note: *You cannot compress a FAT32 drive or removable disk.*

MOUSE

How do I change my mouse behavior?

You can adjust your mouse behavior with the following steps:

1. Click Start and choose Settings | Control Panel.

2. Double-click the Mouse icon to open the Mouse Properties dialog box that you see in Figure 4-18.

3. Click the tab for the behavior you want to change:

   ● **Buttons** allows you to switch the left and right buttons and to change the speed of a double-click.

   ● **Pointers** allows you to customize the pointers that appear in specific circumstances, including animated pointers.

   ● **Motion** allows you to specify whether you want to use pointer trails and adjust the speed at which the pointer moves across the screen.

4. After changing the settings, click OK.

How do I change my mouse driver?

Follow these steps to change the mouse driver using the System Device Manager:

1. Click Start and choose Settings | Control Panel.

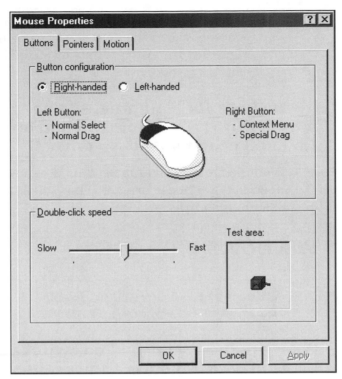

Figure 4-18 Mouse behavior is controlled in the Mouse Properties dialog box

2. Double-click the System icon, and click the Device Manager tab.

3. Click the plus sign opposite Mouse device, select your current pointing device, and click Properties.

4. Click the Driver tab and then click Update Driver. The Update Device Driver Wizard opens, allowing you to either automatically or manually search your local drives, networks, and even the Internet for updated drivers. Click Next.

5. Choose to have Windows conduct a search or allow you to select from a specific location. Click Next.

6. If you chose to have Windows search: Choose the upgraded driver found by Windows or continue using your present driver (if Windows reports that there are no

updated drivers). If you elected to locate the driver yourself, select the new driver to be used from the Manufacturer/Models lists or click Have Disk to use a non-Microsoft driver.

**In Windows for Workgroups I needed to have two mouse drivers—one for DOS and one for Windows. Do I still need two mouse drivers?**

A single mouse driver is used in Windows 98, eliminating the need for two mouse drivers. This will even save you some system resources.

WINDOWS EXPLORER

Note: *The Internet-related features of Windows Explorer, and there are many, are fully covered in Chapter 6.*

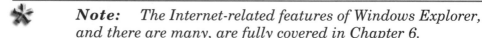**What are the command-line switches that can be used with Windows Explorer in shortcuts and batch files?**

Windows Explorer has several command-line switches that you can use in shortcuts and batch files to set it up in various ways, as you will see later in this section in the answer to the question about opening Windows Explorer at the My Computer level. The switches are entered following Explorer.exe and a space on a command line such as the Start menu Run command, a DOS command line, or the Target command line in a shortcut.

- **/e** specifies that the Explorer view will be used. This is the default view.

- **/n** specifies that a new folder window will be opened. Otherwise the Explorer view is used.

- **,/root,*object*** specifies that the root of the folders displayed will be *object,* where *object* is a drive (network or local) or a folder. Otherwise Desktop is the root. For example, the command

    Explorer.exe /e,/root,*netdrive*

opens an Explorer window with the network drive *Netdrive* as the root drive. This would allow browsing *Netdrive,* but only that drive.

● **/select,*subobject*** specifies that *subobject's* parent folder is opened and selected. For example,

Explorer.exe /e,/select,C:\

opens a Windows Explorer window with My Computer (the parent of C:\) opened and selected. The parent of whatever you specify is what gets opened and selected.

● **,*subobject*** specifies that *subobject* is the initial selected object unless it follows /select. Otherwise your C:\ drive is initially selected.

Is there a fast way to get from the desktop to the My Computer view of my C:\ drive?

Yes, there is. Here are two methods—one for "keyboarders" and one for "mousers":

1. Press CTRL-ESC or the Windows flag key on a Windows-aware keyboard, press R to open the Run dialog box, and type a backslash (\), as shown here:

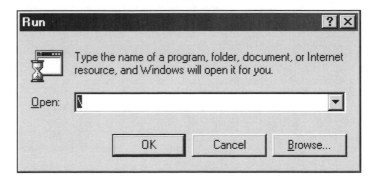

2. Press ENTER.

This method using the mouse takes a preliminary step but once accomplished offers a very quick method:

1. Open My Computer and right-drag (drag the icon with your right mouse button depressed) the C drive icon to the Quick Launch toolbar. (See the questions earlier in

this chapter on using the Quick Launch toolbar and other taskbar toolbars.)

2. Click the C drive icon.

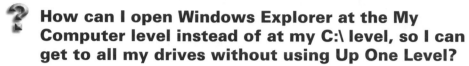

How can I open Windows Explorer at the My Computer level instead of at my C:\ level, so I can get to all my drives without using Up One Level?

To get Windows Explorer to open at the My Computer level, you will need to add command-line switches in the Target command line of the shortcut used to open Windows Explorer. Use the following set of instructions to do that:

1. Create a shortcut for Windows Explorer on your desktop, taskbar toolbar, Favorites folder, or in your Start menu.

2. Right-click the new shortcut, and choose Properties to open the Windows Explorer Properties dialog box.

3. In the Shortcut tab, edit the Target command line so that it reads

   \Windows\Explorer.exe /e,/select,C:\

   (The C:\Windows\Explorer.exe part of the command line may be different on your computer if you installed Windows 98 on a different drive and folder. Leave that part unchanged in your command line.)

   The command-line switches /e,/select, are explained earlier in answer to the question about command-line switches used with Windows Explorer. The ending C:\ should be the first hard drive within My Computer.

4. Click OK and double-click your shortcut (or select it in the Start menu) to try it out. Your results should look like Figure 4-19.

When I use Find Files Or Folders (from the Tools menu), parts of the folder name or the long filename are cut off and I see something like "C:\windows\ sys ...." Is there a way I can see the whole name?

Yes, you can increase the size of the column that shows the folder name by doing the following:

1. Point to the vertical line at the right of the box containing the field name you want to see. The pointer will become a vertical line with arrows pointing to the right and left as shown here:

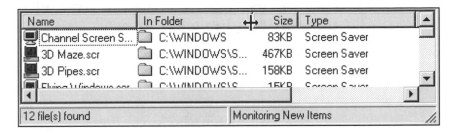

2. Double-click when you see the two-headed arrow. The column will expand to fit the longest name on the list. Or, when the two-headed arrow is displayed, drag the side of the box to the size you want.

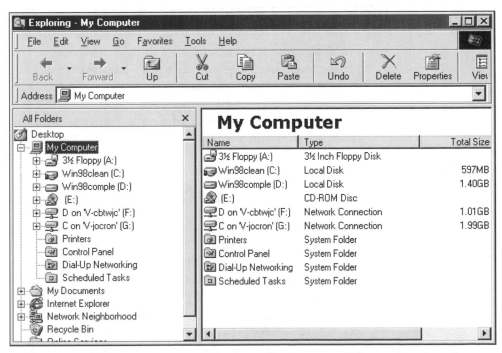

Figure 4-19   You can open Windows Explorer at different levels using command-line switches in the shortcut

 Tip: *You can also change the size of panes in Windows Explorer by dragging them.*

Can I rearrange the order of the fields in the right pane of Windows Explorer?

Yes, you can. Simply drag a field name header into the position where you want it, as shown next. The vertical line between field headers will change color when a dragged header is correctly superimposed on top of, and ready to be moved between, the two headers.

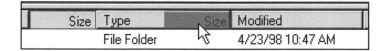

Is there any way I can get a separate window for each drive in Windows Explorer, like I could in File Manager?

No. The only way to get two windows with different drives is to open two instances of Windows Explorer. In Windows Explorer, however, you can select one drive and have it displayed in the right pane, then scroll the left pane so you can see and open the second drive. You can then drag objects from a folder in the first drive to a folder in the second drive.

ACCESSIBILITY OPTIONS AND TOOLS

 Tip: *If you did not install the Accessibility Options during setup, you can still add them to your system. Click Start, select Settings | Control Panel, and double-click Add / Remove Programs. In the Windows Setup tab, place a check mark next to Accessibility Options. Ensure that the check box has a white background (click it a second or third time) to install both Accessibility Options and Accessibility Tools. Click OK. If prompted, insert your Windows 98 CD and follow the prompts.*

How can I adjust the keyboard repeat rate?

You can change the time a key is held down before it begins repeating and the speed at which additional characters are produced in the Keyboard Properties dialog box. While these RepeatKey settings are not officially part of the Accessibility Options, they are important for people who can't lift their fingers off the keyboard quickly. Use the following steps to adjust the RepeatKey settings:

1. Click Start, choose Settings | Control Panel, and double-click Keyboard.

2. Click the Speed tab, shown in Figure 4-20, if it is not already displayed.

   ● To adjust how long a key must be held down before it begins repeating, drag the Repeat Delay slider to the setting you want.

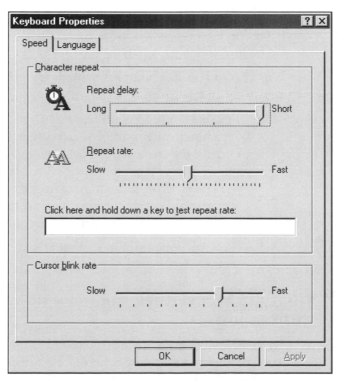

Figure 4-20 Keyboard Properties dialog box allows you to adjust the repeat rate

  ● To adjust how quickly characters repeat when you
     hold down a key, drag the Repeat Rate slider to the
     appropriate setting.

3. Click in the test box and press a key to see if your
   settings work for you. If not, make the necessary
   adjustments and test them again.

4. When you are satisfied with the settings, click OK to
   finalize them.

What are FilterKeys, and how do I implement this feature?

The FilterKeys feature desensitizes the keyboard so that it is
less likely that you will get unwanted keystrokes. Keystrokes
that are not held down for a minimum period are ignored.
This is useful for people who have tremors. The FilterKeys
option is part of the Accessibility Options. Use the following
steps to enable FilterKeys:

1. Click Start, select Settings | Control Panel, and then
   double-click Accessibility Options.

2. From the Keyboard tab, click Use FilterKeys to enable
   the feature.

3. Click Settings to open the Settings For FilterKeys dialog
   box, shown in Figure 4-21, to enable the shortcut
   (holding down RIGHT SHIFT for eight seconds); to ignore
   repeated keystrokes or quick keystrokes and slow down
   the repeat rate; to test the FilterKeys settings; and to
   determine the type of notification that FilterKeys is
   working—a beep or onscreen status display.

4. When you are finished, click OK twice to finalize
   the settings.

What are MouseKeys, and how do I implement this feature?

MouseKeys are part of the Accessibility Options that let users
control the mouse pointer using the numeric keypad as follows:

- Use the arrow keys on the numeric keypad to move the pointer horizontally or vertically.

- Use HOME, END, PGUP, and PGDN to move the pointer diagonally.

- Use 5 in the middle of the keypad as a single click and the + as a double click.

- Use / at the top of the keypad to specify that the left mouse button will be clicked when 5 is pressed. Also at the top of the keypad, use - to specify the right button and use * to specify both buttons.

- Use 0 or INS at the bottom of the keypad to lock down the mouse button for dragging and/or DEL to release the mouse button.

- Hold down SHIFT while you are using the MouseKeys to move the pointer a single pixel at a time.

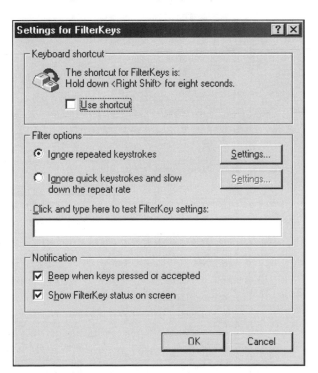

Figure 4-21 FilterKeys ignores unwanted keystrokes

To implement MouseKeys, use the following steps:

1. Click Start, select Settings | Control Panel, and double-click Accessibility Options.

2. Click the Mouse tab and select Use MouseKeys.

3. Click Settings to open the Settings For MouseKeys dialog box, shown in Figure 4-22, to vary the pointer speed and acceleration, to use CTRL or SHIFT to speed up or slow down the speed, or to use NUM LOCK as a toggle to switch MouseKeys on or off.

4. To turn MouseKeys on and off with a shortcut key, select Use Shortcut. This enables you to turn MouseKeys on or off by pressing LEFT ALT-LEFT SHIFT-NUM LOCK.

5. Click OK twice to finalize the settings.

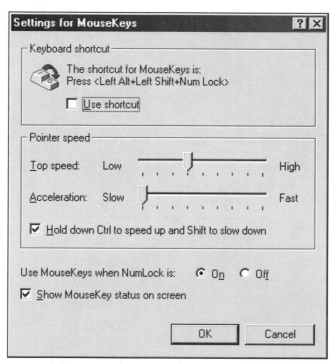

Figure 4-22 Settings For MouseKeys lets you determine how fast the mouse pointer will move

What are StickyKeys, and how do I implement this feature?

The StickyKeys feature, part of the Accessibility Options, allows users to press the keys of a key combination one at a time and have Windows respond as if the keys were pressed together. It is used with the CTRL, SHIFT, or ALT keys. Use the following steps to implement StickyKeys:

1. Click Start, select Settings | Control Panel, and then double-click Accessibility Options.

2. From the Keyboard tab, click Use StickyKeys.

3. Click Settings to open the Settings For StickyKeys dialog box to enable the shortcut (pressing SHIFT five times); to press ALT, SHIFT, or CTRL twice to lock them in for repeated use; to turn off StickyKeys when two keys are pressed at the same time; and to determine notification by sound or on screen when CTRL, SHIFT, or ALT is pressed.

4. When you are finished, click OK twice to finalize the settings.

What are ToggleKeys, and how do I implement this feature?

The ToggleKeys feature, which is part of the Accessibility Options, provides audio cues—high and low beeps—to tell users when CAPS LOCK, NUM LOCK, and SCROLL LOCK keys are pressed. A high tone will be sounded when one of the toggle keys is turned on, and a low tone when they are toggled off. Implement ToggleKeys with these steps:

1. Click Start and select Settings | Control Panel, and then double-click Accessibility Options.

2. From the Keyboard tab, click Use ToggleKeys.

3. Click Settings and select Use Shortcut to enable the shortcut (holding down NUM LOCK for five seconds).

4. When you are finished, click OK twice to finalize the settings.

 Is there a way to quickly enlarge the screen without changing resolution or font size?

You bet. Windows 98 provides a new feature called Magnifier that shows a magnified view of the portion of the screen that is under the mouse pointer, or if you are predominately using the keyboard, under the insertion point. In either case the Magnifier follows the mouse or keyboard commands as they are given. Start Magnifier with these steps:

1. Click Start and choose Programs | Accessories | Accessibility | Magnifier.

2. Select a magnification level (1 being the same level as you see on your screen; 9 being most magnified) and other supporting options. The upper part of your screen displays the magnified area, as shown in Figure 4-23.

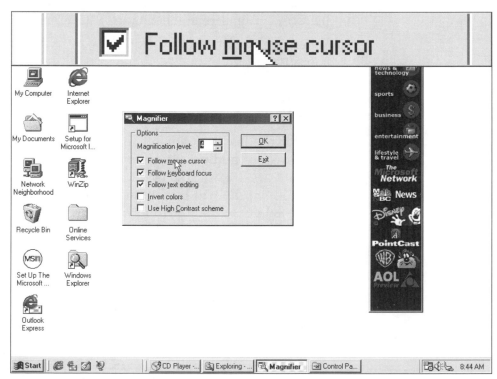

Figure 4-23   Quickly enlarge screen objects using the Magnifier

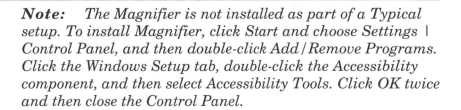

 ***Note:*** *The Magnifier is not installed as part of a Typical setup. To install Magnifier, click Start and choose Settings | Control Panel, and then double-click Add/Remove Programs. Click the Windows Setup tab, double-click the Accessibility component, and then select Accessibility Tools. Click OK twice and then close the Control Panel.*

OPTIMIZING WINDOWS

I've got Windows 98 installed, but it's not performing as well as I had hoped. Is there anything I can do to increase performance?

Windows 98 is self-optimizing, so there isn't much you can do short of buying more memory and a faster CPU. However, here are some things to try:

- Click Start and choose Settings | Control Panel. Then double-click System. Once the System control panel is opened, click the Performance tab and Windows 98 may give you some suggestions on what you can do to increase performance or tell you that your system is configured for optimal performance.

- Defragment your hard drive(s) using the Windows 98 Disk Defragmenter utility (from the Start menu, select Programs | Accessories | System Tools). This can greatly increase disk performance. See Chapter 7 for information on the Disk Defragmenter.

Can I change the time interval, which seems to put my computer to "sleep?"

Sure. Windows 98 provides options for powering down both your monitor and hard drives for common computing situations such as desktop and laptop environments. Adjust these power schemes with these steps:

1. Click Start and choose Settings | Control Panel, and then double-click Power Management.

2. Choose a power scheme that most closely matches your computing style and then choose the intervals for the power-saving shutdown of your monitor and hard drives.

3. Click OK when done.

 Tip: *To display a power meter on the taskbar (especially helpful for laptop users monitoring their battery status) click the Advanced tab and select the related check box.*

In Windows 3.1, a permanent swap file works better than a temporary one. Is it still true for Windows 98?

No. Windows 98 dynamically manages the swap file, which can grow and shrink as necessary. In this sense, its behavior is closer to a Windows 3.*x* temporary swap file. However, it is free of many of the limitations of Windows 3.*x* swap files:

● The Windows 98 swap file does not have to occupy contiguous disk space.

● The Windows 98 swap file can be located on a compressed drive.

● The Windows 98 swap file can be located anywhere the user wants, not just in the root of the boot drive.

It is recommended that you let Windows 98 manage the swap file for you.

How can I view how much of my Windows 98 resources I'm using?

There are a few features you can use to view various internal system resources: Microsoft System Information, Resource Meter, and About Windows.

Microsoft System Information

Microsoft System Information provides a two-pane window scheme similar to Windows Explorer that lets you view a substantial amount of information about your computer, as

shown in Figure 4-24. To open the Microsoft System Information window, click the Start menu and choose Programs | Accessories | System Tools | System Information.

Resource Meter

The Resource Meter gives you a visual indication of the system resources that are being used. If you did a Typical installation you must separately install the Resource Meter through the Control Panel's Add/Remove Programs utility. To start the Resource Meter:

1. Click the Start menu and choose Programs | Accessories | System Tools | Resource Meter.

2. Click OK to acknowledge the message telling you that the Resource Meter will consume some computing resources to run.

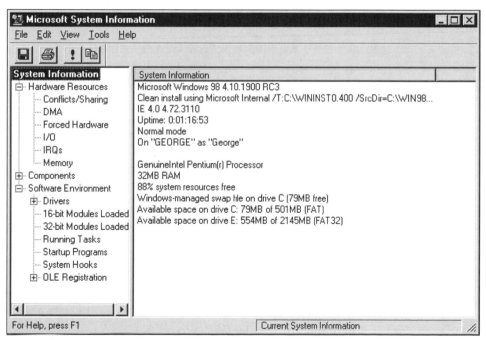

Figure 4-24   The Microsoft System Information window

3. Double-click the taskbar icon to see the meter, as shown here:

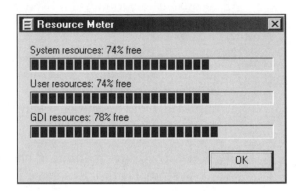

About Windows

The About Windows dialog box gives you a quick snapshot of your system resources usage. You can look at it by opening a folder window, opening the Help menu, and then clicking About Windows 98.

 ## How can I speed up the Start menu?

You can use Regedit to make changes to the Registry that speed up the menu display.

 Warning: *Regedit is a very crude editing tool and gives you no help for what you are doing. It's like doing surgery blindfolded. Incorrect changes to the Registry can cause Windows not to boot. You therefore need to make very sure that you only change what you intend to change and that you understand exactly what to change.* ***Always back up System.dat and User.dat before using Regedit***.

The Registry uses two files, System.dat and User.dat, in the Windows folder. It is strongly recommended that you create backups of these files before modifying the files with Regedit. Use the following instructions to make the backups and then use Regedit:

1. In Windows Explorer, open the Windows folder, right-click System.dat, and choose Copy from the context menu that appears.

2. Right-click a blank area of the right Windows Explorer pane within the Windows folder, and choose Paste to paste a copy of System.dat. It will be named "Copy of System.dat."

3. Repeat steps 1 and 2 for User.dat.

4. Click Start and choose Run.

5. Type **regedit** and click OK to open the Registry Editor.

6. In the left pane, click the plus signs opposite HKEY_CURRENT_USER and Control Panel to open them.

7. Right-click Desktop and select New and String Value, as shown in Figure 4-25.

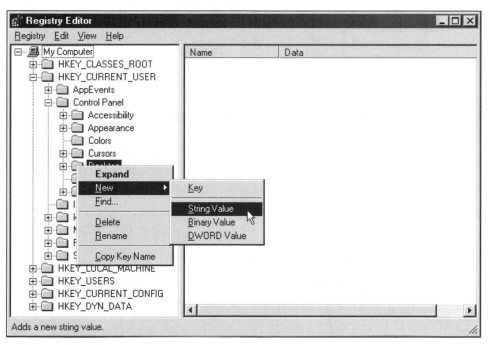

Figure 4-25 Creating a new Registry entry

8. In the new entry that appears in the right pane, type **MenuShowDelay** (all one word) for the name and press ENTER.

9. Double-click the new entry to open the Edit String dialog box. In the Value Data text box, type a value from 10 to 1, with 1 being the fastest. Try **4** and click OK.

10. Exit the Registry Editor (the file is automatically saved) and restart Windows. Take a look at how fast you can access your Start menu items!

If you make a mistake and your system won't boot, boot into DOS, change to the Windows folder, copy Copy of System.dat to System.dat and Copy of User.dat to User.dat, and then boot again.

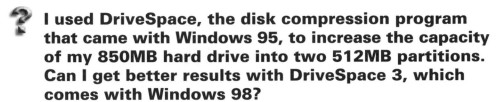

I used DriveSpace, the disk compression program that came with Windows 95, to increase the capacity of my 850MB hard drive into two 512MB partitions. Can I get better results with DriveSpace 3, which comes with Windows 98?

Certainly. DriveSpace 3 is not limited to the 512MB barrier that affected earlier compression routines and can compress drives up to 2GB. You can either maintain your current two partitions and compress both to achieve the approximate 1.7GB maximum total compressed space, or you can Fdisk your drive and return to one 850MB partition, reinstall Windows 98, and compress to a single 1.7GB compressed drive.

 Note: *You cannot compress a FAT32 drive or removable disk.*

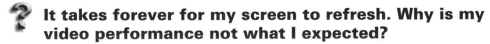

It takes forever for my screen to refresh. Why is my video performance not what I expected?

The controls that are available to change video performance vary, depending on your display adapter card. The controls you do have are reached by opening the Control Panel, double-clicking the System icon, selecting the Performance tab, and clicking Graphics. Depending on your controls, try dragging the Hardware Acceleration slider to each of the four positions and reading the type of problems that setting is optimized to fix.

I increased my virtual memory swap file size to 30MB, and now my system seems to run much more slowly. Why?

By default, Windows 98 will optimize your virtual memory settings for peak performance. When you force a given swap file size, it may adversely affect performance by causing Windows to manage (use) more of a swap file than it would otherwise use in optimal circumstances.

Tip: *For your best performance, let Windows maintain your virtual memory settings.*

Chapter 5

Using Windows 98 (Traditional)

Answer Topics!

Using Windows 98 (Traditional) @ a Glance

Windows 98 could have been easily named Janus 98 in honor of the two-faced Roman god. You can choose an appearance and display functionality almost identical to what you have seen in Windows 95. Or, you can depart from the "traditional" and enter into the world of a Weblike interface, or *Active Desktop,* where your desktop and the online environments of the Internet and intranets merge. This chapter concentrates on the former, as well as the common features that apply to both ways of using Windows 98. Chapter 6 focuses on the Web features.

When you're using Windows 98 and everything is working as expected, you're in fat city! Hopefully, this occurs most of the time. This chapter, however, addresses unexpected situations. Some of the main questions revolve around these areas:

- **Booting Situations** discusses problems that can occur while you are booting or loading Windows 98. Some of the questions involve other operating systems running with or instead of Windows 98.

- **Shortcuts** describes how shortcuts are used and why they sometimes disappear.

- **Drag-and-Drop** covers questions you may have while attempting to drag and drop objects and files.

- **Windows Environment** describes several situations that cause your environment to look or act differently from what you expect. These questions often arise from differences between Windows 98 and Windows 95/3.1, or from a lack of understanding of how Windows 98 now handles certain tasks.

- **WordPad** addresses questions that commonly arise in this Windows 98 text editor.

- **Equipment-Related Problems** discusses problems that can occur with equipment that is standard or nonstandard for Windows 98.

- **Other Problems** covers a variety of questions arising while you are using Windows 98.

Starting Basics

Using Windows 98 begins with finding your way around the computer. You'll learn that it's easy and intuitive. First, you have a Start menu that calls to you, "Start here!" When you do, you'll find options that display programs neatly listed in a menu, documents and files that you frequently use, important settings that control your display and many other elements of your computer; a Find command for searching your files, system Help, and a Run option where you can enter DOS commands. In addition to these basic Start menu options, you can place several other options on the Start menu that let you quickly access the programs and folders you use most frequently. When the number of options exceed the height of your screen, arrows appear at the top and bottom of the menu to allow you to scroll to any hidden options.

On the Start menu and elsewhere in Windows 98, there are a number of tools and convenient ways of getting around that make Windows 98 easy and fun to use. For the first-time user, understanding four facilities of the system is of primary importance in effectively using it. These are the Start menu, the taskbar, the right mouse button, and file management with Explorer, My Computer, and the Network Neighborhood. If you are just beginning, take a minute and look at what you can do with each of these.

- The **Start menu** contains all the information, programs, and tools to get you started using your computer. You open the Start menu by clicking Start, and you can select one of the menu *options* by clicking it. The top five options (below the separator bar, which distinguishes between user options and system options) open a submenu with additional options. You need only point to—you don't have to click—an option if its function is to open a submenu. The purpose of the initial Start menu options (before you add your own) is as follows:

  - **Programs** displays two or more *program groups* at the top of the submenu that, when you point on them, display another submenu listing programs and folders making up that group, as you can see in Figure 5-1. You'll find both Windows 98 groups, such as Accessories and Internet Explorer along with many

valuable small applications or *applets,* and your own groups, perhaps with word processing, spreadsheet, or database programs. At the bottom of the Programs submenu you will have two to four programs (depending on what Windows 98 options you installed) that you simply click to activate.

● **Favorites** allows you access to key Internet features such as "push" technology channels (described in Chapter 6) and any other items you place in your Favorites folder. You can place often-used files, folders, shortcuts, and Internet addresses in this folder. The Favorites folder is accessible throughout Windows 98 in many menus and toolbars.

● **Documents** displays a shortcut to your My Documents folder, a convenient location to store your work, and lists the last 15 documents that you worked on and that were directly activated by double-clicking them or were opened from a shortcut. When you click a document or file that is *associated* with an application, that application will load and the selected file will be opened and ready to use. You will find that this list rapidly fills up with documents, graphics, clip art, and other files that are handy to have at your fingertips.

● **Settings** gives you fast access to the Control Panel, where you can change most of the hardware and user settings (Chapter 4 describes the most common control panels). Settings also gives you access to a Printers folder, where you can control all the printers, local and networked, that you have available, including fax machines. Settings gives you direct access to the taskbar properties, which allows you to vary the taskbar display, even hiding it if you want, and enables you to add programs to the Start menu, either on the top of it or contained within the Programs submenu. You can modify how folder windows behave from the Folder Options selection and control the Web display features of the Active Desktop. Finally, you can go online and check a database of drivers maintained by Microsoft to see if you are using the most current software.

● **Find** allows you to search for files and folders on any disk drive to which you have access, to search for a computer on your

network, or to search for an item on the Internet. You can also access Internet "white pages" where you can attempt to find other people using Internet e-mail. Find is a powerful tool that allows you to search using criteria other than name, such as date, text content, file type.

- **Help** brings up the Windows 98 Help system, which is comprehensive in its coverage of the features and how to use them. You can look at an overview of the Help system, learn some tips and tricks, or be led through a troubleshooting procedure. You can search for an item by subject, indexed alphabetically. Finally, you can search for all references to a subject in a database consisting of all words and phrases in the Help system.

- **Run** provides a command line on which you can type a DOS command or directly initiate a program, or open a folder by typing in its path and name. This is the same as the Run command line in Windows 3.*x*.

- **Log Off** lets you quickly exit Windows 98, allowing other users to log on and use their own profiles on the same computer. Each user profile lets you customize such display items as icons on the desktop and the user options you can add to the Start menu. The Log Off option is also used when you are connected to a network.

- **Shut Down** allows you to gracefully shut down Windows 98 by first saving any open files or reminding you to do so, and then deleting any temporary files that have been in use and are no longer needed. The Shut Down option gives you the option to restart your computer, the equivalent of rebooting, either back into Windows or to DOS. You can protect yourself from losing unsaved information by always using Shut Down when leaving Windows 98 and, only when you are told it's safe, turning off your computer.

- The **taskbar**, which is normally at the bottom of the screen, offers several methods to open your most-used programs and enables you to switch among multiple programs that are already running on your computer. Next to Start is the Quick Launch toolbar, one of many toolbars you can display on the taskbar, which displays a "starter kit" of program icons Microsoft thinks you'll find handy. You can easily drag to it your own program, shortcut, or folder icon. To the right of the Quick Launch toolbar is space for other toolbars and tasks. The taskbar displays each running program as a *task*—a rectangle with the name and icon of the program (see Figure 5-2). After a program is started (see the discussion in Chapter 4 on starting programs), its task appears on the taskbar. When you want to switch from one program to another, you simply click the task for the program you want to use. The program you are switching to opens on the screen. The program you left is still active in memory; it just may not be visible. With the taskbar, you will always know what programs are active, and you'll be able to get to them immediately. As well as the active program tasks, the taskbar contains, in addition to the clock, special status icons that, for example, tell you what maintenance programs you have scheduled to run, or that indicate your connection to the Internet is active, or that allow you to control the volume of your sound system.

- The **right mouse button**, which was largely ignored in Windows 3.*x*, takes a significant role in Windows 98. Most importantly, when you *right-click* an object (a folder, a file, the desktop, or the taskbar), a *context* menu appears that provides options related to the object you clicked on. These context menus, some of which are shown in Figure 5-3, contain many different options. Most of them contain a Properties option that will open a Properties dialog box that gives you information about the object and lets you change its settings. Additionally, you can drag files and folders using the right mouse button and, when you are done dragging, get a context menu that allows you to copy, move, or create a shortcut for the object you dragged.

- **Explorer, My Computer,** and **Network Neighborhood** are the navigating and file management tools within Windows 98. You use them to find a file, a folder, or a networked computer. Chapter 7 discusses these tools more. Explorer is found on the Start | Programs menu. You'll want to place a shortcut to it on the Start menu, the Quick Launch toolbar, or even on the desktop. My Computer and Network Neighborhood are already on the desktop for your quick use.

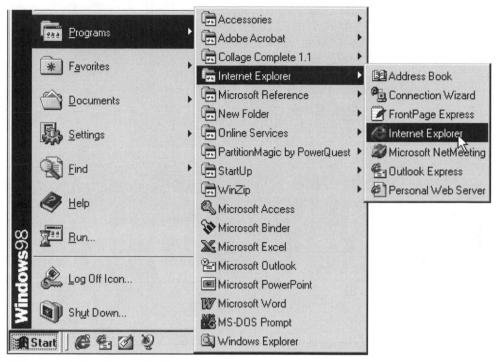

Figure 5-1 From the Start menu you can open a program group and select a program

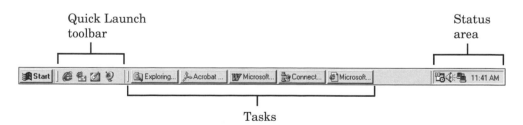

Figure 5-2 The taskbar lets you switch among programs that are running

Desktop context menu

Taskbar context menu

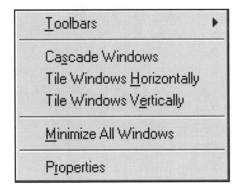

File context menu

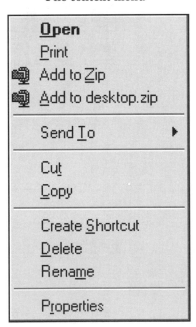

Folder context menu

Figure 5-3 The right mouse button opens context menus such as these

BOOTING SITUATIONS

 I installed Windows 98 to a clean folder instead of updating my current version of Windows 3.*x*. When I boot to my previous version of DOS and then launch Windows 3.*x*, I get a message that states my swap file is corrupt and that I can delete it and create a new one. How can I boot both Windows 3.1 and 98 at different points?

You can do one of three things to rectify this problem:

● Delete the swap file as prompted, and when Windows 3.*x* starts, go to the Control Panel and then click on 386 Enhanced. Click Virtual Memory, and then click Change. Then create a temporary swap file instead of a permanent one.

● You could install Windows 98 on a different drive than the previous version of Windows 3.*x*.

● You could set up a permanent swap file in Windows 3.*x* and then add the following lines to the 386Enh section of the Windows 98 System.ini:

    PagingFile=<Win31xPagingFile>
    MinPagingFileSize=<SizeInk>

<Win31PagingFile> is the swap file (usually C:\386part. par), and <SizeInk> is the size of <Win31PagingFile> divided by 1,024.

 Warning: *FAT32 (32-bit file allocation table) disk formatting does not support dual booting. Windows 98 can be installed using either FAT16 (used in Windows 3.x and earlier versions of Windows 95) or as FAT32 (used in the later, or OSR2, release of Windows 95). If you want to dual boot, make sure you do not choose FAT32. If you do not choose FAT32 you will not be able to take advantage of several of its benefits, such as accessing hard disks or partitions in excess of 2GB.*

How can I boot directly into Safe mode, bypassing the Windows 98 Start menu?

As the computer is booting, you can enter Safe mode by pressing F5 before Windows 98 begins loading. During booting, the computer first checks itself and then displays a list of the computer's components in a rectangle on the screen. After the check, it begins to load Windows. You must wait until the computer has checked itself, and then immediately press F5. You will boot directly into Safe mode.

Tip: *If you press F8 at that time, you will get a menu of booting options. From the menu you can choose Safe Mode (or Safe Mode Command Prompt Only). The Chapter 1 question, "How do I do a clean boot for Windows 98?" describes each of the booting menu options in detail.*

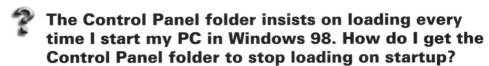 ## The Control Panel folder insists on loading every time I start my PC in Windows 98. How do I get the Control Panel folder to stop loading on startup?

There are three possible ways a folder will be automatically opened at startup. These are as follows:

- The folder was open when Windows 98 was shut down. If so, close the Control Panel and then restart Windows 98. Normally that should take care of it.

- A shortcut to the Control Panel was placed in the \Windows\Start Menu\Programs\StartUp folder. If so, drag the Control Panel icon out of the folder.

- The Win.ini file has a Run=Control Panel statement. Use Notepad to edit the Win.ini file, and change the statement to just Run=.

 ## How do I create a Windows 98 Startup disk if I didn't do it during setup?

Tip: *A Startup floppy disk can be a lifeline if you can't boot from your hard disk. You should create, try out, and keep handy a Startup disk now before you need it.*

You can easily create a *Startup* or *boot disk* from within Windows 98. Follow these steps:

1. Click Start, choose Settings | Control Panel, and double-click Add/Remove Programs.

2. Click the Startup Disk tab, and click Create Disk, as shown in Figure 5-4. Follow the prompts. Make sure you are using a blank high-density disk, because all of the files on the disk will be deleted and replaced with the boot programs.

 Tip: *If you originally installed from a CD-ROM, you'll be asked to insert your Windows 98 CD-ROM to create the Startup disk.*

When I start Windows 98, it comes up with an error message asking me to change my video display settings. How can I find the problem?

To troubleshoot the problem:

1. Reboot your computer.

2. During startup press F8. Select Safe Mode. This starts with the most basic VGA display driver.

3. When Windows 98 is loaded, click Start and choose Settings | Control Panel.

Figure 5-4 Creating a Startup disk after installation

4. Double-click Display and then click the Settings tab.

5. Click Advanced and then the Adapter tab.

6. Click Change to start the Update Device Driver Wizard and click Next.

7. Choose the second option to display a list of drivers to install. Click Next.

8. Choose the Show All Hardware option and click Next to test successively more sophisticated display drivers.

 Note: *If you use a third-party display driver, you may have to get a new driver from the card manufacturer. Most manufacturers offer drivers you can download from their Web sites.*

9. Using Notepad, check System.ini to see what driver is installed by looking at the line

   display.drv=*some.drv*

   where *some.drv* is the driver name you are looking for.

When I reboot the system, I receive the following error message: "Bad or missing Command Interpreter, enter name of Command Interpreter (c:\windows\command.com)." What does this mean, and what do I do about it?

This message can occur when the Windows 98 or the MS-DOS command interpreter (Command.com) is missing or has become corrupted.

To restore the operating system and make the hard disk bootable, do the following:

1. Boot the system using your Windows 98 Startup disk.

2. To move the Windows 98 basic programs to the hard disk from the floppy, type **sys c:** at the MS-DOS command prompt.

3. After the programs have transferred from the floppy disk to the hard disk, remove the disk and reboot the

computer. You may need to reinstall Windows 98, but you will now be able to boot from your hard drive.

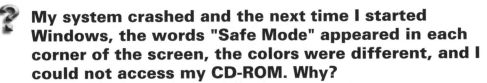 **On one of my PCs I used to have the NT server with a dual-boot configuration. Since then I installed Windows 98 and deleted NT from my hard disk. When I boot, I still must choose between Windows 98 or NT. How do I safely get rid of the dual boot for the deleted NT?**

To eliminate the NT dual boot, do the following:

1. Make sure you have recently backed up your critical files in case this gets messed up.

2. Use your Windows 98 Startup floppy disk (see earlier question on creating a Startup disk) to boot into MS-DOS.

3. Type **sys c:**, which overwrites the NT boot sector on the C drive with a DOS boot sector.

4. Reboot off your hard disk into Windows 98.

My system crashed and the next time I started Windows, the words "Safe Mode" appeared in each corner of the screen, the colors were different, and I could not access my CD-ROM. Why?

If Windows 98 detects a problem during startup or detects that a previous startup did not successfully complete, it then starts in a special troubleshooting mode called Safe mode. This means that all your system files (Config.sys, Autoexec.bat, and all .INI files) are bypassed; no network, printer, or CD-ROM drivers are loaded; and only the standard VGA driver is loaded. This is done so that you can identify the reason for the system crash and make necessary changes.

To figure out what caused the problem, question yourself about what's been happening on your computer. For example: What was the last thing you did before the crash? Did you add a new driver? Retrace your steps and remove the driver. Did you install a printer? Remove it. If you were just working with an application, run ScanDisk (Start | Programs | Accessories | System Tools | ScanDisk). It will report any

problems with your hard drive. Then click Start | Shut Down and choose Restart. If everything is OK, you will get your regular Windows screen. If you are still getting the Safe mode screen, you might have to continue troubleshooting.

What switches are available to start Windows from the command prompt when I need to isolate an error?

Using switches during booting enables you to diagnose problems. When you are having problems bringing up Windows 98, you can use the /d (for diagnostics) switch. This allows you to create an environment to troubleshoot your problem.

Follow these steps:

1. Boot to the MS-DOS environment either by selecting Restart In MS-DOS Mode from the Shut Down Windows dialog box, or by pressing F8 and selecting option 5, Command Prompt Only during startup.

2. At the command prompt, type the following command:

   win /d:*switch*

   where *switch* is one of the following switches:

   - **f**   This disables 32-bit disk access. Use this if the computer seems to have disk problems or if Windows stalls. (This is the same as the statement "32bitdiskaccess=false" in the System.ini file.)

   - **m**   This starts Windows in Safe mode. Use this if you are having trouble booting. You can accomplish the same thing by pressing F5 while booting or by choosing option 3 from the Microsoft Windows 98 Startup Menu reached by pressing F8 while booting.

   - **n**   This starts Windows in Safe mode with networking. Use this if you need network access for your Windows 98 files. You can accomplish the same thing by pressing F6 while booting.

   - **s**   This prevents Windows from using the upper-memory ROM address space between

F000 and FFFF for a break point. Use this if Windows stalls during startup. (This is the same as the "SystemRombreakpoint= false" statement in the System.ini file.)

- **v** This causes the system ROM to handle interrupts from the hard disk controller instead of Windows 98. Use this if you are having disk problems. (This is the same as the statement "VirtualHDIRQ=false" in the System.ini file.)

- **x** This prevents Windows from using any of the upper-memory area A000-FFFF. Use this if you suspect an upper-memory conflict. (This is the same as the statement "EMMexclude=A000-FFFF" in the System.ini file.)

While Windows 98 is loading, an error occurs during video adapter initialization. My computer stalls and I have to press CTRL-ALT-DEL to restart it. How do I change my video driver back to VGA?

To change your video driver, do the following:

1. Restart your computer, and during startup press F8 and choose option 3, Safe Mode.

2. When in Windows 98, click Start and choose Settings | Control Panel.

3. Double-click Display and then click the Settings tab.

4. Click Advanced, and then click Change on the Adapter tab.

5. Click Next when the Update Device Drive Wizard starts and then choose the second option to display a list of drivers. Click Next again.

6. Click Show All Hardware. Under Manufacturers click Standard Display Types, and under Models click Standard Display Adapter (VGA) or Standard PCI Display Adapter (VGA), depending on the type of video card you have (see Figure 5-5). Then click OK.

7. Click Next and then Finish to install the driver

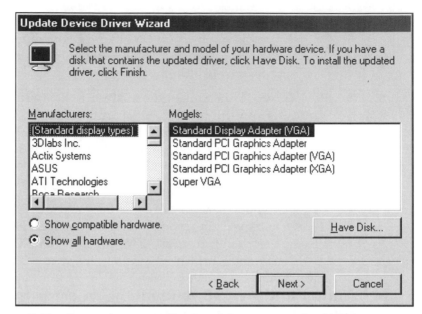

Figure 5-5 Returning your display driver to standard VGA

 Can I warm-boot Windows 98 without rebooting the PC?

Yes. Do the following:

1. Click Start and choose Shut Down.
2. Click Restart.
3. Hold down SHIFT and click OK. This will only restart Windows 98, not the computer (warm boot). This is a lot faster than a normal (cold) reboot.

SHORTCUTS

 How are shortcuts used?

A *shortcut* is a small (under 1K) file that references another file. A shortcut allows you to remotely load a program, open a folder, or access an object (like a printer or a dial-up network connection) by double-clicking the shortcut. You can place a shortcut in a convenient location, for example, on the Start menu (where you only have to single-click it), on the Quick Launch toolbar, or on the desktop. That way, you don't have to search the computer or open a number of folders to find the original object, program, or folder.

There are several ways to create a shortcut, as explained in Chapter 4. Probably the easiest is to right-drag the original file, folder, or object to where you want the shortcut and then select Create Shortcut(s) Here from the context menu. If the file is a program file (a file with an .EXE, .COM, .BAT, or .PIF extension), you can drag it normally (using the left mouse button) to where you want the shortcut, and a shortcut will be created. You can tell that an icon represents a shortcut if the icon contains an arrow, like the one shown here:

Sometimes I create a shortcut and then it seems to disappear. Where does it go?

As a rule of thumb, the shortcut is created in the same folder with the original. If the original is on the desktop, the shortcut will be added to the desktop. In My Computer or Explorer, the shortcut will be created in the same folder as the original. On the other hand, if you are in the Find window and create a shortcut, you may not see it unless you rerun the search. The shortcut to an object, such as a printer or a modem, will by default be placed on the desktop.

DRAG-AND-DROP

How do I drag an item from a Program Manager group to the Windows 98 desktop?

Program Manager, designed to ease the transition between Windows 98 and Windows 3.*x*, does not provide drag-and-drop from its groups to the Windows 98 desktop.

Even though Program Manager ships with Windows 98, it is still a 16-bit application and only has drag-and-drop within its windows.

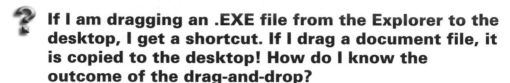

If I am dragging an .EXE file from the Explorer to the desktop, I get a shortcut. If I drag a document file, it is copied to the desktop! How do I know the outcome of the drag-and-drop?

By design, Windows 98 treats program files differently from data files. If you drag an .EXE or .COM file to the desktop, you create a shortcut. If you drag holding down the CTRL key, the file is copied to the desktop. If you drag holding down the SHIFT key, the file is moved to the desktop.

If you drag a data file (a .DOC, .BMP, .XLS, or any type other than .EXE or .COM) to the desktop, the file is moved to the desktop (assuming both locations are on the same drive). You get the same result of moving the file if you drag holding down the SHIFT key. If you drag holding down the CTRL key, the file is copied to the desktop, and if you hold down both CTRL and SHIFT, you will create a shortcut to the data file.

How can I use drag-and-drop with the left mouse button and also with the right mouse button? Is there a difference?

Using the left mouse button and dragging a folder or file, you will have different results depending on the keys you hold down as you are dragging, as follows:

Keys Held	Effect
None	Moves folders and nonprogram files; makes a shortcut of program files (ones with an extension of .EXE or .COM)
CTRL	Copies all selected folders and files
SHIFT	Moves all selected folders and files
CTRL-SHIFT	Makes a shortcut for all selected folders and files

Right button drag-and-drop gives you a context menu when you drop the object, asking if you want to move, copy, or create a shortcut:

Move Here
Copy Here
Create Shortcut(s) Here
_____
Cancel

 Tip: *When transferring files between drives on your computer or on a network, a left mouse button drag copies the file by default. Press SHIFT to move the file.*

 ## How come when I drag a window by its title bar it doesn't follow the mouse pointer, it just shows an outline of the window?

Depending on your preference, you can choose to have the window follow the mouse pointer as you drag. To change the way windows are dragged, do the following:

1. Right-click on the desktop and select Properties from the context menu.
2. Click the Effects tab and select Show Window Contents While Dragging.
3. Click OK.

WINDOWS ENVIRONMENT

 ## How can I access the desktop if it is hidden behind open applications?

Click the Show Desktop icon on the Quick Launch toolbar or right-click an empty area of the taskbar, and choose Minimize All Windows from the context menu; or press ALT-M when the taskbar is selected.

 Tip: *You can restore the windows you closed to their original position by either clicking the Show Desktop icon a second time or, after using Minimize All Windows, right-clicking the taskbar and selecting Undo Minimize All.*

How can I add a program that's on my Start menu to my desktop?

You can easily move or copy one of the user programs from the Start menu to the desktop. You cannot change the programs below the separator bar. Use these steps to add a program to the desktop:

1. Right-drag the shortcut from the Start menu to the desktop.

2. Select Move Here or Copy Here from the context menu.

 Note: *If you do a regular drag-and-drop here, you will move the program to the desktop, not copy it.*

In Add/Remove Programs on the Control Panel (Windows Setup tab), the size in bytes in the Components list is different from the size specified for the Space Required displayed below it. Why?

The two sizes are calculated differently and give you different information. The size you see beside each component listed is the total of the files in that component. The size for the Space Required is calculated by using the cluster size of the hard disk you are installing them on, which varies depending on the size of the hard disk and how it is formatted.

Other than using the Programs menu system, are there any alternative ways that I can run an application?

Yes, there are a number of alternatives. Here are some of them:

● Double-click a shortcut icon created on the desktop by dragging the program's .EXE file there.

● Click an icon on the Quick Launch toolbar, created by dragging a shortcut or program's .EXE file to the toolbar.

- Click an option in the Start menu itself (not the Programs submenu), created by dragging the program's .EXE file to Start.
- Click Start, choose the Run command, type the application's path and filename, and press ENTER.

 Why can't I see my taskbar even when Always On Top is checked in the taskbar Properties Options dialog box?

Sometimes the taskbar is dragged too low on the screen and disappears from view. Place your pointer on the bottom of the screen until it turns into an arrow, as shown here:

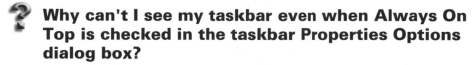

Then drag upward and release the mouse. The taskbar will reappear on the screen.

 Tip: *If you also have Auto Hide enabled, the taskbar will not be visible until you move the pointer to the edge of the screen where the taskbar is.*

 How can I capture my screen in Windows 98?

The PRINT SCREEN key on your keyboard will copy the image on your screen to the Clipboard. You can then paste that image into a document. You can use PRINT SCREEN in the following ways:

- To copy an image of the entire screen, press PRINT SCREEN.
- To copy an image of the window that is currently active, press ALT-PRINT SCREEN.
- To paste the image into a document, select Edit | Paste in the document window.

 When using Explorer, I get an Edit option when I right-click the Autoexec.bat file, but not when I right-click Config.sys. How can I edit Config.sys from the Windows Explorer window?

Windows 98 has attached a special property to .BAT files that brings up the Edit option. You can edit your Config.sys file in Explorer in several ways:

- Double-click the file and then select Notepad as the application to open the file.

- Right-click the file, choose Open With, and select Notepad to open the file.

- Run Sysedit by clicking Start | Run, and typing **sysedit** on the command line. This opens the System Configuration Editor (see Figure 5-6), which opens many of the system files for editing.

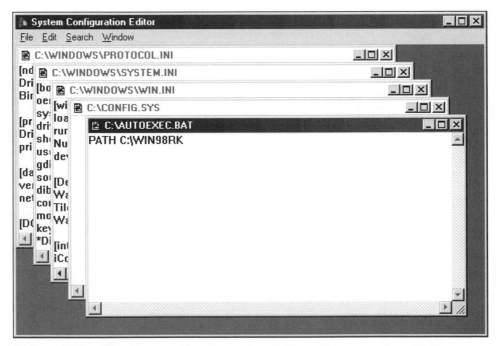

Figure 5-6 The System Configuration Editor allows you to edit your system files

> **_Tip:_** _If you don't see the system files in Explorer, select View | Folder Options. In the View tab select Show All Files. By default Windows 98 will hide files with system and hidden attributes._

How do I get rid of the standard icons on my desktop?

Microsoft provides selective Delete ability for the standard desktop icons. By right-clicking an icon you can tell from its context menu whether Microsoft thinks you should be able to remove it or not. But not to worry; you can even remove those that don't seemingly give you a Delete option by running Tweak UI, a utility that's included on your Windows 98 CD. (See the question in Chapter 4 on Tweak UI for installation instructions.) Take control of your desktop with these steps:

1. Click Start and choose Settings | Control Panel.
2. Double-click Tweak UI, and then click the Desktop tab.
3. Select or clear the check boxes to add or remove desktop icons, as shown in Figure 5-7.
4. Click OK when done.

How can I install a program in Windows 98 when there is no File | Run option?

You may install a program in two ways: by directly loading the program's Install or Setup programs (see the following steps), or by using Windows 98's Add/Remove Programs utility. If you use Add/Remove Programs, you will be guided through placing the program on a menu, perhaps within a program group, and can assign an icon to it.

Follow these steps to directly run the program's own installation procedure:

1. Click Start and choose Run.
2. Type in the command (for example, **a:\setup**), or choose it from the drop-down list if you have recently run Setup from your A drive.

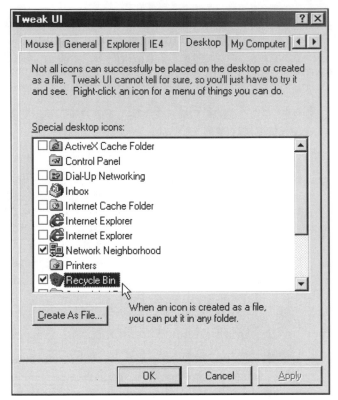

Figure 5-7 Tweak UI lets you really manage your desktop

Follow these instructions to use Add/Remove Programs:

1. Click Start and choose Settings | Control Panel.

2. Double-click Add/Remove Programs, and the Add/Remove Programs Properties dialog box will open, as shown in Figure 5-8.

3. Click Install and follow along as the Installation Wizard leads you through the process.

 Tip: *Only applications written specifically for Windows 95/98 can be completely removed by use of Add/Remove Programs.*

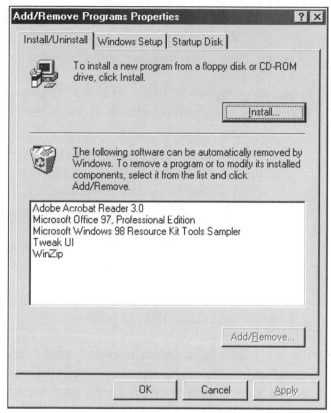

Figure 5-8 Add/Remove Programs leads you through the installation of your programs

How can I move an active window using the keyboard?

To move an active window by use of the keyboard rather than the mouse, follow these steps:

1. Press ALT-SPACEBAR to display a command menu on the active window.

2. Press the DOWN ARROW key once to select Move and press ENTER. A four-way arrow will appear on the active window.

3. Press the arrow keys to move the window in whichever direction you want.

4. When you are finished, press ESC to end the move.

How do I open a file with a different application than the one with which it is already associated?

An option of the right-click context menu contains the Open With option in which you can select the application you want to open the file. Follow these steps to get the Open With command on the right mouse button context menu:

1. In My Computer or Explorer, *left*-click the file to select it.

2. Hold down the SHIFT key and right-click it. The Open With command will appear in the context menu.

Tip: *You must first select the file before SHIFT-right-click will cause Open With to appear.*

I see the terms "real mode" and "protected mode" used a lot in conjunction with Windows 98, but what's the difference between them, and is it really important?

Yes, it is important. *Real mode* was the original way that the 8086 and 8088 processors operated and the foundation on which DOS was built. It was a single-tasking, 16-bit environment limited to slightly over 1MB of address space. The 80286 processor added *protected-mode* instructions, and the 386 and 486 significantly improved on them. These protected-mode instructions, which are 32-bit, provided for *multitasking,* where two or more programs could be in memory at the same time, and allowed addressing up to 4GB in the later processors. (The term "protected" comes from the memory protection routines that are necessary when two programs run in memory at the same time, whereas "real" addressing is what takes place if only one program is running at a time.) DOS never made use of protected mode, and all Intel processors (including the Pentium) have kept the real-mode instructions for that reason. Since all processors have real-mode instructions and it is the initial startup mode, most disk drivers used real-mode instructions. This meant that every time you went from Windows, which runs in protected mode, to the disk driver in real mode, you had to switch the processor from protected to real mode, taking time and going from a more efficient to a less efficient environment. For these reasons, Windows 98 has made a considerable effort to replace real-mode drivers with protected-mode drivers.

 Tip: *Wherever possible, use protected-mode drivers. The easiest way to do that is to use only the drivers that come with Windows 98 by removing any statements in your Config.sys and Autoexec.bat files that load drivers. (Under many circumstances you should be able to completely get rid of your entire Config.sys and possibly your Autoexec.bat files.)*

How can I rebuild Windows 98 default folders?

You can run the Grpconv.exe program that rebuilds the Windows 98 folders (for example, all the folders within the Windows folder). Follow these steps:

1. Click Start and choose Run.

2. In the Run dialog box, type **grpconv /s**. While the program is running, you will see the Start Menu Shortcuts message box appear.

Grpconv.exe is principally used to convert Windows 3.1 program groups to Windows 98 shortcuts in the \Windows\ Start Menu\Programs folder. When Grpconv.exe is used with the /s switch, it rebuilds the default Windows 98 folders.

 As I open multiple applications, my taskbar gets very crowded. How do I see the applications that I am running in the list format?

The easiest way is to drag the inside edge of your taskbar in so you can easily see all of your tasks, like this:

You can also switch to each task individually using ALT-TAB. Or you can press CTRL-ALT-DEL (this is equivalent to pressing CTRL-ESC in Windows 3.*x*), and you will get a list of all running applications with the option to end tasks. Click Cancel to continue without ending a task.

How do I select more than one icon on the desktop at a time?

You can select multiple icons on the desktop in two ways:

● If the icons you want are grouped together, click a blank spot of the desktop and select the icons by dragging the mouse over them, surrounding them with the select rectangle.

● If the icons are not contiguous, press CTRL and click the icons you want.

How can I stop opening multiple windows each time I open a new folder in My Computer?

In your current window, select View | Folder Options, click Settings, and in the Browse Folders As Follows area, choose Open Each Folder In The Same Window, as shown in Figure 5-9.

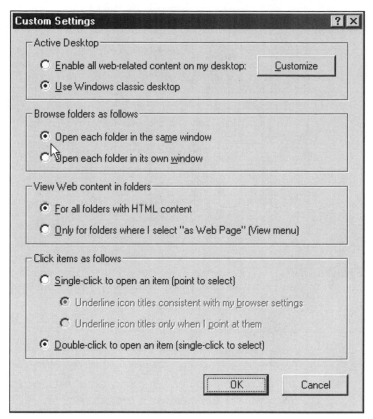

Figure 5-9 The Custom Settings dialog box contains an option for displaying a single window rather than cascading ones

 ### How do I find what system resources are currently available to me?

In My Computer, Explorer, or a number of other windows, open the Help menu and select About Windows 98. The About Windows dialog box opens with both the free system resources and the free physical memory, as shown in Figure 5-10.

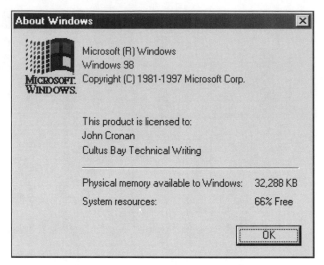

Figure 5-10   The About Windows dialog box, available from
most Windows 98 Help menus, will give you the free
system resources

 Note: *For other ways to see how Windows 98 is operating,
see the question, "How can I view how much of my Windows
98 resources I'm using?" in Chapter 4.*

Why does my taskbar sometimes disappear when I'm running an application?

The Auto Hide feature is enabled. Here are the steps to
clear this:

1. Move your cursor to the edge of the screen where the
   taskbar is located and the taskbar will reappear.

2. Click Start and choose Settings | Taskbar & Start Menu.

3. Clear the Auto Hide box, as you can see in Figure 5-11,
   and click OK when you are done.

Why does Windows 98 change the look of certain parts of my applications and not other parts?

The programming code is often inconsistent throughout an
application, probably because it was written by multiple

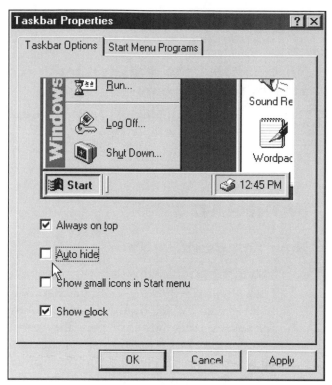

Figure 5-11   If Auto Hide is checked, the taskbar will only be visible when you move the mouse pointer to the edge of the screen

programmers. In some instances an application may use Windows 98 tools to create some parts. For example, in older versions of Access, which uses Windows 98 to create its dialog boxes, the check boxes now come equipped with check marks, and there is a single-click "X" for closing the application in the upper-right corner. Some applications just show a slight appearance change, such as fonts and colors.

 Note: *Microsoft Office 97 has reduced, and the next version will continue to reduce, this problem by making the Office applications more consistent.*

 ## How do I tile or cascade windows in Windows 98?

You can tile or cascade windows to get two or more windows on your screen at one time. Just right-click an empty spot on

the taskbar. You will see the options to Cascade, Tile Horizontally, or Tile Vertically on the context menu.

 ## How do I use the question mark icon on the right side of the title bars?

 This is a Help aid found in dialog boxes. The question mark is known as the "What's This?" button. Click it and the pointer changes to a question mark, as shown here. Click any object in the dialog box, and a short description of the object is shown.

WORDPAD

 ## How do I use WordPad?

WordPad is a 32-bit editor that replaces the Write application that was in Windows 3.*x*. WordPad uses the same file format as Microsoft Word 6 (and Microsoft Word 6 for Windows 95) for saving files, but can open files saved in Word 97 format. It also supports the reading and writing of text files (.TXT) and rich text files (.RTF) and the reading of Write files (.WRI).

To start WordPad, click Start and select Programs | Accessories | WordPad. Alternatively, you can click Start, select Run, type **wordpad**, and press ENTER.

If you create a new document in WordPad, you are given a choice of the type of document you want to create, as shown here:

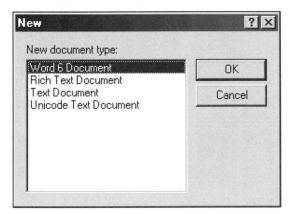

You need to determine what you will do with the document and how much formatting it will have. Word 6 and rich text can handle a lot of formatting, but those formats cannot be used with system files like Autoexec.bat, Config.sys, and Win.ini. If you are writing for international use, consider the Unicode Text Document format, which allows text rendering in languages such as Greek and Chinese.

How do I set a manual page break in WordPad?

There is no provision for page breaks. They are handled automatically.

I am in WordPad, and I am trying to save a file with the name C:\Test.txt, but I am getting an error message: "This filename is not valid." What is going on?

If all characters in the name are valid, the problem might be that all 512 root folder entries are used up. In partitions formatted with FAT16, such as MS-DOS and Win3.x, you could have 512 files and folders defined in the root (C:\) directory or folder. MS-DOS used one root folder entry for each file and folder. In Windows 98 formatted with FAT16, the 512-entry maximum still applies, but you might get to use a lesser number of actual items because Windows 98 uses additional root folder entries to store long filenames and their associated 8.3 aliases, plus the normal files and folders. This means that you can run out of available root folder entries even if you have fewer than 512 files or folders in the root folder. To avoid this problem, save your files to a folder other than the root folder. Folders other than the root do not have the root entries limitation—the only limitation is actual free disk space. This discussion is moot for FAT32 partitions. When Windows 98 is installed, or has been converted, to FAT32 there isn't a maximum number of files and folders defined for the root directory, just the capacity of your hard disk.

EQUIPMENT-RELATED PROBLEMS

 ### How do I add hardware to my computer?

Much of this question depends on what hardware you are adding. If you are adding Plug-and-Play hardware, Windows 98 will most likely handle the installation for you. If you are not using Plug-and-Play, you still have a good chance of Windows 98 handling the installation with no problems. However, if you do have problems, either with Plug-and-Play hardware or without, you can work with the system by finding out where the conflict is (most likely a conflict in how the interrupt request (IRQ), port, or dynamic memory allocation (DMA) addresses are being assigned) and manually assign your new hardware to a different address.

Follow these steps to install new hardware:

1. Click Start, and choose Settings | Control Panel.

2. Double-click Add New Hardware. The Add New Hardware Wizard will lead you through the installation. It will vary depending on the hardware being installed.

If the Wizard is unable to install your hardware, follow these steps to find out why and resolve it:

1. Click Start and choose Settings | Control Panel.

2. Double-click System.

3. Select the Device Manager tab, and select View Devices By Type, as shown in Figure 5-12.

4. Click Print for a list of all your devices and their assigned IRQs, ports, and DMA addresses. Any device conflicts will be flagged for you on the report that is printed.

5. Check your hardware manuals or documentation, and determine what assignments are needed. You now know what is in conflict and what you need.

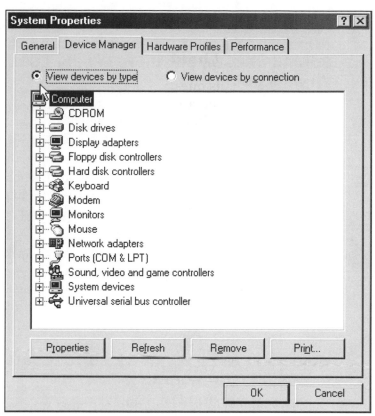

Figure 5-12 The Device Manager provides several ways to see your device assignments

6. Manually assign your hardware to an available IRQ, port, or DMA.

7. Run the Add New Hardware Wizard again with the new settings.

 Warning: *Sometimes with Plug-and-Play, Windows 98 will rearrange a device's resources to make room for new hardware. This is usually just fine. But sometimes software will be looking for a device at a particular IRQ or DMA. You must resolve the conflict by changing the software configuration to the new settings, or changing the hardware assignments to something that will work with the software.*

 I'm having a problem with my Conner external tape drive. The Conner program is attempting to back up 800MB of data, but there is only 500MB of data. What is going on?

The Conner backup program is having problems with long filenames in Windows 98. To back up your data, use the Backup program that comes with Windows 98. You can access Backup by clicking Start and choosing Programs | Accessories | System Tools | Backup. Backup is a 32-bit application that is very easy to use and displays the standard tree and file list view similar to what you see in Explorer.

 Tip: *Not all backup tape drives are supported by Windows 98 Backup. Drives must adhere to QIC (Quarter-Inch Cartridge) 40, 80, or 117 standards. If your tape drive is not supported, contact your tape drive manufacturer for software that works with Windows 98.*

 How can I force Windows 98 to redetect my entire hardware configuration?

To make Windows 98 redetect your hardware configuration, you must boot under Safe mode and then create additional hardware configurations. When you are asked to select one of the configurations during booting, don't select one, which will force Windows 98 to autodetect your hardware. Windows 98 will then create a new configuration based on your current hardware.

Follow these steps to do this:

1. Click Start and select Shut Down. Select Restart and then click OK.

2. As the computer is rebooting, press F8 after the computer resources are listed and before Windows 98 begins to load.

3. Type **3** and press ENTER to bring up Safe mode. A message will be displayed telling you that the computer is running in Safe mode.

4. Click Start and choose Settings | Control Panel. Double-click System to open the System Properties dialog box.

5. Select the Hardware Profiles tab, and click Copy to make a copy of the Original Configuration. Name it **Original Configuration 1** and click OK.

6. Click the Original Configuration to select it and click Rename. Name it **Original Configuration 2** and click OK.

7. Click OK to close the System Properties dialog box.

8. Click Start and select Shut Down. Select Restart and then click OK.

9. During the boot process you will be asked to select between Original Configuration 1, Original Configuration 2, and None Of The Above. Choose None Of The Above. This will force Windows 98 to go through the process of autodetecting the hardware installed.

10. Windows 98 will create a new profile for you called "Original Configuration." It may take a few minutes. You will need to click OK to allow the computer to be rebooted with the new configuration.

11. When the computer is rebooted, you will want to remove the other profiles (Original Configuration 1 and Original Configuration 2).

Do I absolutely have to have a mouse?

It is strongly recommended that you use a mouse in Windows 98 because the whole environment is object-oriented and is strongly tied to pointing and clicking, with both the left and right mouse buttons.

You can substitute the keyboard for many mouse actions by, among other things, using the shortcut keys listed on the command card inserted in this book. Also, the underlined letters in the menus and dialog boxes represent a shortcut—you can hold down the ALT key and press the underlined letter on the keyboard to activate the menu option or dialog box feature.

However, there are a few tasks, such as the following examples, that cannot be performed without a mouse:

● In Explorer, you cannot move the vertical bar that divides the folder tree on the left and list of files on the right without a mouse.

● In Explorer, when you are viewing files in Details view, there is no way without a mouse to change the size of the fields for the filename, type, total size, and free space listings.

● Very long filenames may be truncated on dialog box properties tabs, and you can only see the whole name by holding a mouse pointer over it.

Tip: *Even if you don't have a mouse, you can use the MouseKeys option to simulate the mouse pointer on the keyboard. You can access this option by clicking Start and choosing Settings | Control Panel, and double-clicking Accessibility Options. On the Mouse tab, select Use MouseKeys. (You might have to install the Accessibility Options because they are not installed in every type of setup.)*

Do I need Himem.sys or Emm386.exe in Windows 98?

Windows 98 does need Himem.sys, but you do not need to include it in a Config.sys file. It is automatically loaded through the Io.sys file. If the Himem.sys file is missing or damaged, you will not be able to run Windows 98. Emm386.exe is not required by Windows 98.

Where can I get an accurate view of my computer's memory size?

There are several places where you can see the physical memory you have on your computer:

● As Windows 98 is booting, it displays the memory size.

● In Explorer, My Computer, or any folder window, select Help | About Windows 98. The Physical Memory Available To Windows will be displayed as well as the percentage of System Resources currently available, as shown previously in Figure 5-10.

● Right-click My Computer, and select Properties from the context menu. In the System Properties dialog box, you can select either the General or the Performance tab for the RAM that is recognized by Windows. The Performance tab contains additional important system resource information, as shown here:

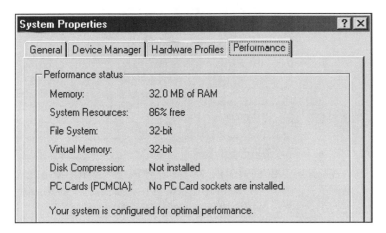

The most comprehensive way to find information on your computer is by opening the Microsoft System Information window. Click Start and choose Properties | Accessories | System Tools | System Information. Opening the folder tree in the left pane displays an incredible wealth of information regarding your computer, as shown in Figure 5-13.

Tip: *From the Tools menu on the Microsoft System Information window you have access to many performance-related utilities that are only available from that menu.*

My SCSI controller isn't working under Windows 98. What can I do?

This is probably due to a conflict between a real-mode driver in your Config.sys file and Windows 98 trying to use a protected-mode driver. (See the discussion on real and protected modes in the "Windows Environment" section

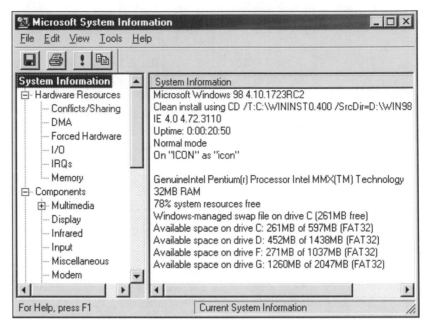

Figure 5-13 The Microsoft System Information utility gives you an in-depth view of your computer's software and hardware environment

earlier in this chapter.) Use either of the following two methods to correct this problem.

- First, try removing the SCSI driver (it probably has "ASPI" in its name) from your Config.sys file so that only the Windows 98 protected-mode driver is loaded.

- Alternatively, edit the Iso.ini file in your Windows folder, and remove the reference to the real-mode driver.

Can I use an upper-memory manager such as QEMM with Windows 98?

There is no need for such utilities. Windows 98 utilizes its internal memory management system, which is superior to QEMM.

My video display blinks (flickers). How do I avoid this?

You probably selected the wrong display type, and your monitor is running at a different frequency than your video card. Use the steps in the earlier question (in the "Booting Situations" section of this chapter) related to changing video drivers to select the correct video device driver. If you don't know the display type, choose Standard Display Adapter (VGA) or Standard PCI Display Adapter (VGA), depending on which type bus your card is using.

 ## I have been changing my video display resolution back and forth, and now suddenly I cannot change it back to what I want. The option is no longer available. How do I restore the original defaults?

Somehow you changed your display type and thereby your video device driver to one that does not have the resolution options of your original driver. You need to reselect your original display type, and the list will be set back to its original defaults. To do that, follow these steps:

1. Click Start and choose Settings I Control Panel, and double-click Display.

2. Click the Settings tab, click Advanced, and then select the Adapter tab. Click Change to start the Update Device Driver Wizard.

3. Click Next and then click Next again to let Windows search for your optimal device driver.

4. Your driver should be on your hard disk so you do not need Windows to search anywhere else. Click Next and Windows will find your missing driver.

5. If Windows doesn't find your driver you can click Back and point to a location other than your hard disk where the driver is located. Alternatively, you can go back a few

more wizard screens and be shown a list of manufacturers and models from which to choose.

6. Click Show All Hardware, select your display adapter, as you can see being done in Figure 5-14; and click Next twice to load the driver.

7. If asked, restart your computer. When you are done, you should be able to select from among your original resolution settings (in the Screen Area section of the Display Properties dialog box Settings tab).

When I insert a Windows 98 CD so that I can add and remove some of my components, a message is displayed that says this is an older version CD and to obtain the latest release of Windows 98. What can I do?

Microsoft had a very extensive beta testing program for Windows 98 which produced several interim builds on CDs

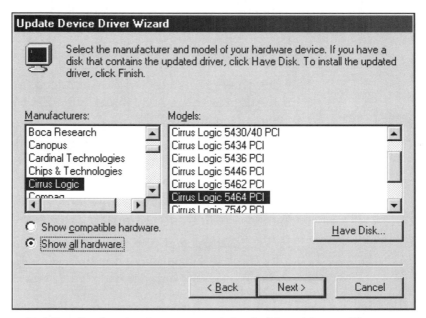

Figure 5-14   Getting back to your original video driver will return your resolution options

for the thousands of beta testers. If you tried to upgrade a newer version with an older build you would get an error message that prevented Setup from continuing. Sounds like you might be trying to use a beta disc instead of the disc you used to install the retail version. Look further for your original CD!

OTHER PROBLEMS

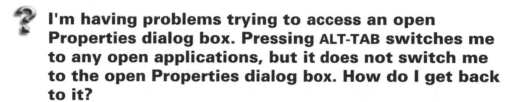 **I'm having problems trying to access an open Properties dialog box. Pressing ALT-TAB switches me to any open applications, but it does not switch me to the open Properties dialog box. How do I get back to it?**

You can use ALT-ESC to switch to a Properties dialog box or to a wizard. ALT-TAB only works with applications.

Are Autoexec.bat and Config.sys files required in Windows 98?

No. Windows 98 does not require these files for operating. However, they are usually included and preserved for compatibility to earlier programs which have not been designed specifically for Windows 98.

How do I close a failed application?

If you cannot use any facilities within the application and you cannot close the DOS window it is running in (or if it isn't a DOS program), use the following steps to close it:

1. Press CTRL-ALT-DEL. Windows will display a list of all running applications so you can specify which one you want to end.

2. If Windows detects that any application is not responding to messages from the system, the text "not responding" appears after the related application in the list. In the Close Program dialog box, select the application you want to close and click End Task.

 Tip: *After you use Cancel or End Task to close the Close Program dialog box, the next time you press CTRL-ALT-DEL, the Close Program dialog box appears again and the computer is not restarted. If you want to press CTRL-ALT-DEL to restart the computer, you must press the keys again while the Close Program dialog box is displayed.*

Warning: *If possible, use Shut Down in the Close Program dialog box or the Shut Down command on the Start menu to quit Windows. This ensures that all current information is saved in the Registry, and that each application is closed correctly before quitting Windows.*

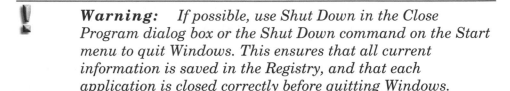 **I have deleted a large number of files over the last couple of days. When I wanted to recover some of them, I could not find the deleted files in the Recycle Bin! How can I avoid this?**

You probably have exceeded the size limit of the Recycle Bin.

Warning: *By default, the system allocates 10 percent of disk space to hold the deleted files in the Recycle Bin. When you exceed this limit, the system purges the oldest files to make space for the newly deleted files. You are not notified when this happens! You can avoid this problem in the future by increasing the disk space allocation.*

Use the following steps to increase the disk space allocated to the Recycle Bin:

1. On the desktop, right-click Recycle Bin and choose Properties.
2. Click the Global tab, as shown in Figure 5-15, and adjust the Maximum Size Of Recycle Bin setting. Click OK when you are done.

 Tip: *Remember also that you can have a separate Recycle Bin for every hard drive (or partition) that you have. To do this, click the individual drive tabs and adjust the disk space accordingly.*

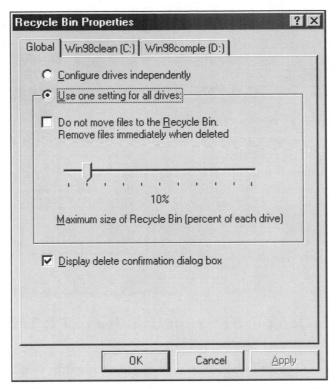

Figure 5-15   You can change the percentage of memory allocated to the Recycle Bin in its Properties dialog box

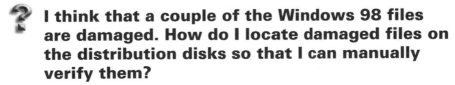 **I think that a couple of the Windows 98 files are damaged. How do I locate damaged files on the distribution disks so that I can manually verify them?**

Unlike Windows 3.*x*, Windows 98 will spare you this effort. You can have the System File Checker do a search for damage of your system files (those with file extensions of .386, .COM, .DLL, .DRV, .EXE, .MPD, .OCX, .SCR, .SYS, or .VXD) or you can even add a file type to check. If any damaged files are found you will be prompted for the correct installation media. Run the System File Checker with these steps:

1. Click Start and choose Programs | Accessories | System Tools | System Information.

2. Open the Tools menu and click System File Checker.

3. Choose to have Windows do a search or browse to a specific file to restore it, as shown here:

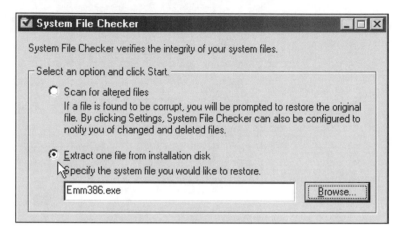

Can I use Norton Utilities or PC Tools for Windows with Windows 98?

You should be very cautious using Norton Utilities, PC Tools, or any other type of disk or file utility that was not specifically designed for Windows 98. The Windows 3.*x* versions of these utilities cannot handle long filenames in Windows 98 and might report the files as corrupt. An attempt to repair the "corruption" will lead to data loss and can seriously damage your whole system. Also, the original version of Windows 95 used an exclusive 16-bit FAT (file allocation table) whereas later OEM (original equipment manufacturer) versions had the option of using either FAT16 or FAT32, as does Windows 98. You need third-party disk management software specifically designed for FAT32 if your hard disk is formatted as such. Verify the compatibility of any utility software to Windows 98 before you permanently alter your file structure.

One of my 16-bit applications has crashed and has not returned the resources it used. How can I refresh the resources without restarting?

Windows 98 will return all 16-bit resources once *all* 16-bit applications have been closed. This includes some screen savers and other 16-bit Windows applications.

Why did Windows 98 put "rem" in front of the SMARTDrive statement in my Autoexec.bat file?

Windows 98 made the SMARTDrive statement a remark so SMARTDrive will not be loaded during startup. Windows 98 replaces SMARTDrive with a protected-mode caching system that shrinks and grows as needed. The SMARTDrive was not totally deleted because you may need it if you boot into your previous DOS.

Note: *If you installed Windows 98 with FAT32 (32-bit file allocation table) or converted a previous Windows operating system using the Drive Converter (FAT32) utility, you cannot dual boot into DOS or Windows 3.x.*

I ran an antivirus utility on Windows 98 and it seemed to see a virus, but it will not remove it from my system. Is there a problem with my antivirus program or my system?

Under Windows 98, many older virus detection software will detect a virus, but it will not remove it from your system. This is because the virus utility uses low-level write commands to repair the damage to the disk. DOS-based virus utilities can only be run by use of the LOCK command. You need to get an antivirus program that supports 32-bit Windows operating systems.

Chapter 6

Using Windows 98 with the Internet (Active Desktop)

Answer Topics!

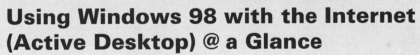

Using Windows 98 with the Internet (Active Desktop) @ a Glance

About the time Windows 95 was being released, Bill Gates made a business decision for Microsoft that would commit the company to using the Internet and its technology as a key ingredient of the company's future. Windows 98 is one result of that decision. If a user elects to take advantage of the Internet access and Web-like features offered in Windows 98, the line between a graphical operating system and an Internet browser becomes very blurry. This is most pronounced in a corporate setting where the use of intranets and dedicated access to the Internet really lets Windows 98 show its full potential. The five sections in this chapter cover Internet and intranet integration, from connecting to the Internet to using tools to create and host your own Web content:

 Connecting to the Internet discusses the types of Internet connection as well as what you need and how to make the connection.

 Exploring the Web covers using the Active Desktop, Windows Explorer, and Internet Explorer to access the Web and local intranets, as well as how to use them securely, in customized ways and in ways that protect children from unsuitable sites.

 Sending and Receiving E-mail looks at the differences among e-mail programs, the way e-mail is addressed, how to include files with e-mail, and ways to add more than words to your correspondence.

 Microsoft Network addresses what Microsoft Network is and how you get started with it, including getting an e-mail address.

Creating and Distributing Web Content explores FrontPage Express, an application for creating your own Web pages, and ways to distribute Web information, including the Personal Web Server and Web site publishing.

 Note: *The multimedia features in Windows 98 that use the Internet are covered in the Chapter 11 section "Using Online Multimedia."*

Note: *If several of the "new" Internet features don't look all that new it's probably because you've kept up with the upgrades and add-ons provided by Microsoft for Windows 95 and Internet Explorer. The Active Desktop available in the standalone version of Internet Explorer 4.0, when combined with the OSR 2 release of Windows 95, can offer a very close resemblance to the Windows 98 interface.*

CONNECTING TO THE INTERNET

 What do I need to access the Internet?

You need to have:

- **A physical connection to the Internet**   This can be a local area network (LAN) connection, a dial-up connection using a modem or ISDN adapter and phone lines, or a direct connection through a router and one or more dedicated phone lines (see the sidebar "Connecting to the Internet" on methods to connect to the Internet).

- **An organization to act as your link to the Internet** This can be an information service such as AOL or MSN, or an independent ISP. (See the questions on methods to connect to the Internet and what to look for in an ISP.) In the case of larger organizations (companies, universities,

or government agencies), they may have the equipment and act as their own link to the Internet.

● **Software to establish the connection over a LAN or a modem/adapter, to handle your e-mail, and to browse the Web** In Windows 98 the connection software is supplied by the networking and dial-up networking components of the operating system. The e-mail can be handled by Outlook Express that is included with Windows 98, by Microsoft Exchange if you are upgrading from Windows 95, by Internet Mail carried over from Internet Explorer 3.*x*, or by a third-party mail client of your choice such as Eudora. (See the question in the "Sending and Receiving E-mail" section on differences among e-mail clients.) Finally, you can access the Web through either the Active Desktop, Internet Explorer, or Windows 98 Explorer, all described in the next section. And, of course, you can always install and use a non-Microsoft browser such as Netscape Navigator.

 ### How do I connect to the Internet?

The simple answer is to double-click the Connect To The Internet icon if it exists on the desktop or on the Internet Explorer icon on either the desktop or in the Quick Launch toolbar. This answer, though, has a number of assumptions implicit in it that may not be correct for you. For that reason a comprehensive sidebar on connecting to the Internet has been included in this chapter.

Connecting to the Internet

How you connect to the Internet depends on the method you choose (see the question in the following section on the methods of connecting to the Internet). You also may need certain information from the organization you are going to use to connect to the Internet before you try to connect (see the question on information needed from an Internet service provider, or ISP).

Methods Used to Connect

There are three methods that you can use to connect to the Internet:

● Using a modem and phone lines to connect to an information service such as MSN or AOL.

● Using a modem and phone line to connect to an independent Internet service provider.

● Using a local area network (LAN) to connect to an Internet provider procured by someone else. This can be your company's own Internet node, an independent service provider, or an information service.

USING AN INFORMATION SERVICE   If you want to use an information service other than MSN, such as AOL, as your Internet link, you will need software provided by that firm. This is included in Windows 98—

simply open the Online Services folder on the desktop, as shown next, and then double-click the service you want to use and follow the instructions. After installing the software, start the program and you'll be prompted on what to do as a new user.

If you want to use MSN, simply double-click the Set Up The Microsoft Network icon on your desktop and follow the instructions to get online with MSN. See the section "Microsoft Network" in this chapter for more on setting it up.

USING AN INDEPENDENT INTERNET SERVICE PROVIDER

Connect to the Internet

If you want to use an independent ISP, all you need to do is double-click the Connect To The Internet icon on your desktop. If this is the first time you have done that, the Internet Connection Wizard will open. You may first be asked to provide dialing settings, depending on how your modem was set up. (After you establish an Internet connection, this icon is removed from your desktop and replaced by the Internet Explorer icon. If you do want to run the wizard again, click Start and choose Programs | Internet Explorer | Connection Wizard.) In the Internet Connection Wizard you'll be asked how you want to set up.

If you don't know an ISP to use, choose the first option; the Wizard (using an 800 number) will search a database for ISPs on the Microsoft Referral Service that you might use. Your computer may be rebooted, and then you'll be shown a list of ISPs. Select the one you want and provide the requested information. That ISP will be automatically called (again using an 800 number), and you'll be asked a series of questions that the ISP needs for you to sign up. If you are asked for a credit card number, it will be over a secure link. In most cases, when you are done, you should be able to immediately use the Internet. Remember that the list of ISPs presented by the Internet Connection Wizard may not all be a local phone number to you. You need to check if they are local or 800 numbers, or long-distance numbers for which you'll be billed extra.

If you do know of an ISP you want to use or if you are connecting over a LAN, click the second option and then click Next. You are asked if you want to use a LAN or a phone line to connect, or if you are using an online information service as described earlier. If you choose a phone line or LAN, you are asked to pick between the two, then you are asked for the telephone number of the ISP you want to use; your user name and password; options for advanced settings; and e-mail, newsgroup, and "white pages" directory service information for the ISP. If you use a LAN to connect, you only need to enter your e-mail information. In most cases, when you are done, you should be able to immediately use the Internet.

Testing an Internet Connection

With an Internet connection set up, you can test it in two ways: by using Internet Explorer to explore the Web and by using Outlook

Express to send and receive e-mail. First, double-click the Internet Explorer icon on your desktop or click the same icon in the Quick Launch toolbar next to Start. You'll see the Dial-Up Connection dialog box open. If all the information is correct, click Connect. You should hear your modem dialing. After connecting, the Internet Explorer will open to an Internet Start page from Microsoft Network. You can explore this site if you wish, or you can enter another Web site by typing the Web address or URL (Uniform Resource Locator) in the Address box.

For example, if you type **cnn.com** and press ENTER, CNN Interactive will open, as you can see in Figure 6-1. You can also use the File | Open dialog box as an alternative to typing in the Address box.

Tip: *You can also access the CNN Web site by subscribing to its channel. Channels provide "push" content that automatically updates information on your computer so you can view when offline and possibly not incur connect charges. See the Channel Guide on your desktop for the Web sites that Windows 98 provides links to.*

From CNN you can click a link to go to other Web sites, or you can enter another URL. When you are done, click the Close button in the upper right of the window. You should remain connected to the Internet.

The second thing you can do to test your Web connection is to send and receive e-mail. Have a friend use your e-mail address to send you some mail. Then double-click the Outlook Express icon. Click OK to accept the default file location. The Outlook Express window will appear, as shown in Figure 6-2. Click Send and Receive on the toolbar. If you are not already connected to the Internet, you will be directly connected. If you have mail, it will be downloaded to your Inbox. Click Read Mail in the right pane or double-click the Inbox folder in the left pane. If you got mail from your friend, you can open it, and after reading it, click Reply on the toolbar to send a message back to that person.

If you are connected to the Internet just to get mail, you'll be automatically disconnected when you are done downloading it. If you remain connected from Internet Explorer, you'll need to manually disconnect. Do that by right-clicking the Connect icon on the taskbar next to the clock and then clicking Disconnect.

Figure 6-1   Typing a URL in the Address box and pressing ENTER opens that Web site

How do I find an Internet service provider (ISP)?

Probably the best sources for a local ISP recommendation are your friends and acquaintances. Ask people if they are on the Internet and if so, how they are connected. See how happy they are with the service. How often do they get a busy signal, how often is it really slow (this may be the fault of the Internet itself and not the ISPs), and how good is the support? If this approach doesn't work, go into a couple of computer stores and ask them who the good local ISPs are. Ask which ISP the store uses.

Other sources are the yellow pages and newspaper ads. Some areas have computer-related newspapers, which not only have ads for ISPs, but may also rate them.

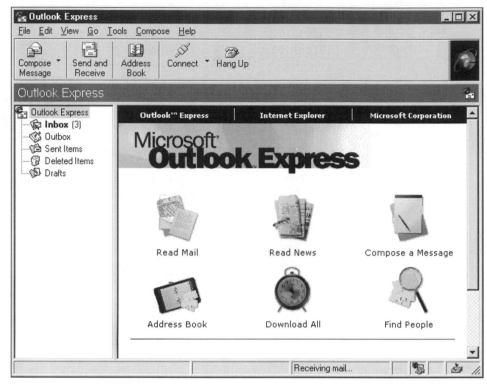

Figure 6-2 Send and receive e-mail from Outlook Express

What should I look for in an ISP?

An ISP is your link to the Internet. You go through them for all that you do on the Internet. This includes your Internet e-mail, your exploring or "surfing" of the World Wide Web (the Web), and the posting of your own Web pages for others to see. Therefore the primary issue is easy, unobstructed access. This translates to the following criteria:

- **Local phone lines**   Look for phone lines without long distance charges where you are (or will be if you travel much with a computer).

- **A high ratio of incoming lines and modems to the number of users**   One line and modem for seven users is a good standard, one for ten is tight, and anything lower than that (say one line and modem for 12 users) is not acceptable.

- **A large enough connection to the rest of the Internet to handle the ISP's users**   A T-1 line will max out if a little over 50 users at 28.8Kbps are all trying to access the Internet at exactly the same time. The key is the last part of that statement: "all trying to access the Internet at *exactly the same time*." With "average usage," many firms believe that between 1,000 and 1,500 users can be accommodated on a single T-1 line. But the next two considerations significantly affect this.

- **Redundancy in their connection to the Internet**   An ISP needs to have at least two separate links to two separate Internet nodes, so that if one goes down, it still has the other. While it could use a fractional T-1 or an ISDN line, for an ISP of any size (a thousand or more users), it should have at least two T-1 lines connected to different Internet nodes.

- **Load balancing among the outgoing lines and their Internet nodes**   An ISP with two or more outgoing lines needs to be able to balance the load among those lines and be able to switch away from a node that is becoming a bottleneck. Such equipment is available in the routers currently on the market, but it is newer and expensive.

In addition to easy and unobstructed access to the Internet, there are a number of other factors to consider when choosing an ISP. Among these are

- **Attractive pricing and services**   The price of Internet access is obviously related to the services that it buys. A low price that doesn't provide the services you need is worthless, while a full-service price that gives you more than you need is a waste of money. You have to look at an ISP's offerings and decide if the price is commensurate with the services being provided. This requires that you look at and compare several ISPs. An industry norm is $19.95 per month for unlimited access (although not a full-time connection) up to 33.6Kbps (many ISPs offer 56Kbps at the same or slightly higher price) and generally includes a personal Web page and one or more megabytes of storage. You often can get a discount if you pay for a year in advance, but make sure you want to stay a year.

● **A "busy-free" service policy**   If you get a busy signal very often when you connect to your ISP, you have lost the access that you wanted. This is normally controlled by the ratio of lines and modems to users, but it can be enhanced by an ISP guaranteeing not to exceed a certain number of busy signals monthly—or even no busy signals. The guarantee has to mean something, like a credit on your monthly bill, for it to be worthwhile.

● **Users complementary to your use**   If you are a business user, you want an ISP geared to business users, with a large percentage of business customers. If you are a home user, you want an ISP that is geared to that market. This generally addresses the type of services that are available, the pricing, and the type and amount of support.

● **Plentiful and easy-to-reach support**   The optimum support is a toll-free line staffed 24 hours a day, seven days a week, with a guarantee that they will get back to you in three hours or less if they are busy when you call. Very few ISPs provide this service, and many charge extra if you want it. Is the probably less-than-optimum support good enough for you? Does it supply what you need? If you only use the Internet in the evening and weekends, and service is only available during business hours, it's not what you need.

● **Web page services commensurate with your needs** If you want to put your own Web page up on the Internet, does your ISP provide what you need? Consider factors such as the amount of disk space you can use and the amount of traffic you can have on your page before they start charging you. ISPs normally provide limits on both of these. If you want to use a Web page authoring program such as FrontPage Express or its big brother, Microsoft FrontPage, to create your Web page (and it's probably the easiest way to do so), then you want your ISP to support the FrontPage server extensions.

What information do I need from my Internet link before I can connect to the Internet?

Depending on how you choose to connect to the Internet, you may need to talk on the telephone with the organization that will act as your link and get certain information that you will use as you are setting it up. With AOL, CompuServe, and MSN, the information you need is generated and given to you as you are signing up. With some ISPs, you need only a phone number (see the earlier question on how to find an ISP). All the other information is generated during sign-up. If you must call your ISP on the phone, ask for the following information:

- **Phone numbers** you are to use with various modem speeds.

- **User name or ID and password**, for example, "georgem" and "owl*4567." (Can you use the same user name/ID and password for both logging on to the Internet and for e-mail, or do you need different ones, and what are they?)

- **Provider's domain name**, for example, "provider.com."

- **Provider's primary and alternate DNS** server numbers, for example, 123.12.34.56.

- **Your e-mail address** and your Internet mail server, for example, "georgem@provider.com" and "provider.com."

Ask your ISP if they require a terminal window for authentication (most do not). If so, have them explain how to set up a script to handle that. Also ask if they automatically assign you an IP number (most do), or if they give you a permanent number (a *static* IP) and what that number is.

 I didn't have a modem when I first set up Windows 98; now I do. How do I manually set up a dial-up Internet connection?

You can manually set up a connection for using the Internet in two major steps. First, you must install and configure a modem, as described in Chapter 10. Then you have to install Dial-Up Networking. To install and set up Dial-Up Networking, follow these steps.

1. If you did a Typical Windows 98 Installation, Dial-Up Networking is already installed on your computer and you only need to set up a dial-up connection, which you can do beginning with step 2 next. If you do not have

Dial-up Networking (look in My Computer for the Dial-Up Networking folder), you can install if from the Windows 98 CD. To do that, click Start, choose Settings | Control Panel, and double-click Add/Remove Programs. Click the Windows Setup tab, double-click the Communications component, and then select the Dial-Up Networking check box. Click OK twice.

2. Open My Computer and double-click Dial-Up Networking. If you do not have a dial-up connection, the Welcome to Dial-Up Networking message will be displayed. Click Next.

3. If you already have a dial-up connection, the Dial-Up Networking folder will be displayed. In that case, double-click Make New Connection. The Make New Connection Wizard will be displayed.

4. If you don't have a modem installed the Install New Modem Wizard will open. This will go through the process of installing and setting up your modem as described in Chapter 10.

5. Type a name for the computer you will be dialing, and verify that the modem you want to use is selected and is properly configured by clicking Configure. It will display the Modems Properties dialog box as described in Chapter 10.

6. Click the Options tab. If you need to enter your user name and password when you sign on to the Internet, then click Bring Up Terminal Window After Dialing. When you are satisfied with the modem properties, click OK and then click Next.

7. Enter the Area Code, Telephone Number, and Country Code as needed. Click Next.

8. Click Finish to complete the installation.

9. In the Dial-Up Networking dialog box, right-click your new connection and click Properties. The connection's Properties dialog box will open.

10. Click the Server Types tab, shown in Figure 6-3.

11. Make sure that PPP: Internet, Windows NT Server, Windows 98 is selected as the Type Of Dial-Up Server. If NetBEUI and IPX/SPX protocols are enabled, click them to disable those protocols. TCP/IP should be enabled (checked).

12. Click the TCP/IP Settings button. The dialog box that opens has very important settings that only your Internet provider can tell you how to set. Discuss these settings with your Internet provider and set them accordingly (see the earlier question on what to ask your ISP).

13. When you have made the TCP/IP settings, click OK twice to return to the Dial-Up Networking folder.

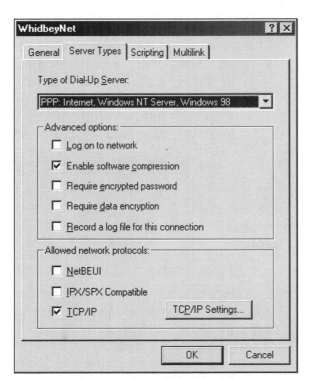

Figure 6-3 Setting up a dial-up connection to an Internet server

> ╋ ***Tip:*** *Remember the TCP/IP Settings dialog box, reached from your dial-up connection's Properties on the Server Types tab. The TCP/IP Settings dialog box contains a number of settings that can cause you grief. In particular, if your Internet provider does not have a strong opinion on whether to Use IP Header Compression (second from the bottom check box), disable it by removing the check mark.*

The PPP protocol is installed by default because it is the most flexible, being able to work over NetBEUI, IPX/SPX, and TCP/IP. Now use the connection with these steps:

1. From the Dial-Up Networking window, double-click the Internet connection you just created. The Connect To dialog box will open.

2. Enter your User Name and Password, check on the correctness of the Phone Number, and click Connect. You should hear your modem dial and will see a message that the system is trying to connect to your Internet provider. If the Terminal window opens, you will need to enter your user name and password again, possibly type **ppp**, and then press F7 to close the terminal window. Finally, you should see a connected message like this:

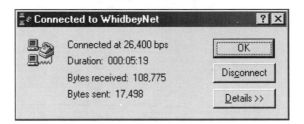

Once you have gotten the connection message, you can start your Web browsing and Internet mail packages. You can use Outlook Express for Internet mail or a mail client that you install separately.

If you did not get connected, look at the Windows 98 Help Troubleshooter for your modem and for Dial-Up Networking. If that does not help, go over all of your settings with your Internet provider.

What are the differences among the methods to connect to the Internet?

There are a number of choices that you have when you look at connecting to the Internet. Among your choices are the following:

- **A LAN connection or a telephone connection**   If you are on a local area network (LAN) with a connection to the Internet, you can go through your LAN to connect to the Internet. That is probably the fastest and least expensive way, barring the availability of a TV cable or satellite connection. Without a LAN, TV cable, or satellite connection, you must use a telephone connection.

- **A dial-up telephone connection or a direct dedicated-telephone connection**   A dial-up connection is the standard modem connection to any phone jack. A direct dedicated connection is a dedicated phone line open all the time between you and the organization linking you to the Internet. It is normally terminated on your end with a *router* that can be connected to a LAN or directly to several computers. A direct connection is definitely faster, but it is also a lot more expensive. Therefore, unless you share a direct connection with a number of people, which reduces some of the speed benefit, a direct connection is normally too expensive. In addition to standard modems, you also have the choice of ISDN adapters, which, like modems, can be dial-up or dedicated. If Windows 98 detects that you have an ISDN adapter on your machine, the ISDN Configuration Wizard will help you set it up, as does the Install New Modem Wizard, described in Chapter 10.

- **Information services or independent Internet service providers (ISPs)**   *Information service providers* such as America Online (AOL) or Microsoft Network (MSN) provide Internet access as well as their own value-added content, generally at a higher price. Independent ISPs only provide Internet access at lower prices. One other benefit of information services is that

they have local phone service in many cities in the world, so that if you travel a lot, you are more likely to find a local phone connection.

What does "bandwidth" mean when talking about the Internet?

Bandwidth refers to the data-carrying capacity of your connection to the Internet or any Internet link in terms of the number of bits per second (bps) that can be carried. Normal dial-up service today is either 28.8Kbps or 33.6Kbps, with the 56Kbps V.90 standard finally shaking out the confusion between the early X2 and 56KFlex standards. ISDN (Integrated Services Digital Network) dial-up service is either 64Kbps or 128Kbps. Direct connection service ranges from 64Kbps for a single channel ISDN direct service, to a 1.54Mbps T-1 line and a 44.74Mbps T-3 line. The common discussion relating to bandwidth is the need to increase it from today's standard of 28.8Kbps to at least 1.54Mbps.

I have heard people talk about a firewall in relation to the Internet. What is it and how is it used?

The purpose of a *firewall* is to protect an intranet within an organization from being accessed across the intranet's connection to the Internet. A firewall is most often a separate computer that sits between an intranet and the Internet. This computer stops and validates any request made from outside to inside the intranet. If it passes the inbound tests, then the firewall computer itself makes the request of the intranet and makes sure that any information going out meets certain criteria. Only after the outbound tests are passed is the information given to the Internet requester.

EXPLORING THE WEB

What can Active Desktop do to make my computing behave in a more unified manner?

The Active Desktop allows you to blend the way you use your local resources with the way you use a browser to navigate

the Web. As more and more new people are introduced to computing, the main attraction for many is the fascination with the Web—so why learn two conventions? The Active Desktop is mainly a subset of Internet Explorer 4.0 taken out of its normal window and integrated into your desktop. Start to view your desktop as a Web page by right-clicking your desktop, and choosing Active Desktop | View As Web Page from the context menu. Now you customize how several Web features appear on your desktop such as the Channel Bar, which appears by default. By selecting Customize My Desktop from the Active Desktop menu, you open the Web tab of the Display Properties box, shown in Figure 6-4, which provides the gateway to even more options:

- **Add New Active Desktop Items** Select the View My Active Desktop As A Web Page check box, and then click

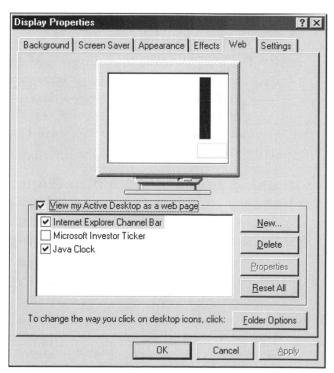

Figure 6-4 Customize how your Web-centric desktop appears

New to gain Web access to a gallery of other Active Desktop features, as you can see here:

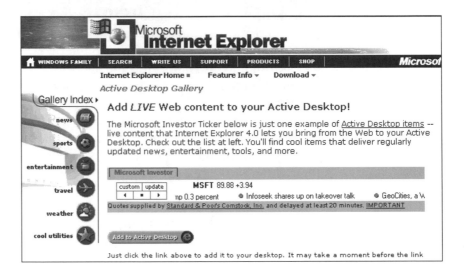

● **Use Single Click to Select Items** Click Folder Options and then click Web Style to activate all Web Active Desktop features, including using the Web-style of single-clicking to launch programs from icons and select files and folders in Windows Explorer. You can further modify these features by clicking Settings and choosing exactly which features you want to use and which you want to remain in the "classic" Windows 95 style.

 I'm using single click, but in Windows Explorer whenever I click a file after selecting it to rename it, Explorer tries to open or execute the file. How can I easily rename files when using single click?

You can always select a file by pointing at it and then choosing Rename from the File menu (as you can do with double-click mode). You can also point at the file and press F2. However, we find the easiest way to rename a file is to right-click it and select Rename from the context menu. The filename is then selected for editing.

 A friend of mine says he can view the Web with Windows Explorer. I told him he might be able to *open* Internet Explorer from Windows Explorer, but I never heard of what he's describing. Who's right?

You both are, but he's probably more right. As with any version of Windows you can navigate to the applicable folder and launch the executable file for a program in its file management program (Program Manager or Window Explorer) so you're correct, but in Windows 98 Explorer you can transform the window into several forms that at first glance look just like Internet Explorer. The Internet integration features of Windows 98 Explorer include

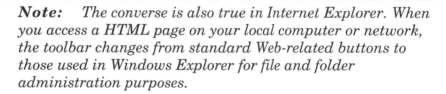

- **The Explorer bar**, which has been commonly called the "left pane" of the Windows Explorer window. It can now display several Web-related bars in addition to the file and folder structure familiar to Windows 95, as shown in Figure 6-5. The Explorer bar options are found on the View menu.
- **The Web toolbar**, which replaces the standard toolbar in Windows Explorer to provide access to Web features.

Note: *The converse is also true in Internet Explorer. When you access a HTML page on your local computer or network, the toolbar changes from standard Web-related buttons to those used in Windows Explorer for file and folder administration purposes.*

- **The Address bar** where you can type Web addresses.
- **Customized menu options** that offer Web features such as changing the Folder Options choice on the View menu to Internet Options.

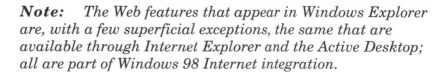

Note: *The Web features that appear in Windows Explorer are, with a few superficial exceptions, the same that are available through Internet Explorer and the Active Desktop; all are part of Windows 98 Internet integration.*

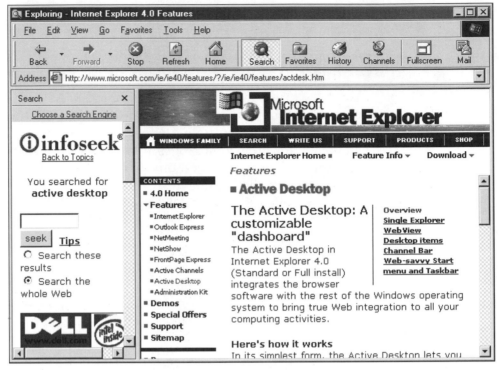

Figure 6-5 Searching the Web from Windows Explorer

 I like the Web-style look for most of my windows, but in Windows Explorer I want it to look as it did in Windows 95. How can I eliminate the Web-page look?

In Windows Explorer, as with any folder window, you can choose whether to include Web content in the window. There are several settings you can adjust to provide just what you want.

Global Settings

Here's how you can globally affect the Web content of folder windows:

1. In a folder window, click Folder Options on the View menu and then click Settings.

2. Under View Web Content in Folders, choose to view all folder windows in Web-style or only those you choose.

Individual Folder Window Setting

For an individual folder window, in the View menu remove or add the check mark next to As Web Page to display HTML content if it's available.

Customizing Web Content in a Folder Window

You can also customize the Web content of a folder window by adding HTML content or a background image with these steps:

1. In a folder window, click Customize This Folder on the View menu.

2. Choose one of the three options in the Customize This Folder Wizard. You can create or edit content, add a background graphic, or remove any customization.

What is the difference between a subscription and a channel, and how do you use them?

The terminology can be confusing because you actually "subscribe" to a channel as well. The easiest way to look at it is to think of subscriptions as automatic updates to a standard Web site where you define the schedule that pages are downloaded to your computer for, generally, online viewing (you can also manually update pages by clicking Refresh on the Internet or Windows Explorer toolbar). Channels are self-contained sites that use their own Channel Definition Format (.CDF) to define content that comprises the channel. They are also downloaded on a schedule of your choosing, but are generally meant for offline viewing.

Subscribing to a Web Site

Here's how to subscribe to a Web site:

1. In Internet or Windows Explorer, connect to the Web site that you want to be updated.

2. On the Favorites menu, click Add To Favorites to open the Add Favorite dialog box.

3. Choose one of the subscription options to either just be told that changes have occurred or actually have the page downloaded and also be notified.

4. Click Customize to have an e-mail notification sent to you when changes occur.

 Tip: *A red "gleam" is added to the Web page icon when a change has been made to the page.*

Subscribing to a Channel

Here's how to subscribe to a channel:

 1. Click the View Channels icon on the Quick Launch toolbar, next to Start.

2. The Microsoft Active Channel Guide opens, which provides access to more than three thousand channels (as of the writing of this book in early August 1998), as shown in Figure 6-6.

3. Click Search to enter the Search page where you can find a channel of your choosing. Once you connect to a channel, follow its instructions for subscribing.

Administering Your Subscriptions

In any folder window, including Internet and Windows Explorer, click Manage Subscriptions on the Favorites menu. Any channel or Web site you have subscribed to is shown in the right pane of the Subscriptions window, as shown in Figure 6-7.

To update content, select an individual link and click Update on the toolbar, or click Update All. Be aware that if you have many links or if any have a lot of graphics to download, you might be transferring data for some time.

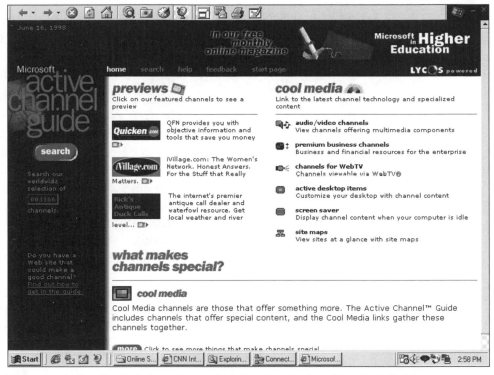

Figure 6-6 Search for channels from the Active Channel Guide

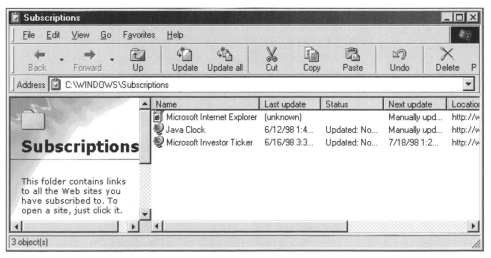

Figure 6-7 Manage your subscribed channels and Web sites from the Subscriptions window

I have a hard time using a mouse, but Web pages are so "mouse-centric." Is there a way to access the Web content without using the mouse?

Yes, the Internet Explorer browser integration into Windows 98 has several accessibility options that provide optional ways to access and view Web content. These include using your keyboard in place of the mouse, enlarging the font that is used in a page, and viewing alternative text in place of images.

The most important set of keys to navigate a Web page are TAB and SHIFT-TAB. These keys scroll a Web page forward and backward from the Address box to the first hyperlink on the page, to the next hyperlink, and so on. As each hyperlink is selected, a narrow border appears around it. You can then activate the hyperlink by pressing ENTER. See Table 6-1, for other possibilities.

You can change the size of the font used by the Internet or Windows Explorer by opening the View menu, choosing Fonts, and selecting the size you want to use, as shown next.

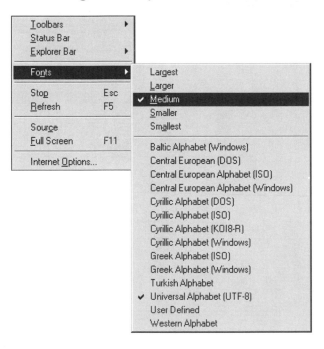

Key	Function
BACKSPACE or ALT-LEFT ARROW	Go back to the previous page
CTRL-N	Open another Internet Explorer window
CTRL-O	Open a new Internet address, file, or folder
CTRL-P	Print the current page
CTRL-S	Save the current page
CTRL-TAB	Go from one frame to the next
ENTER	Activate the selected hyperlink
ESC	Stop downloading the current page
F5	Refresh the current page
SHIFT-BACKSPACE or ALT-RIGHT ARROW	Go forward to the next page
SHIFT-CTRL-TAB	Go backward from one frame to the next
SHIFT-F10	Go up the page from one hyperlink to the next

Table 6-1   Keyboard Alternatives for Web Navigation

Finally, most Web authors include alternative text with the graphic images they place on a Web page. If you move the mouse pointer over the image, a tooltip will appear displaying the alternative text, as you can see in the next illustration.

My company would like to send some proprietary information over the Internet, but we are concerned about security. What can we do to assure that information sent over the Internet is secure?

Assuring the security of Internet information has three elements, all of which must be handled satisfactorily for you to achieve your objective. The elements are

● Authenticating the sender, the receiver, and the data transferred, so both parties know that the other party and the information are as represented

● Securing the transmission of information so that it cannot be read by an unintended recipient

● Limiting access to Web pages and the server containing them so the pages aren't changed

Much of what needs to be done to implement Web security must be done at the Web server. This is especially true with the limiting of access. To handle the server-side questions, you'll need to work with your network administrator or ISP. If you want to set up your own Windows NT server, an excellent reference is Tom Sheldon's *The Windows NT Security Handbook* (Osborne/McGraw-Hill, 1997). Another good source is the Microsoft Security Advisor at **http://www. microsoft.com/security**.

The security features that you can control are described in the sidebar "Internet Explorer Security Features."

Can I control what my children see on the Web?

Yes. Internet Explorer has a ratings feature that allows you to control access to Web sites based on the PICS Internet rating system. This allows you to choose the level of language, nudity, sex, and violence that you feel is

Internet Explorer Security Features

The security features in Internet Explorer that you can control are in the Security, Content, and Advanced tabs of the Internet Options dialog box, which you can open from the View menu. In the Security tab, shown in Figure 6-8, you can do the following:

- Determine the level of security that you want based on one of four zones:
  - **Local Intranet** for all Web sites on your intranet, those that bypass a proxy server, and all network paths that use a Universal Naming Convention (UNC) address.
  - **Trusted Sites** for sites that you feel you can trust.
  - **Internet** for sites on the Web that you haven't placed in another zone.
  - **Restricted Sites** for sites that you find of questionable security.
- Choose from three preset levels that give various degrees of protection and warnings, and you can also customize a level by selecting Custom and clicking Settings.

  In the Content tab, you can do the following:

- View and change the certificates on your computer for yourself and for software publishers, and the certification authorities that you will accept. If you have your own certificate, then others will know that you are who you say you are. If you accept the certification authorities, then you can see the certifications of information and programs you download.

  Your personal certification requires that you be certified by a certification authority. In other words, a *certification authority* will certify that you are who you say you are. With Internet Explorer, you

can get a free Class 1 certification or "Digital ID" from VeriSign, Inc. at **http://digitalid.verisign.com/ms_client.htm**. At this site you can see what the difference is between a Class 1 and Class 2 certification and the associated costs.

In the Advanced tab, shown in Figure 6-9, you can do the following:

- Make cryptography settings by determining the type of encryption that you will allow. This enables Internet Explorer to automatically encrypt and decrypt information transferred between you and a secure server using the https service. Under most circumstances, all three protocols are valid means of securely transmitting information.

- Determine what kinds of security conditions you want to be warned about. While the warnings are worthwhile to keep you informed, they also can get annoying if they are not telling you something you care about.

- Control the type of software that can be downloaded and run on your computer. A number of Web sites have small ActiveX and Java programs that they download and run on your computer. You can prevent various types of programs from being downloaded, or prevent the running of those programs.

If you are a U.S. or Canadian citizen, you can download a version of Internet Explorer that implements a 128-bit encryption key. This is all but impossible to break and therefore provides a very high level of security. The normal version of Internet Explorer, and the only version available outside of the United States and Canada (this may be changing), uses a 40-bit encryption key, which for an experienced hacker, is possible to crack.

Tip: *You can determine which type of encryption you have by opening the Help menu and choosing About Internet Explorer. In the second line under the title you should see "Cipher Strength:" and either "40-bit" or "128-bit." A Typical installation of Windows 98 will give you the 40-bit version. Download the 128-bit version from **http://www.microsoft.com/ie/download**.*

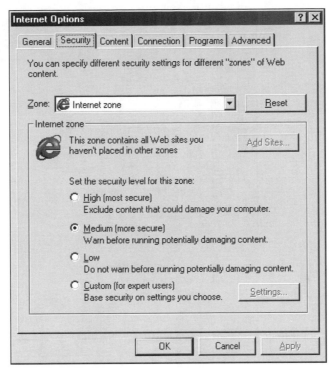

Figure 6-8 Security tab of the Internet Options dialog box

acceptable. You can also block access to sites that aren't rated, and set passwords that allow access to blocked sites. To set the level of material that users are allowed to see, follow these instructions:

1. In Internet Explorer, open the View menu, choose Internet Options, and click the Content tab.

2. Click Enable under Content Advisor, enter and confirm a password that must be used to change the ratings, and click OK.

3. The Content Advisor dialog box will open. (If you have previously set the password, you'll need to click Settings to open the Content Advisor.) Click one of the four content areas (Language, Nudity, Sex, or Violence), and

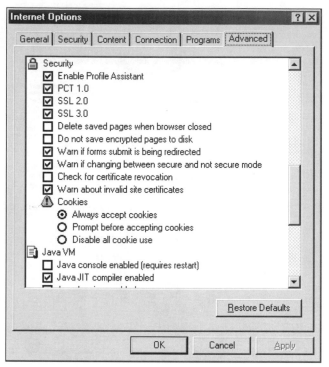

Figure 6-9 Advanced tab of the Internet Options dialog box

a five-position slider bar will appear, as you can see in Figure 6-10.

4. Move the slider to the highest level of content that you want to allow users of the computer to be able to see. If you want more information of the meanings of each level, click More Info at the bottom of the Content Advisor dialog box.

5. Click each of the other content areas and set the desired level.

6. When you have completed setting the desired levels, click the General tab.

7. Determine if you want users to see sites without ratings and if you want to use a supervisory password to allow users to see sites that would otherwise be blocked. You can also change the supervisory password.

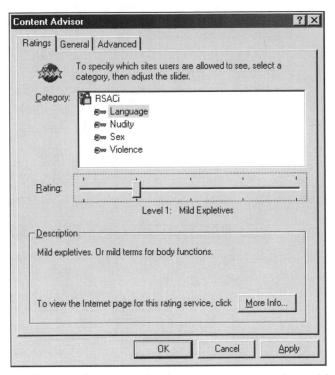

Figure 6-10 Setting the level of content that can be viewed in the Internet Explorer

8. When you have made your settings, click OK twice to close both the Content Advisor and Internet Options dialog boxes.

 What are "cookies" and are they harmful?

Cookies are small pieces of information that are placed on your computer by a Web site to identify your computer to that site. When you first visit a Web site, you may be asked for identifying information such as your name, company name, and so on. The Web site then places this information in a cookie and stores it on your computer. The cookie also contains the domain name and path of the Web page that created it, as well as an expiration date and security flag. The next time you visit that Web site, the Internet Explorer first

looks to see if you have a cookie for the site, and if you do, it will send the information to the site as it is connecting to it.

As a general rule, cookies are not harmful and are actually helpful in that they can save you the time of identifying yourself every time you visit the site. If you would like to be warned before accepting cookies on your computer, you can accomplish that with these steps:

1. In Internet Explorer, open the View menu, choose Internet Options, and click the Advanced tab.

2. Click Prompt Before Accepting Cookies, as shown here:

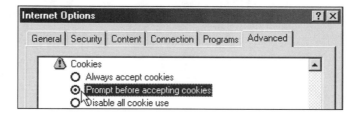

3. Click OK to close the Internet Options dialog box.

 How can I get the latest version of Internet Explorer?

At the time this is written (summer 1998), the latest English language version of the Internet Explorer for Windows 98 and Windows NT 4.0 is Version 4.01 with Service Pack 1. It is available for download from **http://www.microsoft.com/ie /download**.

 I would like to change some of the ways the Internet Explorer looks and behaves. What customization capabilities are available in Internet Explorer?

There are a number of changes that you can make to customize the Internet Explorer, including changing the size, position, and contents of the toolbar; organizing the list of favorite sites; and setting up your start page and links. Here are some things that you can do directly:

● Place the mouse pointer on the bottom of the toolbar area below the Address box and drag that area up and down. You can see how you can enlarge the toolbar, as shown in the first illustration, or shrink it to a single row without labels, as you can see in the second illustration.

● Click the ridged area on the left of the Address or Links bar to maximize and minimize these bars.

● Place the mouse pointer on the Address or Links labels, and drag those bars to place them in various positions.

● Place the mouse pointer on the ridged area of the Address, Links, or toolbar, and drag those bars to make them smaller or larger.

● Change what Web site is automatically opened when you start Internet Explorer by displaying your preferred Web site in the Internet Explorer, selecting View | Internet Options, clicking the General tab, and in the Home Page section clicking Use Current.

● Add Web sites that are pointed to on the Links bar by dragging the icon next to the current page's URL in the Address box to the position on the Links toolbar where you want it. Delete a link by right-clicking it and choosing Delete from the context menu.

● Organize how Web sites are displayed in your Favorites list by selecting Favorites | Organize Favorites, and then moving, renaming, deleting, and placing in new or existing folders the Web sites that are listed.

 I have several Web sites that I want to be able to quickly open. What is the best way to do that?

Probably the easiest way to handle this is to put shortcuts to these Web sites on your desktop. Then all you need to do is double-click the shortcut to open Internet Explorer and display the Web site, if you are connected to the Internet. Use these steps to create the shortcuts:

1. Connect to the Internet and start Internet Explorer.

2. Enter the URL or address of the site for which you want to create a shortcut and press ENTER. Your site should be displayed in Internet Explorer.

3. Right-click the home page of the site after it opens and choose Create Shortcut from the context menu. A message will appear telling you that a shortcut is about to be placed on your desktop. Click OK. A shortcut to the Web site will appear on your desktop, like this:

CNN
Interactive

 I view several foreign Web sites. Does Internet Explorer support international character sets, and if so, how?

Yes, Internet Explorer supports a large number of international character sets by default, and you can download additional support packs for Chinese (Traditional or Simplified), Japanese, and Pan Euro for Eastern European support. To view e-mail and Web pages with the special characters in French, German, Spanish, and the Scandinavian languages, you don't have to do anything special—the characters will automatically be displayed. For many Eastern European languages you can select one from Fonts on the View menu. For Far Eastern languages and others, you can add them to Internet Explorer by following these steps:

1. Click Internet Options on the View menu.

2. Click Languages on the General tab.

3. Click Add in the Language Preference dialog box and select the language support you want. Click OK.

4. Change the priority of a language by moving it up or down in the list using the buttons on the right side of the Language Preference dialog box, as shown next. The closer a language is to the top of the list, the greater its priority to be used on pages that offer more than one language.

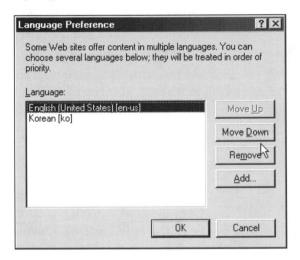

5. Click OK twice to close the open dialog boxes.

 Tip: *You can get many full-language versions of Internet Explorer (where all the labels and menus are in another language) in addition to the ability to support another language in the English language version from* ***http://www.microsoft.com/ie/download***.

 ### What are some ways I can access intranet and Internet addresses?

There are several avenues you can use to open Web material on your screen. Some of the factors to consider are:

- Personal preference
- Location of the material (Web or intranet)
- How much of the address is known
- Whether you've visited the site previously

Explore the following methods. Most can be used in the Active Desktop and Windows Explorer; all are available in Internet Explorer.

- **Typing an address in the Address box** and pressing ENTER is the most direct path to a known intranet or Internet address. Although this can be somewhat tedious for longer addresses, there are several features available to make it easier.

- **AutoComplete** attempts to finish addresses based on the characters you type for sites you have already visited. As you type the full address, either from "http:", or at any point in the address, AutoComplete will begin to fill in text and give you options to modify what it chooses. After AutoComplete adds some text (it will be highlighted) you can press UP or DOWN ARROW to rotate through a list of recently viewed sites, or you can right-click in the highlighted text, select Completions from the context menu, and choose an address from the submenu, as shown next. And you can just type a company name, such as "microsoft" and AutoComplete will add the prefix "http://www." and suffix ".com" for you after you press CTRL-ENTER.

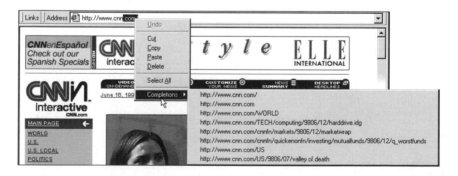

- **The History list**, accessed by clicking the down arrow at the right end of the Address box, displays a list of recently visited sites you can return to. You can open a History bar in a separate pane that categorizes your visits into days and weeks. Click History on the toolbar.

 Tip: *You can clear the entries that appear in the History list or modify how long they appear there by clicking Internet Options on the View menu and clicking the General tab.*

- **The File menu** provides two ways to easily access HTML pages. First, you can click Open to display a dialog box where you can type or browse for a file or page. Browsing in the Open dialog box is the best way to find files on your intranet or network. Also, toward the bottom of the File menu are listed recently opened pages you can click and immediately revisit.

- **Forward and Back buttons** on the toolbar provide a page-by-page chronological method of viewing pages, or you can click the down arrow next to either button to display a list of recently visited pages and jump directly to them.

- **Favorites** allow you to save "bookmarks" of sites you want to return to. On the Favorites menu, click Add To Favorites to add the current page to your list, or choose an existing favorite from the bottom of the menu. You can organize your favorites into folders as your list grows. You can open the Favorites bar by clicking the Favorites button on the toolbar

- **The Links toolbar** lets you drag and drop URL icons from the Address box (or any other location such as a folder) to the toolbar where you have quick access to them.

- **Search** connects you to a Microsoft site that lists several search engines, as shown in Figure 6-11, that you can use to type keywords, or in some cases, drill down through categories of content to find content and e-mail addresses.

- **The Explorer bar** provides several bars (or panes) that you can use to search for sites, launch favorite sites, see a history of your surfing, open channels, and view files and folders on the computer and network (Windows Explorer only).

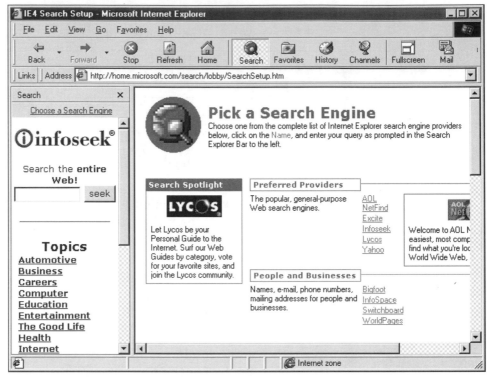

Figure 6-11 Locate Web sites and people from Microsoft's search site

SENDING AND RECEIVING E-MAIL

What does Windows 98 offer for an e-mail client?

Outlook Express, Windows 98's messaging and newsgroup client, allows you to send and receive e-mail and connect to and respond to newsgroup articles. Outlook Express is derived from Internet Mail, which was offered with earlier versions of Internet Explorer, and its big brother, Microsoft Outlook; however, in several messaging areas this prodigy has surpassed its more encompassing sibling. Open Outlook Express with these steps:

1. If you haven't already run the Internet Connection Wizard, do so with the instructions in the "Connecting to the Internet" section earlier in this chapter. The Internet Connection Wizard performs the double-duty of

establishing a connection to your Internet service provider as well as connecting to your mail server.

2. Double-click the Outlook Express icon on your desktop or click the same icon on the Quick Launch toolbar.

Tip: *Windows 98 Internet tools and programs can be opened by clicking Start and choosing Programs | Internet Explorer.*

3. Click OK to accept the default Outlook Express file location.

4. If prompted to connect, click OK, or you can click Connect on the toolbar when the Outlook Express window appears, as shown in Figure 6-12.

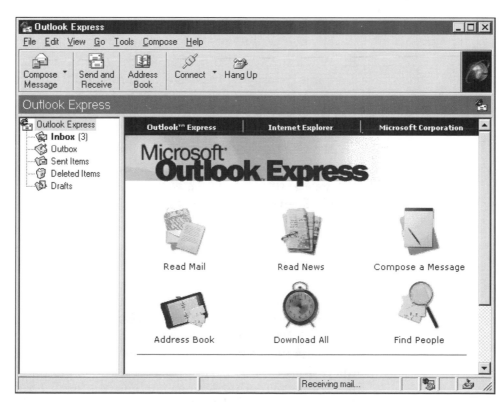

Figure 6-12   Outlook Express provides ease of messaging and newsgroup reading with several of the latest bells and whistles

Tip: *If you set up multiple e-mail accounts, you can choose which one to connect to by clicking the down arrow next to the Connect button and choosing the connection you want.*

5. Click Read Mail in the right pane to open the Inbox, where new messages are received. To force a "look" on your mail server to see if you have any new messages to download (or send messages from your Outbox) click Send And Receive on the toolbar.

6. Click a message in the upper-right pane and see its preview in the pane below. Double-clicking a message in the upper pane will open a message in its own window.

7. Create a message by clicking Compose Message on the toolbar. You can include a background design to your messages by clicking the down arrow next to the Compose Message icon and choosing one of the stationery themes.

8. When through composing, sending, receiving, and reading e-mail, close any message windows and then click Close in the upper-right corner of the Outlook Express window. You also might have to close your Internet connection by double-clicking the Connection icon next to the clock on the taskbar and choosing Disconnect.

 I used Microsoft Internet Mail in earlier versions of Windows. Can I bring my messages into Outlook Express?

Yes, but with some qualifications. Outlook Express provides several formats that can be used to import message folders from other mail clients; however, you may have to perform an intermediate step to get the data in a format that is recognized. For example, Outlook Express has an import format for Microsoft Internet Mail for Windows 3.1, which may or may not work for you. The best approach is to try and import directly, and if that doesn't work, export within your mail client to another format such as Microsoft Exchange or Microsoft Outlook, and then import that result to Outlook Express. Import with these steps:

1. Click the Outlook Express icon on the Quick Launch toolbar (or double-click the Outlook Express icon on your desktop).

2. Open the File menu, point to Import, and click Messages.

3. Select your mail client from the list and click Next.

4. Follow the prompts in the wizard and your messages should appear in folders in the left pane of the Outlook Express window.

How do I get an e-mail address, and what form does it take?

The organization through which you connect to the Internet will assign you an e-mail address. Your address will be of the form: *youraccountid@domainname.domaintype.* The *domaintype* in the United States is one of six three-letter suffixes: .COM for commercial accounts, .NET for Internet infrastructure organizations such as ISPs, .GOV for federal government organizations, .MIL for military organizations, .EDU for educational organizations, and .ORG for other organizations not covered by the other suffixes. Outside of the United States, the suffix is a two-letter identification of the country, such as .CA for Canada, and .UK for the United Kingdom. The *domainname* identifies the organization providing the connection to you. For example: McGraw-Hill is *mcgraw-hill.com*, the United States Department of the Treasury is *ustreas.gov*, and NCF Communications, Inc., an ISP, is *ncfweb.net*. The *youraccountid* depends on your Internet connection. If you are connected using CompuServe, this is commonly a number; if you are connected through an ISP, they may prescribe an account ID such as "johnc" or "jclark," or they may allow you to pick your own.

Can I get my own domain name, and if so, how?

Yes. A *domain name* is the part of the e-mail and Web address that ends in ".com" or ".net," for example, "microsoft.com" or "whidbey.net." The easiest way to get a domain name is to ask your ISP. For a fee, normally a one-time payment of a couple hundred dollars and a much

smaller monthly amount, your ISP can set you up with your own domain name so you can be "*you@yourdomain*.com." You don't need your own domain for either e-mail or a Web page, but if you want to promote something, putting that in your domain name can be beneficial.

Domain names are all registered in the United States with InterNIC, a cooperative activity of the National Science Foundation, AT&T, and Network Solutions, Inc. You can go directly to InterNIC (**http://rs.internic.net/rs-internic.html**) to obtain a domain name. The fee is $75 for the first two years and then $35 per year thereafter, but you will need to have a host such as an ISP for the name, so you might as well go to your ISP to start with.

An important service provided by InterNIC is the online directory of registered domain names at **http://rs.internic.net/cgi-bin/whois**. By using this directory, you can check out a domain name to see if it is being used, as shown in Figure 6-13. If you do not find an existing user of the domain name, you will get the message "No match found for *domainname*.com." Otherwise the search results will be displayed like this:

 Note: *In Canada, domain name registration is through Cyberspace Research, in North York, Ontario, at **http://www.csr.ists.ca/w3can/forms/registration.html**.*

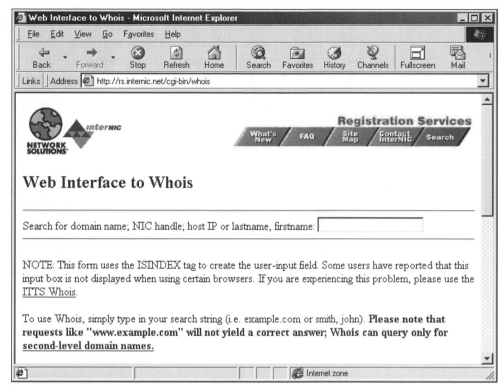

Figure 6-13 InterNIC's Whois Web page, which allows searching for existing domain names

 I would like to include a document with an e-mail message. I know I can copy and paste it in the message, but is there a way to send the file?

 Yes. You can attach any file to an e-mail message and send it with the message. In Outlook Express this is accomplished while you are creating a message (the New Message window is open) by clicking the Insert File button on the toolbar. When you click this button, the Insert Attachment dialog box will open where you can select the drive, folder, and file that you want to send. Other e-mail programs work similarly, but may offer more features. For example, in Microsoft Outlook 98 you can attach not only files, but other Outlook items such as other messages, contact information, and notes.

 I keep getting messages with acronyms like ROFL and odd little faces like :-7 that I don't understand. Where can I find out what these mean?

ROFL stands for "rolling on the floor laughing" and viewed sideways the little face, called a "smiley," indicates a wry statement. The best sources on acronyms and smileys are the acronym and smiley dictionaries at **http://magicpub.com/ netprimer**.

 What are the differences among e-mail programs?

With Windows 98 you get a free e-mail client program, Outlook Express. It provides a full-featured facility for creating, sending, receiving, and storing e-mail that is sent and received over the Internet. Windows 98 also provides an address book, where you can set up e-mail and other contact information for people you regularly correspond with, as you can see in Figure 6-14.

If you used either Microsoft Internet Explorer prior to version 4.0 or Netscape Navigator, there is a mail program that is available and provides almost the same services that are available in Outlook Express. Also, if upgrading from Windows 95, you may still be using Microsoft Exchange. The only difference besides support for newer Internet technology is that Exchange can also be used for LAN mail and for some information services mail. See the section "Microsoft Exchange" in Chapter 10 for some questions related to this legacy product.

There are also a number of other mail programs available on the Internet. Probably the most widely used is Eudora. There is a free version, Eudora Light for Windows. A more full-featured version, Eudora Pro for Windows can be purchased and downloaded from the Web site, **http://www.eudora.com**, (not including disks or paper manuals). You can also download for free Eudora Web-Mail, which uses any browser as a mail client shell and the account is provided for free. More and more companies, such as Yahoo!, are offering free e-mail accounts. The only

Jenny Diver Properties ☐ ? ☒

Personal | Home | Business | Other | NetMeeting | Digital IDs |

Enter personal information about this contact here.

Name

First: Jenny   Middle: [   ]   Last: Diver

Display: Jenny Diver ▼   Nickname: [   ]

E-Mail Addresses

Add new: [   ]   Add

✉ **scubawomen@underwater.com   (Default E-Mail)**   Edit

Remove

Set as Default

☐ Send E-Mail using plain text only.

OK   Cancel

Figure 6-14   Keep an online "rolodex" of information for your contacts

question is whether these products will remain available and free. When you live and die by e-mail, as we do, you sleep better at night, despite the monthly bill, knowing your tried-and-true ISP is always there handling your e-mail.

Microsoft Office 97 includes Outlook (and you can upgrade to Outlook 98, released in the spring of 1998) which beautifully handles e-mail from and to many sources. It also provides scheduling, contact lists, task lists, and a number of ways to automatically create journal entries, all integrated with e-mail, as you can see in Figure 6-15. Outlook is our e-mail because it allows us to use Microsoft Word to create and read e-mail and because it provides the ability to do group scheduling and task assignments with the mail system.

Note: *See* Microsoft Outlook 98 Made Easy, *by Carole and Martin Matthews (Osborne/McGraw-Hill, 1998).*

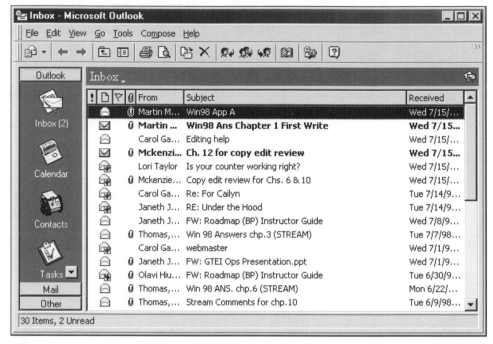

Figure 6-15 Microsoft Outlook 98—e-mail and a lot more

 I have been using Eudora to handle my e-mail and would like to switch to Internet Explorer. How can I transfer my address book and message file to Internet Explorer?

You can import your mail messages and the address book after the first startup of Outlook Express by opening the File menu and choosing Import.

MICROSOFT NETWORK

 What is Microsoft Network?

Microsoft Network is Microsoft's information service. It provides a multitude of services, such as bulletin boards, chat sessions, forums, opportunities to buy products, and information on a wide variety of subjects, including computing, science, business, education, and many others. You can connect to and use the Internet from within Microsoft Network. You can also connect to Microsoft Network through the Internet. It is one of several online services you can subscribe to such as America Online, AT&T WorldNet Service, CompuServe, and Prodigy Internet (all available from the Online Services folder on your desktop).

How do I set up and use MSN?

The Microsoft Network (MSN) is both an information service that allows you to search and retrieve information that it provides, as well as an Internet service provider that gives you access to the Internet. To use MSN, you need a modem with a phone connection in addition to Windows 98. To set up and use MSN, follow these steps:

1. Double-click the Setup The Microsoft Network icon on the desktop. You may be prompted to insert your Windows 98 CD.

2. If you have not already installed MSN, follow the prompts to do so. After you have completed installation, double-click the MSN icon on your desktop. You will be connected to MSN where you will finish setting it up.

3. If this is your first time using MSN you will have to tolerate several steps to possibly update your MSN software, receive special offerings, and other administrative tasks. Eventually, Internet Explorer will open with the On Stage home page, shown in Figure 6-16, your gateway into MSN and all that it offers. From On Stage you have access to your e-mail account, several search engines, categories of Web sites, and links to other Microsoft sites, including MSNBC News. The best way to learn about MSN is to just start exploring. If you get lost and want to return to the On Stage home page, click the Microsoft Network icon next to the clock, point to On Stage, and click On Stage Home Page. The context menu, shown next, also provides quick access to many MSN features and lets you know how long you've been

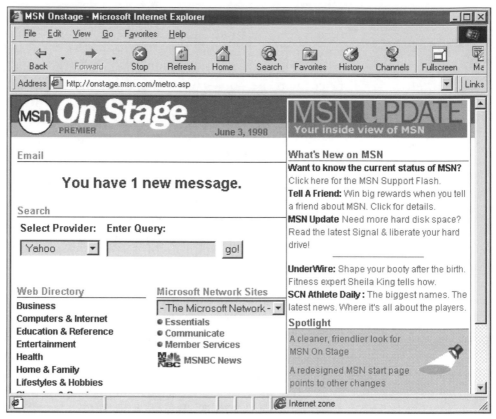

Figure 6-16   The MSN On Stage home page

online, how to change your account options, and a link to disconnect from MSN.

If I sign up on the Microsoft Network, how do I know my e-mail address?

> Your Internet e-mail address on MSN is your *memberid@ msn.com*, or within MSN, just *memberid*. Your *memberid* is the one you use to sign on to MSN.

CREATING AND DISTRIBUTING WEB CONTENT

My boss assigned me the job of exploring how to create a Web page for our office. What does Windows 98 offer for creating Web pages and working with Web pages?

> Windows 98 provides three tools that will allow you to create Web content, publish (or copy) your Web material to a Web server, and host your own limited Web or FTP (file transfer protocol) server. Following is an overview of these three programs.

 Note: Providing thorough information on using these tools is beyond the scope of this book. See FrontPage 98: The Complete Reference *by Martin Matthews and Erik Poulsen (Osborne/McGraw-Hill, 1998) for an in-depth primer on creating and publishing Web material.*

Personal Web Server

> To host Web content you need software that provides the necessary file handling functions for a Web site that uses browsers as *clients* to access a *Web server*, where the site content is stored. Windows 98 provides the Personal Web Server (PWS) to allow you to host Web content in a limited fashion. The PWS contains the necessary FrontPage Extensions that allow the more advanced features of FrontPage Express to be displayed properly in the browsers of people viewing your Web content. Install the PWS with these steps:
>
> 1. Click Start and choose Programs | Internet Explorer | Personal Web Server.

2. Read the instructions that are presented, insert your Windows 98 CD in your drive, and follow the installation instructions. A Typical installation is recommended unless you are experienced in setting up a Web server.

3. Restart your computer when prompted. The PWS icon located next to the clock on the taskbar lets you know the server is active.

4. Double-click the Publish icon on your desktop or right-click the PWS icon and click Properties on the context menu. The Personal Web Manager opens, as shown in Figure 6-17.

5. Click Web Site on the sidebar to open a wizard that leads you through creating your own home page and Web site.

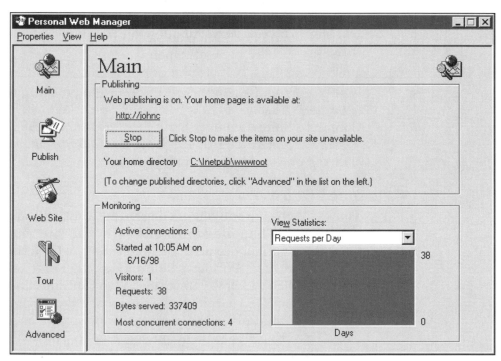

Figure 6-17   Use the Personal Web Manager to control your Personal Web Server

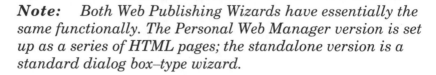

Personal Web Manager. You can also install a standalone Web Publishing Wizard with these steps:

Note: *Both Web Publishing Wizards have essentially the same functionally. The Personal Web Manager version is set up as a series of HTML pages; the standalone version is a standard dialog box–type wizard.*

1. Click Start, choose Settings | Control Panel, and double-click Add/Remove Programs

2. Click the Windows Setup tab, double-click Internet Tools, select Web Publishing Wizard, and click OK twice.

3. Start the Web Publishing Wizard by clicking Start and choosing Programs | Internet Tools | Web Publishing Wizard.

Chapter 7

File Management

Answer Topics!

File Management @ a Glance

File management, the handling of information written onto and read off of disks, was the primary focus of the first operating systems. Operating systems today do many other things, but file management remains critically important. It is a major area of enhancement in Windows 98 over the previous combination of Windows 3.*x* and DOS 6.*x*, and a continuing level of improvement started in Windows 95. Windows 98 provides a full 32-bit file system, many protected-mode drivers (see Chapter 5), long filenames, and Windows Explorer, in addition to many smaller enhancements. The result of all these changes is a file system that is easier to use, more intuitive, and faster than its predecessors. Windows 98 almost transparently provides these basic services, without which computing would be useless.

Here are the areas explored by this chapter:

- **Disk Backup and Copy** describes how to make copies of disks and back up your data.

- **Maintaining Your File System** answers questions on how to keep your system optimally tuned for maximum performance.

- **Automating Tasks** covers the scheduling tools that ensure your programs are run when you want them.

- **Working with Disks** explores some of the basic disk operations such as formatting and labeling.

- **Folder and Filenames** answers questions about using filenames and which characters are valid.

- **File and Folder Operations** covers a broad spectrum on how to organize your data structure by moving, copying, and removing files and folders.

- **Viewing Files and Folders** discusses the several methods you can use to view your data.

- **File Allocation Table (FAT vs. FAT32)** provides a primer on the two file storage schemes, including how to convert from FAT to FAT32.

 Note: *The questions described in this chapter assume you are using the default method of single-clicking to select items and double-clicking to open them. The alternative method, which behaves more like the functionality of a Web browser, is described in Chapter 6.*

DISK BACKUP AND COPY

 How do I copy a disk?

You can copy a disk in either My Computer or Windows Explorer. Follow these steps:

1. Double-click My Computer on the desktop. Alternatively, open Windows Explorer by holding SHIFT while double-clicking My Computer or clicking Start and choosing Programs | Windows Explorer.

2. Right-click the floppy disk drive to be copied. This will open the context menu shown here:

3. Click Copy Disk. The Copy Disk dialog box will be displayed, as shown here:

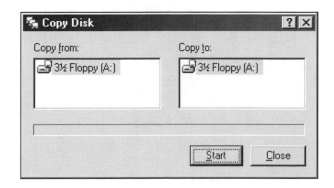

4. From the Copy From list, select the disk drive to be used as the source of the copy (if you have more than one).

5. From the Copy To list, select the disk drive to be used as the destination of the copy (if you have more than one).

6. Click Start and follow any prompts.

 ## Can I restore backups made from previous versions of Microsoft Backup?

No. The Windows 98 Backup program only restores backup files that it has created.

Note: Microsoft Backup is not installed as part of a Typical setup. To install Microsoft Backup, click Start and choose Settings | Control Panel and double-click Add/Remove Programs. On the Windows Setup tab, scroll down to the System Tools component and double-click it. Select Backup and click OK twice to install the program files. You will need to restart your computer.

 ## Can I schedule unattended backups using Microsoft Backup?

Yes, but the scheduling is not performed by Microsoft Backup. It's handled by the Scheduled Tasks utility (see questions related to Scheduled Tasks and the Maintenance Wizard later in this chapter). To allow unattended backups by eliminating prompts, verify the following:

1. Open Microsoft Backup by clicking Start and choosing Programs | Accessories | System Tools | Backup and clicking Close when the first wizard dialog box appears.

 2. Click the Job Options button on the toolbar and click the Report tab.

3. Make sure the Perform An Unattended Backup check box is selected, as shown here:

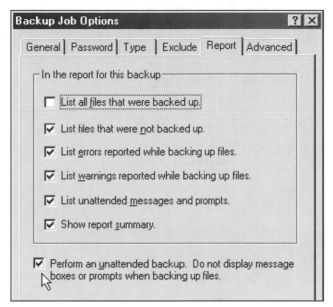

File Management Tools

Here is a brief summary of some of the more important file management tools in Windows 98.

- **Backup**, accessed through Start | Programs | Accessories | System Tools, compresses selected files and stores them on multiple floppy disks, magnetic tape, or larger removable disks.

- **Disk Defragmenter** rearranges how files are stored on your hard disk to minimize the time it takes to access data.

- **ScanDisk** checks your files and the physical make-up of your hard disk, and informs you of problems and recommended courses of action to fix them.

- **Scheduled Tasks/Maintenance Wizard** provides automatic scheduling to run disk maintenance programs, as well as any executable file on your computer.

● **Disk Cleanup** examines your hard disk and provides several options to remove files that you probably don't need any longer.

● **DriveSpace 3/Compression Agent** is accessed through Start | Programs | Accessories | System Tools. DriveSpace 3 provides disk-wide compression that can double your hard disk storage space, while the Compression Agent allows you to selectively adjust the compression level used on specific files.

● **Drive Converter (FAT32)** allows you to convert your hard disk file allocation table from FAT (or FAT16) to the more efficient FAT32, freeing up unused, but inaccessible, space on your disk.

● **Cut and Paste** can be used to move or copy a file, as well as text or graphics within a file. Use CTRL-X to delete or cut, CTRL-C to copy, and CTRL-V to paste. You can also click the Cut, Copy, and Paste buttons (shown here) in a folder window's toolbar.

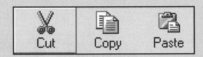

● **Drag-and-Drop** allows you to move or copy files or *folders* (*directories* in DOS and Windows 3.x) by pointing on them with the mouse, pressing and holding a mouse button, and dragging them from one location to another. Using the right mouse button gives you a menu, shown next, when you release the mouse button ("drop" the object), whereas the left mouse button does different things depending on the type of file and the keyboard keys held down (see discussion in Chapter 5).

> **Move Here**
> Copy Here
> Create Shortcut(s) Here
> ─────────────
> Cancel

- **Windows Explorer**, **My Computer**, and **Network Neighborhood** are your primary access to files and folders within Windows 98. They allow you to locate files, folders, disks, and computers on a network; to look at files and folders in different views; to open, copy, move, delete, and rename files and folders; to create folders and shortcuts to files and folders; to format and copy disks; to share disks and folders; and to map disks on a network.

> *Note:* *The integration of Internet Explorer in Windows 98 provides yet another whole environment for accessing files. These features are described in Chapter 6.*

- **Folder Window** is the standard window used by Windows Explorer, My Computer, Network Neighborhood, and all folders that are opened. Figure 7-1 shows you its standard features.

- **Long Names** of up to 255 characters can be used in Windows 98 and can include spaces and all other characters *except* \ / : * " ? < > and |. You can give files descriptive names that are easily remembered, rather than the eight-character names with three-character extensions required in Windows 3.*x* and DOS.

- **My Briefcase** is used to synchronize files that are being modified or edited on another computer. This is a way to keep multiple copies of a file up to date.

- **Recycle Bin** holds deleted files until it's emptied (or full, in which case the older files are deleted). You can cut, copy, paste, and restore files from this folder.

- **Renaming Files** can be done by clicking the filename to select the file, clicking again to open the name for editing (or pressing F2), and then typing the new name. It is fast and efficient. (The click-slowly-twice method doesn't work if you are using single-click to open items. In that case you have to point on the filename to select it and then press F2 to open the name for editing. Choose between single- or double-click methods by opening a folder window's View menu and choosing Folder Options | Settings.)

Folders   Address box

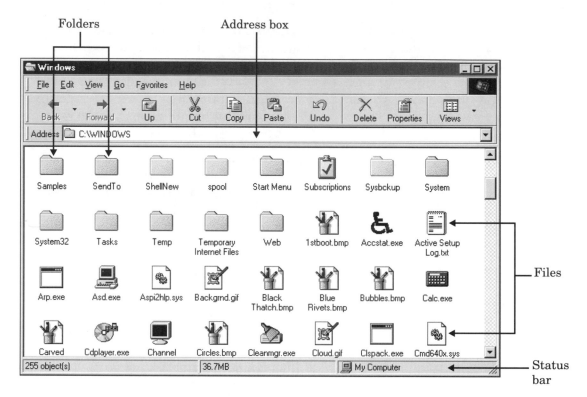

Figure 7-1 The folder window is the primary tool for file management functions in Windows 98

MAINTAINING YOUR FILE SYSTEM

 ### What is Defrag and how do I use it?

The Disk Defragmenter (which has the filename Defrag.exe) is a system utility that optimizes disk performance by reorganizing the files on a drive. When your disk begins to get full and you continue to save files, the files are broken up into segments, which are spread out over the disk in any unused space. Defrag's reorganization gathers up the segments and places them in one contiguous location. This considerably speeds up disk access. Additionally, Defrag can rearrange your most used files to be in the same area as their associated program files, thereby decreasing disk access time even more. Defrag can run from within Windows and even while you are performing other tasks—although this is *not* recommended, since Defrag restarts every time you write something on the disk. You can defragment your local hard drives, compressed drives, and floppy drives. You cannot use Defrag on network drives or CD-ROM drives.

We recommend that you run Defrag regularly—at least monthly—if you use your PC fairly often.

 Tip: *Use the Maintenance Wizard, described later in this chapter, to set up Defrag to automate this task for you.*

Follow these steps to start the Disk Defragmenter:

1. Click Start and choose Programs I Accessories I System Tools I Disk Defragmenter.

2. Click the down arrow to open the drive drop-down list, and select the disk drive to be defragmented. It will default to your C: hard drive. Click Settings to set some options for how the defragmenting will be done. Click OK to start the Defrag process.

3. The Disk Defragmenter will examine your disk and, if it's less than 10 percent defragmented, display the percentage of fragmentation in your disk and recommend whether you should defragment the drive. If you decide to proceed, click Start and a message box will open, giving you the status as shown here:

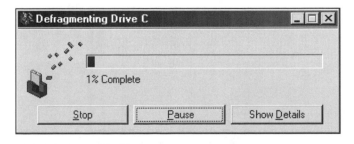

 Tip: *If you enjoy watching grass grow, click Show Details in the Disk Defragmenter dialog box and watch a pictorial representation of your hard disk being defragmented.*

 Windows 98 seems to have two versions of ScanDisk. What is the difference in the two versions?

One version of ScanDisk on the Windows 98 startup disk is a DOS program that checks your hard drive for errors before allowing setup. The other is a Windows-based version that can be run through Explorer or from the Start menu. Both versions check the File Allocation Table (FAT), long filenames, system structure, folder structure, surface damage (bad sectors and lost allocation units), and any DriveSpace or DoubleSpace volume and compression.

After Windows 98 has been installed, you can use ScanDisk from your Accessories menu with these instructions:

1. Click Start and choose Programs | Accessories | System Tools | ScanDisk. The ScanDisk dialog box will be displayed, as shown in Figure 7-2.

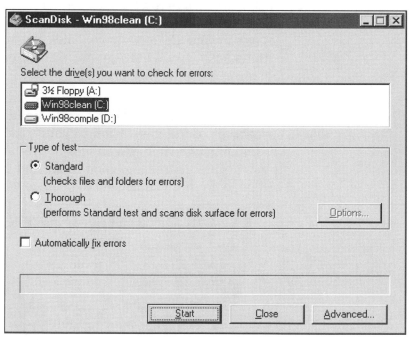

Figure 7-2 ScanDisk searches your disk drives for errors

2. Select the disk drive to be checked.

3. Click the Type Of Test: Standard or Thorough. If you choose Thorough, you can click Options to select the area of the disk to be scanned. Also under Options you can choose whether to perform write testing and to repair bad sectors in hidden or system files.

4. If you want the errors automatically fixed without alerting you, click Automatically Fix Errors.

5. If you want to change some of the default settings ScanDisk uses, click Advanced.

6. Click Start to begin the error checking.

Is there an easier way than going through the maze of menus if I want to run the drive utilities such as ScanDisk and Defrag?

There are two other ways to manually start the disk utilities: from the Start menu Run option and from the disk's Properties dialog box. See the next section, "Automating Tasks," for unattended methods that can run these utilities.

Follow these steps to use the Run option:

1. Click Start and choose Run.

2. Type **scandskw** to start ScanDisk, or type **defrag** to start the Disk Defragmenter, and in either case, press ENTER or click OK.

Follow these steps to use the Properties dialog box:

1. Open My Computer or Windows Explorer.

2. Right-click the drive you want to work on and choose Properties. The Properties dialog box will appear. Click the Tools tab as shown in Figure 7-3.

3. Click Check Now to run ScanDisk, Backup Now to run Microsoft Backup, and Defragment Now to run the Disk Defragmenter.

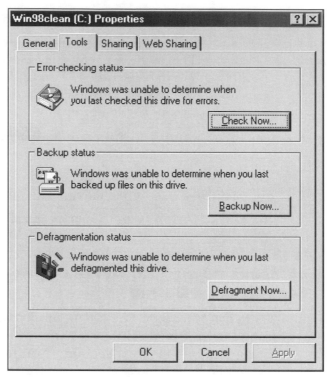

Figure 7-3 The Tools tab of the disk's Properties dialog box provides access to some of the important disk utilities

Is there an easy way I can get rid of files that I no longer use or need to free up disk space?

Windows 98 provides just what you're looking for—Disk Cleanup, a utility that scans your hard disk for temporary files, your Recycle Bin, and program files you have downloaded (and probably have already run) that you can delete. Run Disk Cleanup with these steps:

1. Click Start and choose Programs | Accessories | System Tools | Disk Cleanup. Select the drive you want to clean up.

2. Select the types of files to delete. You can read a description of what type of files each category deletes in the Description list box and you can view the files Disk Cleanup recommends can be deleted by clicking View Files, as you can see here:

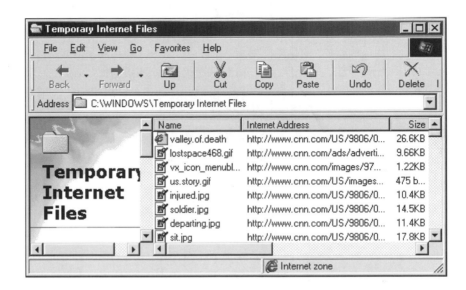

3. Close any folder windows you opened and then click OK in the Disk Cleanup dialog box to delete the types of files you selected.

In the other two tabs you can get quick access to the Add/Remove Programs control panel where you can remove unwanted programs, start a conversion utility to change your file allocation table to FAT32 (reducing cluster size and gaining more usable disk space), and automatically run Disk Cleanup when you run low on disk space.

Tip: *Run the Maintenance Wizard to have Disk Cleanup check your disk on an unattended schedule.*

AUTOMATING TASKS

 Everything I read says I should do periodic maintenance on my system, but I never seem to get around to it. Does Windows 98 offer me any assistance?

 Yes it does, in the form of the Scheduled Tasks utility. Microsoft even tries to get everyone to use it by placing its icon next to the clock by default.

See how to schedule a task, recurring or on a one-time basis, with these steps:

1. Double-click the Task Scheduler icon on the taskbar, or alternatively, click Start and choose Programs | Accessories | System Tools | Scheduled Tasks.

2. In the Scheduled Tasks window, shown in Figure 7-4, double-click Add Scheduled Task in the Name column to start the Scheduled Task Wizard. Click Next.

3. Choose a program from the list box or click Browse and locate a program file you want to run. Click Next.

4. Change the name for the task if you want and select when you want it to be run. Click Next.

5. Set up the time, periodicity, and day of the week you want to run the task. Click Next.

6. Click Finish to add the task to the list of tasks to be run.

 Note: In order for the Task Scheduler to accomplish the tasks you have mandated, your computer must be turned on *during the times that you have scheduled.*

Supporting options for the Task Scheduler, such as being notified if a task is not performed, are available on the Advanced menu.

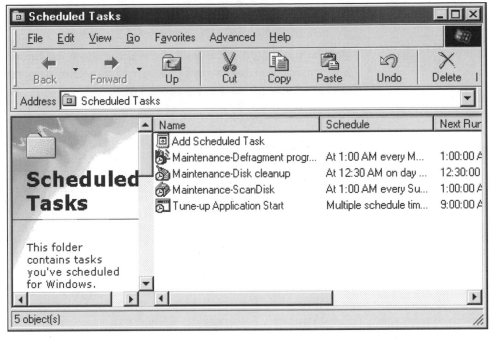

Figure 7-4 Automate the running of programs and utilities

 I want to keep my system tuned without having to figure out which programs to use to do it. Is there a one-stop method to accomplish this?

Yes, you're in luck. You can run the Maintenance Wizard which will quickly set up three primary disk utility programs and include them in the Task Scheduler for you (see the preceding question). Run the Maintenance Wizard as follows:

1. Click Start and choose Programs | Accessories | System Tools | Maintenance Wizard.

2. Accept the default Express method and click Next.

3. Choose a time to have Windows run the utilities. Pick a time that your computer will be turned on. Microsoft

recommends you leave your computer on all the time and choose the nighttime option. Click Next.

4. Before you click Finish you can choose to have the Disk Defragmenter, ScanDisk, and Disk Cleanup run in advance of your scheduled time.

WORKING WITH DISKS

 ### How do I format a disk in Windows 98?

You can format a disk from either My Computer or Windows Explorer using these steps:

1. Insert a disk into the floppy drive.

2. On the desktop, double-click My Computer, or open Windows Explorer by selecting Start | Programs | Windows Explorer.

 Tip: *You can also open Windows Explorer by pressing SHIFT and then double-clicking My Computer, or by pressing the Windows symbol key (on the left side, bottom row of a Windows 95-style keyboard) and the E key.*

3. Right-click the disk drive that contains the disk and choose Format.

4. Choose the Capacity and Format Type, or just accept the defaults that Windows 98 is offering if you are not sure (if the capacity is incorrect, you will have another chance to change it). Type in a Label if you want one on the disk. You can also select No Label, Display Summary When Finished, and Copy System Files (which will produce a bootable disk).

5. Click Start.

 Warning: *Formatting a used disk erases all data on it, and the lost data cannot be restored.*

 How can I label a disk?

You can label a disk while formatting it, as described in the previous question. You can also label a disk after it has been formatted by following these steps:

1. If you want to label a floppy disk, place it in the disk drive.

2. Double-click the My Computer icon, or open Windows Explorer by selecting Start | Programs | Windows Explorer.

3. Right-click the disk drive, floppy or hard, and choose Properties. Select the General tab if it is not already selected, as shown in Figure 7-5.

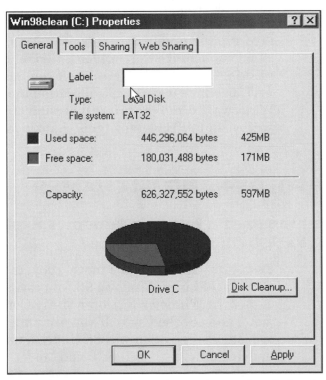

Figure 7-5   The General tab of the disk's Properties dialog box allows you to label a disk

 Tip: *If you click the Tools tab, you can find out the last time the disk was error-checked, backed up, or defragmented. If these tasks haven't been performed recently on the disk, you can run the disk tools ScanDisk, Disk Defragmenter, and Backup from this dialog box.*

4. Type the text for the label in the Label text box and then click OK.

 After I ran a disk utility (an older version of Norton Utilities, for example), all my long filenames disappeared. Why?

You have to run a disk utility that supports long filenames, or the utility will look at the information in the Virtual File Allocation Table (VFAT) that stores the long filename, consider it corruption or garbage, and clean it up. Be sure to use Windows utilities that are long filename–aware. Also, consider utilities that are FAT32-aware if you have converted from FAT16, which was the file allocation table scheme used in Windows 3.*x* and the original version of Windows 95. See the section on FAT32 later in this chapter for more information.

FOLDER AND FILENAMES

 I renamed a folder in Windows Explorer. Can I get back to the original name?

Yes. After you perform a move, copy, or rename operation on a file or folder in Windows 98, you can undo it. Just press CTRL-Z. In Windows Explorer or My Computer, open the Edit menu and choose Undo. If you are undoing a rename operation, the option will be Undo Rename; if you are undoing a move, it will be Undo Move.

Tip: *You can undo the last ten copy, move, or rename operations that you performed.*

After I restored a tape backup, I lost my long filenames. Why?

Not all tape backup programs support long filenames. Windows 98 includes a backup utility, Microsoft Backup, that supports long filenames and many tape drives. You access it by clicking Start and choosing Programs | Accessories | System Tools | Backup.

What are the valid filenames I can use in Windows 98?

Filenames in Windows 98 can be up to 255 characters in length and can use all of the valid DOS filename characters, plus additional characters. Windows 98 filenames are not case-sensitive, but the case is preserved. Also in Windows 98 you can have any number of characters after a period and multiple periods, so long as the total number of characters does not exceed 255. In addition to the normal letters and numbers on your keyboard, the special characters shown here are valid in DOS and Windows.

Symbol	Description
$	Dollar sign
%	Percent sign
'	Apostrophe or closing single quotation mark
`	Opening single quotation mark
-	Hyphen
@	At sign
{	Left brace
}	Right brace
~	Tilde
!	Exclamation point
#	Number sign
(	Opening parenthesis
)	Closing parenthesis
&	Ampersand
_	Underscore
^	Caret

The special characters shown next are valid in Windows 98 only.

Symbol	Description
	Space
+	Plus sign
,	Comma
.	Period
;	Semicolon
=	Equal sign
[	Opening bracket
]	Closing bracket

To see the DOS 8.3 name corresponding to a long filename, right-click the file and then click Properties. On the General tab, you will see the long filename at the top of the dialog box and the MS-DOS name in the middle, as you can see in Figure 7-6.

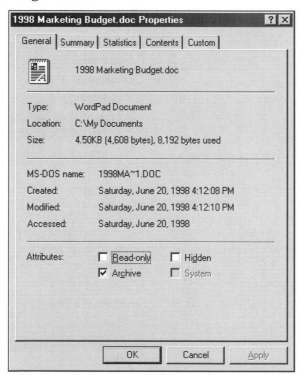

Figure 7-6　A file or folder's Properties dialog box shows both the long and short filenames

FILE AND FOLDER OPERATIONS

 Can I add new options to the Send To menu that I get when I right-click a file?

Initially, the Send To menu shows the floppy drives and other destinations that you have installed, as shown in Figure 7-7. However, you can specify any other disk and/or folder as a destination by adding shortcuts to the \Windows\SendTo folder. For example, adding a shortcut to the Recycle Bin saves time and avoids the prompt "Are you sure you want to send *filename* to the Recycle Bin?" Alternatively, any other folder such as a temporary folder can also be used.

To add a disk and/or folder to the SendTo folder, follow these steps:

1. In the right pane of the Windows Explorer window, locate the drive, folder, or device (such as a printer) to place in the SendTo folder.

2. In the left, or All Folders, pane, locate \Windows\ SendTo, but do not select it. Simply display it on the left of the Windows Explorer window.

3. Drag the drive and/or folder from the right pane to the \Windows\SendTo folder in the left pane.

Now when you right-click a file and select Send To, the new destination will appear.

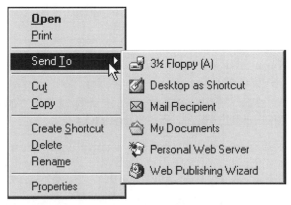

Figure 7-7   The Send To menu initially shows the destinations you have installed

 Note: *The left pane of Windows Explorer can take on several views. Collectively, the pane is called the Explorer Bar and besides the default All Folders view you can choose from the View menu four Web-related views, as well as displaying no pane. The Web views are described in Chapter 6.*

 Tip: *Here is a bonus. If you have different but related places to send a file, you can create another level of submenu. You place an additional folder (not a shortcut) in the SendTo folder—for example, a Customers folder. Then, within that folder, place shortcuts to all your customers' individual folders, naming each shortcut appropriately. As a result, when you right-click a file icon, your Send To quick menu will show the new Customers option. When you move to it, you will see a submenu listing all your customers' shortcuts. (You may want to remove the "shortcut to" text from the icons in the SendTo folder.)*

How do I check my free and used disk space in Windows 98?

Follow these steps:

1. Double-click My Computer on the desktop.
2. Right-click the disk drive you want to check.
3. Choose Properties from the context menu.
4. Choose the General tab. The disk space, free and used, will be displayed.

How do I copy files and folders in Windows Explorer or My Computer to a different name in the same folder? For example, I want to copy Win.ini to Win.old. How do I do this?

You can make such a copy with the following instructions:

1. In Windows Explorer or My Computer, right-click the file you want to copy.

2. Choose Copy from the context menu, as shown here:

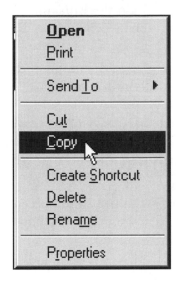

3. Right-click an empty area inside the same folder you copied from, and choose Paste. This will create a copy of your file at the end of the folder. If the original was called Win.ini, the copy will be called "Copy of Win.ini."

4. Type the name you want in place of the default name.

 Tip: *If you prefer to work from the keyboard you can also use CTRL-C for copy and CTRL-V for paste.*

Can I create a copy of a file on my A:\ drive without using a second disk or copying the file to my hard drive?

Yes, so long as there is enough room on your floppy to hold the copy. You can use the technique discussed in answer to the earlier question on how to check free and used disk space, or you can do the following:

1. Open My Computer, double-click the A:\ disk drive, and select the file or files you want to copy.

2. Open the Edit menu and choose Copy.

3. Open the Edit menu again and choose Paste. A copy of the selected file or files will be created with the words "Copy of" in front of the filename.

4. Select the name and type the name you want over the default name.

When I delete a shortcut from my desktop, it is placed in the Recycle Bin. How can I just delete a file and not have it go into the Recycle Bin?

First, select the file and then hold down the SHIFT key and press the DEL key. You can also right-click the file and then hold down the SHIFT key before selecting Delete from the context menu.

Warning: *Of course, if you delete a file without sending it to the Recycle Bin, it cannot be restored.*

How do I drag one file to another folder using just Windows Explorer?

To drag a file from one folder to another using only one instance of Explorer, use the following steps:

1. Locate the file or folder you want to move in the right pane of the Windows Explorer window.

2. Drag the file or folder into the left, or All Folders, pane near but not on top of the top or bottom border of the pane. This will cause the pane to scroll, either up or down, depending on whether you moved to the top or bottom (this is called *nudging*). When you see the destination folder, drag the file or folder you are moving to it.

I am getting an error message: "This folder already contains a file ...." What does that mean?

An example of this message is shown in Figure 7-8. It's telling you that you are trying to place two copies of the same

file in the same folder, and asking if you want to replace the original file with the one you are trying to copy or move there. You cannot have more than one file with exactly the same name in the same folder. You can replace the existing file with the new one by clicking Yes. Alternatively, you can click No and copy or move the file to a different location or modify its filename.

Where do I find the Recycle Bin files?

There is a hidden system folder, Recycled, in the root folder of every drive. This folder stores the deleted files.

The following are procedures that you can use when working with the Recycle Bin:

- If you delete or rename this folder in Windows Explorer, Windows 98 will re-create a new one when you restart Windows 98. Of course, the new Recycled folder will not contain your previously deleted files.

- If you rename the old Recycled folder back to its original name, all the previously deleted files will be displayed in the Recycle Bin again.

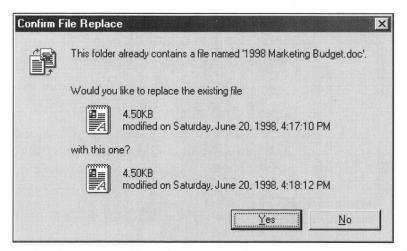

Figure 7-8 A message like this appears when you try to place two files with the same name in the same folder

 ## What is the Recycle Bin?

The Recycle Bin holds deleted files. These are automatically placed there when you delete a file by pressing DEL or by selecting Delete from the Edit menu or a context menu. Items in the Recycle Bin can be cut, copied, pasted, or dragged to another location; or they can be restored to their original location by double-clicking Recycle Bin, opening the Edit menu, and choosing Undo Delete. Items remain in the Recycle Bin until it is emptied by right-clicking it and choosing Empty Recycle Bin; however, if you exceed the disk space allotted for the Recycle Bin, older files will be permanently removed to make room for newer ones and you will not be warned of this.

✚ ***Tip:*** *In Windows 98-compliant applications, such as Microsoft Word 97, if you right-click a file in the Open dialog box and choose Delete, the file will be placed in the Recycle Bin.*

 ## What are some tips and tricks for quickly moving and copying files?

If you drag an object, varying the use of SHIFT and CTRL while you drag, you'll get the results described next.

- If you drag a file or folder *without* using SHIFT or CTRL, you will have these effects:
  - Dragging within the same drive will move the object.
  - Dragging to a different drive will copy the object.
- The exceptions to this are if you drag a program file (one with an .EXE or .COM extension) without using SHIFT or CTRL. Then
  - Dragging within the same drive will create a shortcut.
  - Dragging to a different drive that is not removable will create a shortcut.
  - Dragging to a different removable drive will create a copy.

- Using SHIFT only always moves the object.
- Using CTRL only always copies the object.
- Using SHIFT and CTRL together while dragging always creates a shortcut.

 Tip: *Certain folders do not allow objects to be dragged to them, such as the Control Panel and Printers folders. Dragging to other folders always creates a move regardless of SHIFT and/or CTRL status, such as dragging to the Recycle Bin.*

 ## What is My Briefcase?

My Briefcase is a tool that you can use to synchronize files on different computers. You can change a file and then make sure that a copy on another computer is also changed. To install the Briefcase on your desktop use the Windows Setup tab on the Add/Remove Programs control panel (My Briefcase is installed by default when you choose a Windows 98 Portable setup).

To use My Briefcase, follow these procedures:

1. Using Windows Explorer or My Computer, drag the files you want to maintain or keep synchronized from folders on your computer to My Briefcase in Explorer or on your desktop. That places a copy of the files in the folder named My Briefcase. If this is your first time using the Briefcase, you will see a Welcome to... message that gives a quick overview of the steps involved.

2. Drag the My Briefcase icon to a floppy disk that you will use to transport the files to another computer.

3. Update your files in My Briefcase on the other computer, making sure that updates are saved to the My Briefcase folder.

4. When you're finished working on the files on the other computer, insert the updated floppy disk into your main computer.

5. Double-click My Briefcase, and the My Briefcase window will be displayed, as shown in Figure 7-9.

Chapter 7 File Management

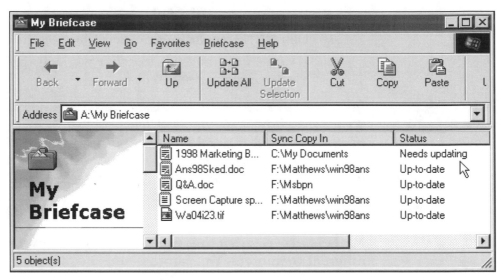

Figure 7-9 My Briefcase tells you when two copies of a file are not in synch

6. From the Briefcase menu or the toolbar, select Update All to update your files on the main computer. Select Update Selection if you only want to update some of the files.

7. Confirm the action you want to perform, as shown next. The files on the main computer are automatically revised.

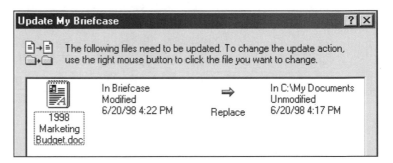

 Tip: *When you edit a file in My Briefcase, you are changing the file in the Windows\Desktop\My Briefcase\ folder, not the original file in another folder. However, that original file is linked with the My Briefcase file, and when you choose Update All or Update Selection, you will update the original file.*

How can I select multiple folders or files?

The method used depends on whether or not the files are contiguous.

For contiguous files use one of these methods:

- Click just above or to the right of the first item (not on an item), hold down the left mouse button, and drag the resulting selection box to include all items you want to select.

- Click the first file in a group, press SHIFT, and then click the last file in the group. All files in the group will be selected.

  For noncontiguous files, click each file while holding CTRL.

How can I select noncontiguous files from a list one at a time?

Hold the CTRL key and click the files.

Why is a shortcut not created when I drag a file from File Manager to the desktop?

File Manager is a Windows 3.*x* application. It does not support the functionality of creating shortcuts. Nor does it support dragging and dropping in any form outside of its windows. Use My Computer or Windows Explorer to create shortcuts.

VIEWING FILES AND FOLDERS

What is a folder?

A folder is a directory, as that term was used in earlier versions of Windows and DOS. It is a subdivision of a disk in which you can store files or other folders.

How do I make a new folder?

Making a new folder is easy. Use the following steps:

1. Open Windows Explorer or My Computer and open the folder which will contain the new folder (the contents of the folder should either appear in the folder's own window or in the right pane of Windows Explorer).

2. Right-click an empty area in either the folder window or the right pane of Windows Explorer.

3. Choose New | Folder, as shown next. The new folder is created and placed in the parent folder.

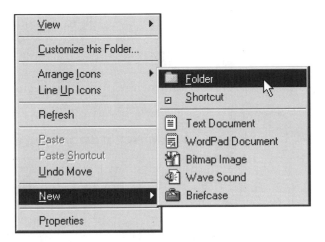

4. Type the name over the New Folder default name and you're done.

I have changed the property of a file to hidden, but it still shows up in Windows Explorer. What's wrong?

You have Windows Explorer (and any folder window) set to display hidden files. To change that, do the following:

1. Open Windows Explorer's View menu and choose Folder Options.

2. On the View tab, under Hidden Files, choose Do Not Show Hidden Files.

3. Click OK.

? How do I clear out the files from the Documents menu?

To remove files from the Documents menu, do the following:

1. Click Start and choose Settings | Taskbar & Start Menu.
2. Click the Start Menu Programs tab, and click Clear in the Documents Menu section, as shown in Figure 7-10.

? How do I know which .DLL files are being called by a given program?

Right-click the program file (a file with an .EXE or .COM extension) in the right pane of the Windows Explorer window and choose Quick View. The Import Table will show you the list of .DLLs being called by the program, as shown in Figure 7-11.

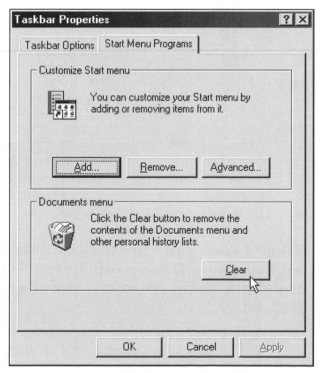

Figure 7-10 Remove the contents of the Documents menu by clicking Clear

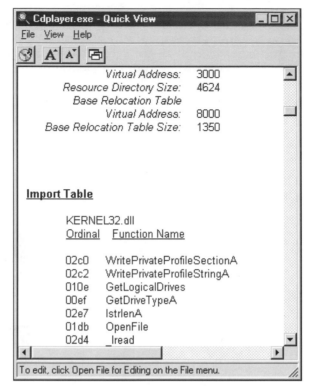

Figure 7-11 The Quick View Import Table of a program file will tell you the .DLL files loaded by a program

---

Note: *Quick View is not installed as part of a Windows 98 Typical setup. To install Quick View, open the Add/Remove Programs control panel, select the Windows Setup tab, and then select the Accessories component. Click Details, select Quick View, and click OK twice.*

 When I save a file in Microsoft Word 6.0, it does not appear under Documents in the Start menu. If I save the same file in WordPad, the file shows up on the list! Why?

The documents will only show under Documents in the Start menu if they were saved by a 32-bit application. Word 6.0 is a 16-bit Win3.*x* application and does not support the Windows 98 environment in this way. If you use Word 95 or 97 you will see your documents on the list.

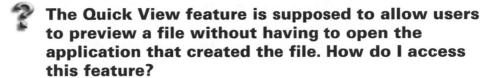

The Quick View feature is supposed to allow users to preview a file without having to open the application that created the file. How do I access this feature?

To use Quick View to see a file, follow these instructions:

1. Right-click the file in Windows Explorer or My Computer.

2. Select Quick View, as shown here:

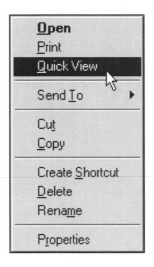

If the file extension cannot be opened by Quick View, this context menu option will not be available. If you don't get the Quick View option at all (try it on a .DOC or .TXT file), Quick View may not be installed. To see if it's installed, use these steps:

1. Click Start and choose Settings | Control Panel.

2. Double-click Add/Remove Programs, and click the Windows Setup tab.

3. Select Accessories and then click Details. If Quick View doesn't have a check mark next to it, as shown in Figure 7-12, it means that it was not installed during the initial setup. In this case, just click this item to select it, choose OK, and follow the prompts, if any, for your Windows 98 media.

Figure 7-12 Select Quick View by placing a check mark next to the name

 What file formats can I see in Quick View?

The following are among the file formats Quick View can open:

File Extension	File Format
.ASC	ASCII text
.BMP	Windows bitmap
.CDR	CorelDRAW!
.DOC	Microsoft Word for DOS 5 and 6
	Microsoft Word for Windows 2 through 8
	WordPerfect 4.2 through 6.1
.DRW	Micrografx Designer
.INF	Setup information
.INI	Windows initialization

File Extension	File Format
.MOD	MultiPlan 3 through 4.1
.RTF	Rich text format
.SAM and .AMI	AmiPro
.TXT	Text
.WB1	QuattroPro
.WKS, .WK1-.WK4	Lotus 1-2-3, 3 and 4
.WPD	WordPerfect document
.WPS	Works word processing
.WQ1	QuattroPro 5 for DOS
.WRI	Write
.XLC and .XLS	Excel 4 through 8

Other viewers might be available from the manufacturer of a specific application.

 How do I find a file when I have forgotten its name?

The Find command for a file will first try to find a file by its filename, so if you have forgotten its name, you must use another search criterion. You can search for files created on a certain date, or search for text contained within the file.

Follow these steps:

1. From the Windows Explorer, select Tools | Find | Files Or Folders.

2. To search by date, click the Date tab. Type the date or the date range that the file was last created or modified.

3. To search by text string, click the Name & Location tab. Type in the text string to be searched for.

4. To search by file type, click the Advanced tab. Type in the type of the file (such as **.doc**) and the size of the file if you know it.

5. Click Find Now to begin the search.

 Note: *You can combine searches by filling in all the known parameters on the three tabs, for instance, date and text string.*

 I often use Find to search for the same files. How can I save and reuse my criteria?

You can save your search criteria with these steps:

1. Click Start, then select Find | Files Or Folders.

2. Fill in the details of the search, such as the filename to search for and the disk and/or folders to search in.

3. After all of the search parameters have been entered, click Find Now to perform the search and confirm that the criteria produced the desired results.

4. When the search is complete, open the File menu and select Save Search. Your search will be saved on the desktop with a filename that contains the search criteria and the file extension of .FND.

Tip: *You can also save the results of a search, not just the criteria, by selecting Options and then Save Results.*

To use a saved search, simply double-click the Find file (one with an extension .FND) on the desktop.

 I thought I moved some files around in My Computer, but they still show up in the old place. Why does this happen?

You probably haven't done anything to cause the screen to be refreshed. Press F5 and the display will be refreshed.

 I really prefer File Manager from Windows 3.*x* to Windows Explorer. Is there any way to get it back?

Sure. Do the following to restore the File Manager:

1. Right-click the desktop.

2. Choose New | Shortcut.

3. Type in the filename **winfile.exe** and choose Next.

4. Type in the name of the shortcut, **File Manager**, and then click Finish. A shortcut to the Windows 3.*x* File Manager will appear on your desktop, as shown to the left.

How do I search for a document that contains a specific word?

Using Find, you can conduct a search using specific text for the criteria. Use these instructions:

1. Click Start and choose Find | Files Or Folders. (Alternatively, you can start by selecting Find from the Tools menu in Windows Explorer.)

2. In the Name & Location tab go to the Look In field and type or select from the drop-down list the disk drive or the path to be searched. Click Include Subfolders if you want the search to be extended to these. If you do not know the name of a folder or disk drive you want to search, click Browse and find it that way.

3. Type the keyword or phrase for which you want to search in the Containing Text box, as shown in Figure 7-13.

4. Click Find Now to activate the search.

 Tip: *You can quickly open Find by pressing F3. The currently active drive and folder will be the basis for the search, so if you select the drive and folder first and then press F3, you will get exactly the Find dialog box you want.*

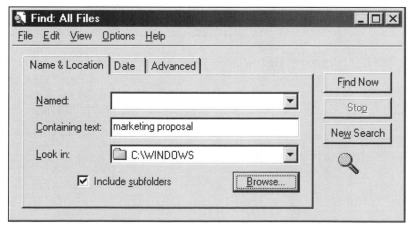

Figure 7-13 Find allows you to search for a document containing specific text

 When I save a search that contains a wildcard, the filename of the search contains different characters in place of the wildcard. Why does this happen?

This is because wildcards (asterisks and question marks) are not valid characters to use in filenames. Windows 98 replaces asterisks with the @ symbol and question marks with !, the exclamation point, but only in the filename. When you use the saved search, the original criteria with the wildcards reappear as you can see in Figure 7-14.

 In My Computer, how do I select the details that appear in a folder?

To select a file or folder in My Computer or Windows Explorer, you must click the filename or the icon itself. You cannot click the details that appear to the right of the icon and filename in Details view. My Computer and Windows Explorer are designed this way so you can select multiple files and/or folders by pointing to the upper right of the

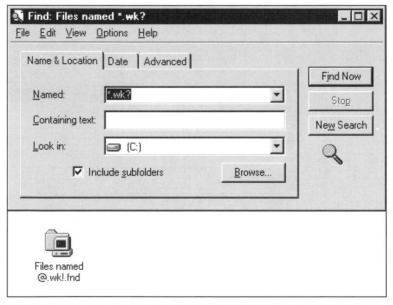

Figure 7-14 Although wildcards are replaced in the filename of a saved search, the actual search criteria remain unchanged

objects, pressing and holding down the mouse button, and dragging a selection rectangle to the lower left of the objects.

In Windows 98, is there any way I can still view files by type without using File Manager?

Yes, there are two ways you can see all files of a certain type together: by sorting the files by type and by excluding the files you don't want to see.

To sort the files by file type in My Computer or Windows Explorer, use these instructions:

1. Open the View menu and choose Arrange Icons.

2. Click By Type, as shown in Figure 7-15.

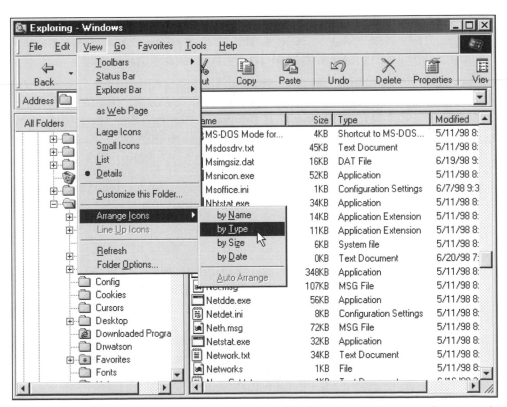

Figure 7-15   Any Windows Explorer or My Computer view can be sorted with the Arrange Icons option

Tip: *In Details view you can sort by clicking the headings at the top of the columns.*

You can exclude certain system file types from being viewed and therefore see only the files that were not excluded. The following steps show how:

1. In either Windows Explorer or My Computer, open the View menu and select Folder Options, and then click the View tab.

2. Under Hidden Files, click Do Not Show Hidden Or System Files. This will hide all of the system and hidden files, leaving only the files that you might normally use.

3. Click OK. You'll only see the file types that were excluded from the "hidden files" list.

How do I view only one type of file (for example, only .DLL files) in Windows Explorer?

You can look at all your .DLL files in two ways, either using Windows Explorer directly or using the Find option in either the Windows Explorer Tools menu or the Start menu.

Follow these steps to sort Windows Explorer so all the .DLL files in a given folder are together:

1. Open Windows Explorer and select the folder in which you want to see the .DLL files.

2. Open the View menu and select Details to see the file types.

3. In the right-hand pane, click Type in the column heading above the files. This will sort the files in ascending order on the file type or file extension as shown in Figure 7-16.

Tip: *If you click a column heading once, you will sort the files in ascending order; if you click twice, you will sort in descending order.*

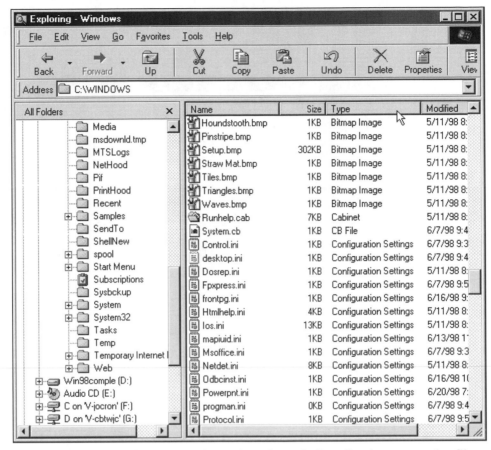

Figure 7-16 Clicking the column headings in Details view sorts the files by that column

Follow these steps to use Find to gather together the .DLL files in all folders:

1. In Windows Explorer, select Tools | Find | Files Or Folders.

2. In the Name & Location tab, type ***.dll** in the Named box. Choose the disk or folder to be searched in Look In. Use Browse if you are not sure.

3. Click Find Now. Your results will look like those shown in Figure 7-17.

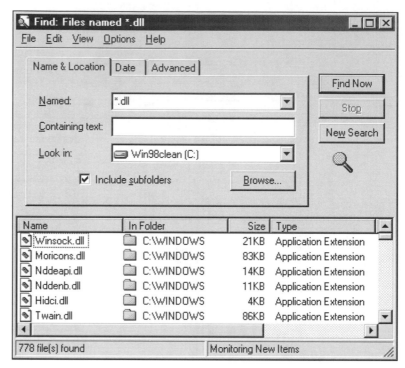

Figure 7-17 The Find option can gather similar files across many folders

 Can I rearrange the columns in Windows Explorer Details view to see the Modified column next to the Name column?

Sure. You can move columns into the position and order you want. Simply place your mouse pointer in the column heading of the column you wish to move, and drag it between the columns where you want it, as shown here:

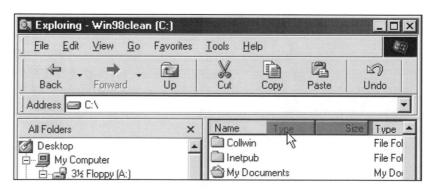

FILE ALLOCATION TABLE (FAT VS. FAT32)

 I am getting errors trying to save from a Windows 98 application to another folder on my PC. I have a configuration that allows dual booting between Windows 98 and Windows NT. I know it is not a matter of insufficient disk space, because the FAT partition that I created under NT is 4GB. Why am I getting these errors?

Windows 98 only supports a 2GB primary partition when formatted using the 16-bit FAT (the file allocation table system referred to as FAT16 or just FAT) that was standard in Windows 3.*x*/DOS and early versions of Windows 95. Windows 98 can be formatted in either FAT or FAT32, the 32-bit file system. Windows NT can create FAT partitions of up to 4GB. The reason is that for Windows 98 on a FAT partition (like MS-DOS), the maximum cluster size is 32K, while for Windows NT it is 64K. (The maximum number of clusters in both cases is 64K.) This means that Windows 98 can create a maximum drive of 32K × 64K = 2048MB (or 2GB). For Windows NT, the numbers are 64K × 64K = 4096MB (4GB).

 Tip: *Fdisk in MS-DOS or FAT (or FAT16) in Windows 98 can create extended partitions of more than 2GB and then create several logical partitions of under 2GB. But it cannot create primary partitions over 2GB.*

Tip: *FAT32 theoretically can support up to 2TB (terebytes). Practically speaking, however, unless your BIOS supports interrupt 13 extensions, only 7.9GB can be fully addressed. To determine whether your BIOS supports the interrupt 13 extensions, you must consult the documentation for the motherboard and drive.*

 When I upgraded my Windows 95 system to Windows 98, Setup gave me the opportunity to convert to FAT32, which I declined. Can I convert now that I have Windows 98 installed?

Yes, by using the Drive Converter (FAT32) utility. Do so with these steps:

1. Click Start and choose Programs | Accessories | System Tools | Drive Converter (FAT32).

2. In the first Drive Converter dialog box click Details, which will open the Help topic on FAT32, as shown in Figure 7-18. We strongly recommend you read this to learn about the restrictions FAT32 imposes on you.

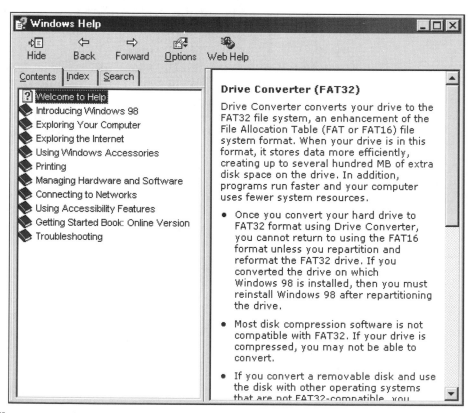

Figure 7-18 Help provides a good description of the advantages and disadvantages of converting to FAT32

3. Close or minimize the Help window and click Next.

4. Select the drive you want to convert, click Next, and follow the prompts to convert your disk.

! ***Warning:*** *Once you convert a disk to FAT32 you cannot uninstall it. You will have to reformat the disk and re-install any programs, including Windows 98, that were on it.*

When I use my Startup disk to start my computer I can't see my hard disk. Why?

If your hard disk is using FAT32 and your Startup disk is not, the Windows system files on your floppy disk will not be able to recognize the file structure on your hard disk. Chances are you created the Startup disk with Windows 95, but not with the OSR2 (operating system release 2) version, or with Windows 98, both of which are FAT32-compliant. There are a couple of ways to resolve this problem.

Create a New Startup Disk from Windows 98

1. Click Start and choose Settings | Control Panel and double-click Add/Remove Programs.

2. Click the Startup Disk tab and then click Create Disk.

3. When prompted, insert a floppy disk and click OK.

Copy Windows 98 System Files to Your Startup Disk

1. At a MS-DOS prompt (either press F8 during booting, but before Windows 98 loads and then choose Command Prompt from the menu, or click Start and choose Programs | MS-DOS Prompt), type **sys a:**.

2. Insert your Startup disk and press ENTER.

Can I view FAT32 media from my drive where I have Windows 98 FAT installed?

Yes and no. You can see FAT32 drives across a network, but you cannot see FAT drives on your own computer, including floppy disks.

Chapter 8

Printing

Answer Topics!

Printing @ a Glance

After entering information into your computer and saving it, the next most important job is printing it. Sometimes this is the most troublesome and often the most time-consuming of the tasks. You may have problems associated with the mechanical device, with connecting it to your computer, with using the correct software drivers, and with scheduling and handling the print queue. If you are printing over a network, all of these problems can increase exponentially. If that weren't enough, with today's printers you also have to worry about fonts—loading, using, managing, and removing them. Refer to the sidebar "Printing Enhancements in Windows 98" for more specific information about features that deal with common printer problems.

This chapter covers the following:

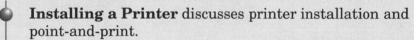

- **Installing a Printer** discusses printer installation and point-and-print.

- **Using a Printer** gives information about printing from Windows Explorer, using drag-and-drop to print, printing offline, changing the print order, and printing from various applications.

- **Fonts** covers viewing fonts, the number of fonts that can be installed, and installing additional fonts.

Printing Enhancements in Windows 98

Windows 98 addresses all of the major printing concerns and goes a long way toward making printing truly easy. Among the many enhancements in Windows 98 are the following:

- **Easier printer installation** and setup is made possible with Plug-and-Play, the Add Printer Wizard, and point-and-print. With a plug-and-play-compliant printer, all you need to do is plug it in and start Windows 98; the rest is done for you. With the Add Printer Wizard, you are quickly led through the setup process step by step. Using point-and-print, you use the Network Neighborhood to locate a shared printer on the network and then double-click it. This starts the Add Printer Wizard to complete the process.

- **Faster printing** is a reality as a result of a 32-bit printing system, bidirectional communications, enhanced metafile (EMF) spooling, and support for the extended capabilities parallel port (ECP). Windows 98 replaces the Windows 3.*x* Print Manager with a faster 32-bit protected-mode print spooler using 32-bit virtual device drivers for the popular printers. With the printers that can support it, these device drivers will more closely interact with the printers through bidirectional communications and the extended capabilities parallel port. Using the enhanced metafile encoding scheme, Windows 98 can quickly spool a print job to the disk and then, with very little use of system resources, feed the job to the printer. This gets the user back to his or her work sooner and provides true background printing.

- **More printing support** is provided with Image Color Matching (ICM), deferred printing, improved font handling and flexibility, and the sharing of printers through a NetWare server. Using ICM, you can better match the colors on the screen with those produced with a color printer. If you are using a portable computer or are for some other reason disconnected from your printer, you can use deferred printing to hold the print job until you are next connected to a printer, at which time the job will automatically be printed. Windows 98 provides for font substitutions, enhanced and more accurate font generation, and the ability to store and print many more fonts.

INSTALLING A PRINTER

 How do I install a new printer on my computer in Windows 98?

You can install a new printer using the Add Printer Wizard from your Printer's dialog box. The wizard will prompt you in the installation of your printer. Use these steps:

1. Click Start and choose Settings | Printers.

2. Double-click Add Printer. The Add Printer Wizard window will be displayed.

3. Click Next. Choose Local Printer.

4. Click Next. The lists of Manufacturers and Printers will appear, as you can see in Figure 8-1.

5. In the Manufacturers list, select the manufacturer's name and in the Printers list, double-click the model you want to install, or select the model and click Next.

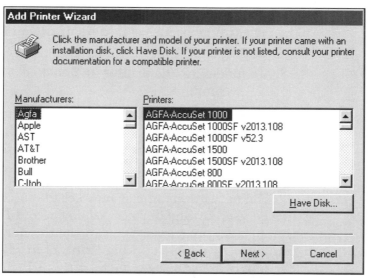

Figure 8-1 Windows 98 gives you a wide choice of printer manufacturers and models from which to choose

6. Select the port it will use. The LPT1 parallel port is the most common choice.

7. Click Next. The wizard will prompt you for a friendly name (type a name that easily identifies the particular printer).

8. Decide if this printer will be your default printer and click Next.

9. Decide if you want to print a test page and then click Finish. Windows begins to copy the necessary files. If the files are already installed, you can use them or choose to install new files. You can install new files from Windows source files, files downloaded from the Internet, or from a disk from the manufacturer.

I keep hearing about point-and-print. How does it work?

Point-and-print allows you to easily install a printer driver on your computer so you can use a shared network printer. Here's how:

1. Double-click the Network Neighborhood to open it.

2. Browse through your network by opening (double-clicking) various computers until you find the printer you want to use.

3. Double-click the printer and click Yes to install it on your computer.

4. Answer the various questions from the Add Printer Wizard, clicking Next and finally clicking Finish. The print queue for the network printer will open. Click Close.

The network printer is now set up on your computer and can be used by any of your Windows (and DOS, if you selected that option) programs. You can see the new printer on your computer by double-clicking Printers in My Computer or by clicking Start and selecting Settings | Printers. In both cases, the Printers folder will open and display a new networked

printer, one with a cable beneath it, as seen in the lower right area of the dialog box shown here:

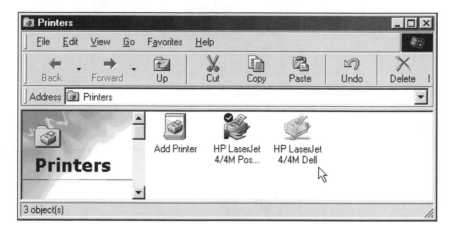

 How do I make my printer available to others on my network?

What you are asking is how to "share" your printer. Any printer connected to any computer on a network can be set up to be used by other workgroup members. You can also selectively share it by assigning a password to it and providing that password to only those who you want to use it. See how to share a printer with these steps:

Tip: *In order to share printers you must have selected printer sharing in your networking settings. Open your Network control panel, click File And Print Sharing, and verify you have selected the second check box. If not, select it, click OK twice, and restart your computer.*

1. Click Start and choose Settings | Printers.
2. Right-click the printer you want to share and click Sharing from the context menu.
3. Select Shared As and provide a comment and password if you want. See the question later in this chapter on adding and viewing comments.

4. Click OK. A "sharing hand" will appear below the printer's icon, as shown here:

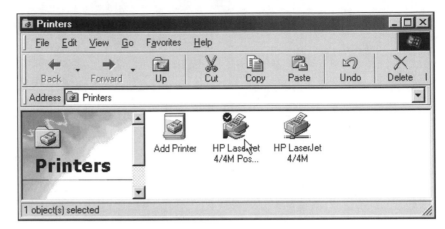

USING A PRINTER

I have sent a number of files to the printer. One of them is urgent. How can I change the order in which the files will be printed?

To change the print order, do the following:

1. Double-click the printer icon on the right of the taskbar next to the clock, as shown to the left. Your printer's print queue window will open, as you can see in Figure 8-2.

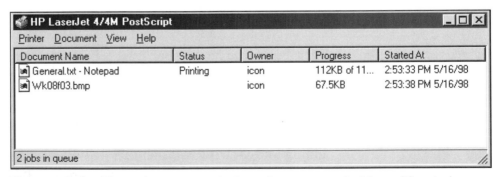

Figure 8-2 The print queue window shows you what is waiting to be printed and in what order

2. Select the file you want to print sooner and drag it up to the top of the queue.

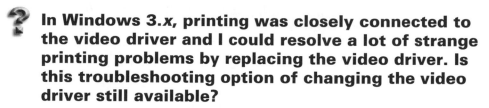 **In Windows 3.x, printing was closely connected to the video driver and I could resolve a lot of strange printing problems by replacing the video driver. Is this troubleshooting option of changing the video driver still available?**

In Windows 98, printing and video display are completely independent. The Windows 98 video driver and the Windows 98 printer drivers get graphical display information from separate sources and not from a common graphical device interface (GDI), as was the case in Windows 3.x.

This is true only for the native 32-bit Windows printer drivers. If you are using Windows 3.x printer drivers, the printer drivers would still access the common GDI for printing information. In this case, changing the video driver might directly affect printing.

In Windows 3.1, the colors on the printout did not match the colors on the screen. Does Windows 98 improve color printing?

This has been addressed by a Windows 98 feature called Image Color Matching (ICM), which provides the user with real WYSIWYG (what you see is what you get) color. Applications that directly support ICM will match the formatting of the printed output to colors on screen based on the specifications of the printer and display. Even older applications that are not ICM-aware (Windows 3.x applications) would benefit from this, because the ICM can be enabled directly through the printer driver. The printer driver has to be a native 32-bit Windows driver that supports color printing.

How do I set the default printer for Windows 98?

1. Click Start and select Settings | Printers.
2. Right-click the appropriate printer, and click Set As Default in the context menu.

Tip: *In most applications you can set a printer to be the default printer for all Windows applications by choosing the printer in the application's Print dialog box and selecting Set As Default.*

I have been told that drag-and-drop printing is the quickest way to print. Is this so? How do I do it?

Yes, it is the fastest way to print. If you create a shortcut to your printer on your desktop, you can drag a file from My Computer or Windows Explorer and drop it on the printer shortcut. This will send the document to the printer without your having to open the application that created the file. To create a shortcut to a printer, follow these instructions:

Printers

1. From My Computer, Windows Explorer, or the Control Panel, double-click Printers. The Printers folder will open.

2. Drag the printer for which you want a shortcut to the desktop.

3. Answer Yes, indicating that you want to create a shortcut.

4. Rename the shortcut if you wish.

Tip: *Drag-and-drop printing only works for documents that have a registered association with an application and have a printing option defined.*

To see if drag-and-drop printing has been defined for a type of file, use these steps:

1. From Windows Explorer or My Computer, open the View menu and choose Folder Options.

2. Click the File Types tab, and select the file type you want to check in the Registered File Types list box.

3. Click Edit. The Edit File Type dialog box will open, as you can see in Figure 8-3.

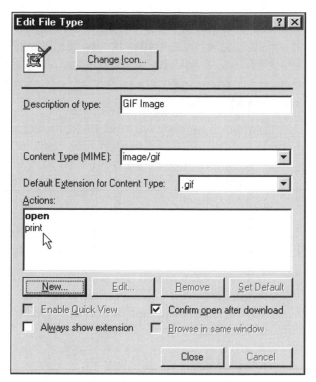

Figure 8-3   The drag-and-drop actions available for a file type are listed in the Edit File Type dialog box

4. Check to see if the list of Actions includes Print. If so, drag-and-drop printing will work with that file type.

5. If Print is not shown in the list of Actions in the Edit File Type dialog box, you can add it to the list by clicking New, typing **Print** in the Actions text box, and clicking Browse to select the application you want to use to print the job.

What is EMF?

EMF is an enhanced metafile. It is a nondevice-specific picture of what is being sent to the printer. A print job can be quickly captured as an EMF on disk and then sent to the printer in the background. Spooling with an EMF allows you to get back to work faster after printing a file and to do more while the EMF is being sent to the printer.

 Since Windows 98 does not use a "Print Manager" but sends the pages to be printed in a queue as metafiles, will my printer be required to have enough memory to print a full page of my graphics in metafile format?

No, your printer will not need additional memory. The Windows 98 EMF format (see the earlier question about EMF format for additional information) increases the actual printing speed, but does not require the printer to hold or process more information.

 Sometimes I print a document, but nothing comes out. How do I avoid this problem?

If you are trying to use a network printer or one that is sometimes not connected to your computer, check to make sure the printer has not been set to work offline. Use these steps to do that:

1. Click Start and choose Settings | Printers, or open My Computer and double-click Printers.

2. Right-click the printer you are trying to use. The printer's context menu, shown here, will open.

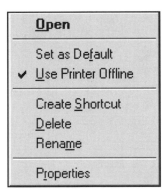

3. If Use Printer Offline is selected and you can in fact connect to the printer, deselect the Use Printer Offline option.

If you are using a local printer and having the problem, check all the obvious things like the cable being connected to the port you think you are using, the printer being turned on

and online, and the driver you are using being the correct one for your printer. Windows 98 has an excellent printer troubleshooting section in online Help. The next set of steps will open it for you:

1. Click the Help menu in the Windows Explorer, My Computer, or Printers window and select Help Topics. Windows Help will open.

2. In the Contents tab, click Troubleshooting, click Windows 98 Troubleshooters, and then click Print. The Print Troubleshooter will open, as shown in Figure 8-4.

3. Click the button that best describes your problem, click Next, and follow along as additional questions are asked until your problem is fixed. See the sidebar for other things you might do.

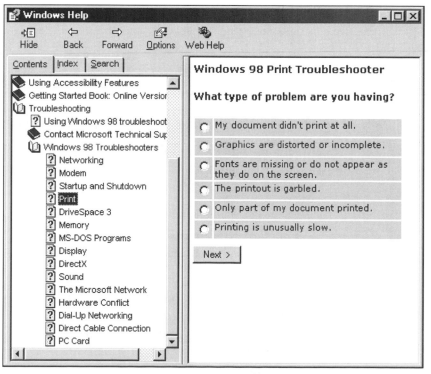

Figure 8-4 The Print Troubleshooter will help you solve your printing problems

Other Things You Might Do

If you're still having printing problems, try out these suggestions:

● Empty the Recycle Bin. See Chapter 7 for several questions on using the Recycle Bin.

● Delete .TMP files in your Temp folder, usually C:\Windows\Temp. This is a common problem for printing.

● Reboot your computer.

● If your printer is a network printer, the print queue may be hung up on the server end. Wait for the print jobs to be processed, and if that doesn't work, contact the system administrator in charge of the server.

● Check the printer path. Check the Details tab in the Properties dialog box (click Start | Settings | Printers) of the printer you are trying to print to.

● Make sure the correct printer is selected in the application you are printing from. Check the Print dialog box (or Print Settings dialog box in some applications) to see which printer is selected.

 How can I print a file from Windows Explorer?

If printing has been defined as an option in a file type's registration, then there are three ways to print that file type from Windows Explorer:

● Drag the file from Windows Explorer, and drop it on a shortcut to a printer that you have created on your desktop. (See the earlier question about drag-and-drop for how to do this.)

● Right-click a file and select Print from the context menu that opens.

● Right-click a file and select Send To | Printer if you have added a shortcut to your printer in your \Windows\ SendTo folder.

To add an item to the Send To list, use the following steps:

1. Create a shortcut to a printer on your desktop as described earlier in the drag-and-drop question.

2. Open Windows Explorer and then the \Windows\ SendTo folder.

3. Right-click the right pane of the Windows Explorer window, which should be the \Windows\SendTo folder.

4. Choose New | Shortcut from the context menu that appears.

5. Click Browse in the Create Shortcut Wizard that appears.

6. Select Desktop in the Look In drop-down list and All Files in the Files Of Type list. Your printer shortcut should appear in the list of objects on the desktop.

7. Double-click the printer shortcut and click Next.

8. Type the name you want to use and click Finish. Your printer will now appear in your Send To list.

When I print from my DOS application, I get an error message and I can't print. Why does this happen?

This happens because you only configured the printer to print from Windows applications. You will need to reconfigure the printer to print from DOS applications by deleting the current driver and using the Add Printer Wizard to install a new driver with support for DOS. Use these steps to do that:

1. Click Start and choose Settings | Printers.

2. Select the printer you want to reconfigure, press DEL, and answer Yes, you are sure you want to delete the printer.

3. Double-click Add Printer and click Next.

4. Select Network Printer and click Next.

5. Type in or browse for the path to the printer; select Yes, you print from MS-DOS-based programs, as you can see in Figure 8-5; and click Next.

6. Click Capture Printer Port; select the device, such as LPT3; click OK; and click Next.

7. Type in a name for the printer, decide if you want to make it your default printer, and click Next.

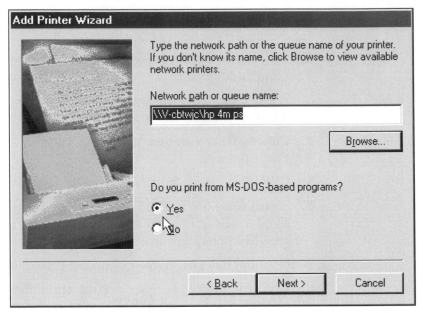

Figure 8-5 You must establish the capability to print from DOS applications while you are setting up the printer

8. Print a test page if you wish and click Finish.

Tip: *DOS programs cannot print directly to a network printer. You must map the network printer to a port address on your computer (such as LPT3, as was done in step 6) that DOS can print to.*

 ### How do I print from Lotus Notes under Windows 98?

When you install a network printer on your computer, the default port is the path to the printer in the form *server*\ *printername*. This works fine with many products. Notes, like DOS applications, is looking for a port address such as LPT3, as opposed to just *server**printername*. You can fix this problem by capturing the network printer to a port address on your computer. Use these instructions to do that:

1. Click Start and choose Settings | Printers.

2. Right-click the icon for the printer you want to use and choose Properties.

3. Click the Details tab and then select Capture Printer Port.

4. In the Device list, select the port address that you want to use.

5. Select or type the network path for the printer, select Reconnect At Logon, as shown next, and then click OK.

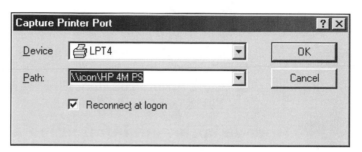

6. In the Print To The Following Port box, select the port you mapped, and click OK.

If I print offline, will I lose my print job if I turn off my laptop?

No, the whole idea behind deferred printing is that you can process the print job while not being actually connected to the printer. The job is spooled to the disk, and an EMF (enhanced metafile) print output is created. It will stay on your hard disk until you connect to a printer. Then when you connect to the printer and turn Use Printer Offline off, your print job will be completed and the temporary spool file deleted.

I used to be able to print offline on my laptop computer, but then I changed something in my settings and this option is gone. What did I do?

If you have turned off spooling in your printer properties, you cannot print offline. Follow the next set of steps to turn this back on:

1. Click Start and select Settings | Printers to open the Printers folder.

2. Right-click the printer and select Properties from the context menu.

3. Click the Details tab and then Spool Settings. The Spool Settings dialog box will open, as shown in Figure 8-6.

 Tip: *The Spool Settings dialog box allows you to begin printing after one page has spooled (which increases printing speed) or after all pages have spooled (which gets you back to your application faster).*

 Note: *If you have shared your printer on a network, you will not be able to turn spooling off.*

4. Click Spool Print Jobs So Program Finishes Printing Faster and click OK twice.

How do I print out information about my computer configuration?

To print your computer configuration information, use the following steps:

1. Right-click My Computer.

2. Choose Properties and click the Device Manager tab.

3. Select Computer and then click Print.

4. Make sure System Summary is selected in the Print dialog box and click OK.

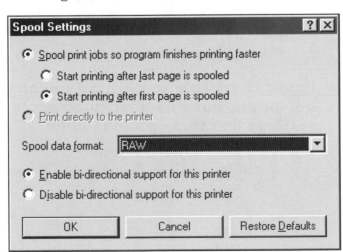

Figure 8-6 The Spool Settings dialog box allows you to turn print spooling on and off

How can I print to a file, and can I do it from Windows Explorer?

You can send your output to a file and print later from a different PC. You must either create a new printer, or change the configuration of one of your existing printers so that you have a printer defined that prints to a file. Then you can use one of the techniques in the earlier question about printing from the Windows Explorer. Here's how you change the configuration of an existing printer to have it print to a file (if you want a new printer to serve that purpose, use the Add Printer Wizard, as described in the question about installing a new printer):

1. Right-click the printer you want to reconfigure, and select Properties. The printer's Properties dialog box will open.

2. Click the Details tab, and open the Print To The Following Port drop-down list box.

3. Select FILE, as shown in Figure 8-7. Click OK.

Tip: *You cannot print to a file with a printer that you share. If you choose to use a shared printer to print files Windows will unshare it.*

When you issue the Print command, the print job will be sent to a file and you will be prompted for a filename, as you can see here:

Print To File		? X
File name:	Folders:	OK
*.prn	C:\My Documents	Cancel
	c:\	Network...
	My Documents	
Save file as type:	Drives:	
Printer Files	c: win98clean	

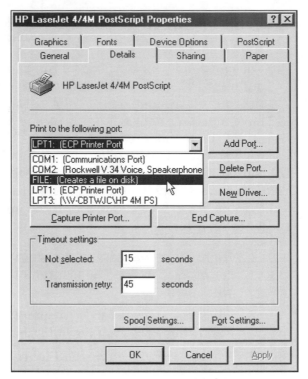

Figure 8-7 You can direct printer output to a file or a fax as well as to an actual printer by changing the port you are printing to

To print the file later, use these steps:

1. Click Start and choose Programs | MS-DOS Prompt to open a DOS window.

2. At the DOS prompt, type **copy c:\\<*path*>*filename lpt1***, where <*path*>*filename* is the full path and name of your file, and *lpt1* is your printer port. Make sure you are printing using the same type of printer you selected when you printed to a file.

I was trying to print to a file (for example, Device Manager information) but it isn't readable. What happened?

When Windows 98 prints information to a file, it uses printer language output rather than straight text format. To print to

a file and have it in a readable format, you have to print to the Generic Text Only printer. To install the Generic Text Only printer, do the following:

1. Click Start and choose Settings | Printers.

2. Double-click Add Printer, and click Next.

3. When you are prompted, click Local Printer, and then click Next.

4. In the Manufacturers box, select Generic; in the Printers box, select Generic/Text Only.

5. Click Next and in the Available Ports box, select FILE, and click Next.

6. Enter the name you want for the printer, and answer No to using this printer as the default printer for Windows-based programs.

7. Click Next. Answer No to testing the printer and click Finish.

I thought I should be able to print to a printer connected to a UNIX machine because I am running TCP/IP and can see the UNIX box. Why am I not able to do this?

In Windows 98, you cannot print directly to a printer on a machine running UNIX only. You can print to a printer on a Windows NT server or on a NetWare server that is also running UNIX. For example, you can connect to a UNIX printer through a Windows NT machine and then share it to Windows 98 clients.

Can I change the spooling options for my printer?

Yes. Do the following:

1. Click Start and select Settings | Printers.

2. Right-click the appropriate printer, and choose Properties from the context menu.

3. Click the Details tab and then click Spool Settings to go to the Spool Settings dialog box.

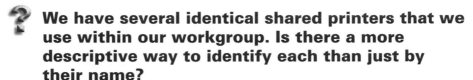

4. You can choose whether to spool print jobs or print directly to a printer, when to start printing after spooling, what spool data format to use, and whether to use bidirectional printer support. Make any changes and click OK when done.

Refer to the question earlier in this chapter about printing offline on your laptop computer for additional information.

We have several identical shared printers that we use within our workgroup. Is there a more descriptive way to identify each than just by their name?

Sure. You can attach a comment to each printer that lets you add information such as its physical location and any settings it has for specialty work. Workgroup members then can read the comments from within Network Neighborhood. See how to add and view comments with these steps.

Adding Comments to Shared Printers

1. Click Start and choose Settings | Printers.
2. Right-click on the printer that you want to add a comment for and click Sharing from the context menu.
3. Type in your information in the Comment box and click OK.

Viewing Comments on Shared Printers

1. From your desktop, double-click Network Neighborhood.
2. Change your view to Details by choosing it from the View menu. Any standalone network printer (or computer) will show comments next to its name. If the printer is a local printer to a computer on the network, double-click the computer to show its shared resources, as shown here:

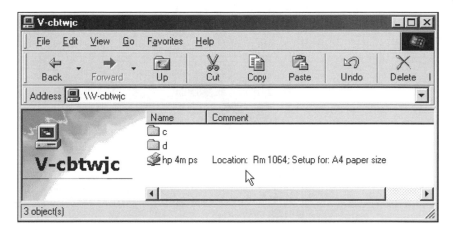

FONTS

How do I add new fonts?

Use the following steps to install new fonts.

1. Click Start and select Settings | Control Panel.

2. Double-click Fonts, and choose Install New Font from the File menu.

3. In the Add Fonts dialog box, browse to the location of the new fonts you want to add. The fonts in the folder will appear in the List Of Fonts box, as shown in Figure 8-8. Select the fonts you want to add and choose OK.

Tip: *Fonts are copied to the \Windows\Fonts folder on your hard drive by default. If you want to use fonts from another location (for example, a Fonts folder on a network server) instead of copying them to your hard drive, clear the Copy Fonts To Fonts Folder check box.*

What is the maximum number of TrueType fonts that I can install on my PC?

Because Windows 98 uses the Registry to store fonts, there is no limit to the number of TrueType fonts that can be installed. You can select and use nearly 1,000 different fonts and styles on any document without any problems.

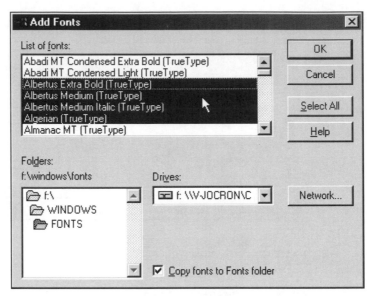

Figure 8-8 Select one or more fonts to add to your computer's font inventory in the Add Fonts dialog box

How do I preview my fonts without actually having to format text in an application?

You can see the fonts without using them in text by doing the following:

1. Open My Computer and double-click Control Panel.
2. Double-click Fonts.
3. Double-click the font you want to see. The font's dialog box will open, as shown in Figure 8-9.
4. Click Print to print the sample fonts, and click Done when you are finished.

Tip: *To print samples of several fonts in the Fonts folder, select all the desired fonts at once while holding down* CTRL, *open the File menu, and choose Print. (You'll have to click OK in the Print dialog box and Done in the font's dialog box for each of the fonts to complete the printing.)*

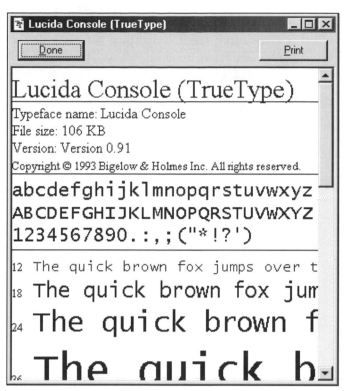

Figure 8-9   You can see what a font looks like by double-clicking it

 When I remove a font, Windows 98 deletes the file and places it in the Recycle Bin. In Windows 3.*x*, if font trouble occurred, I could "remove" the font without removing the file from the hard disk. Does this functionality still exist in Windows 98?

Windows 98 accomplishes the same end by moving the fonts to the Recycle Bin. You can then return the font to its folder by opening the Recycle Bin, selecting the file, and choosing Restore from the File menu. The upside of this method is that all of your deleted files, including font files, are located in one central clearinghouse, and when you decide to permanently remove files from the Recycle Bin you free up disk space. The

downside is that you could inadvertently empty your Recycle
Bin of font files you might want to use again. If you choose
the option of not using the Recycle Bin, once a file is deleted
it's really deleted.

**I want to change the font I'm using to something
that looks reasonably close to it. Is there an easy
way to look at similar fonts?**

Sure. You can have similar fonts grouped together so you can
narrow your search. See how to group your installed fonts
with these steps:

1. Click Start and choose Settings | Control Panel and
   double-click Fonts.

2. Open the View menu and click List Fonts By Similarity.

3. Choose a font to compare to by selecting it from the
   List Fonts By Similarity To drop-down list box. Your
   installed fonts will be categorized according to how
   similar they are to your selected font, as shown in
   Figure 8-10.

Tip: *You can further "boil down" your list by choosing Hide
Variations from the View menu, which eliminates the bold
and italic versions of a font family from the font list.*

**Occasionally, my monitor displays a font with very
rough edges that makes it hard to read. Is there
anything I can do to improve the appearance of
onscreen fonts?**

Yes there is. You can have Windows 98 try and smooth out
what sometimes are referred to as the "jaggies," or jagged
edges, that often distort a font. Here's how to improve your
font's appearance:

1. In Windows Explorer, My Computer, or any folder
   window, open the View menu and choose Folder Options.

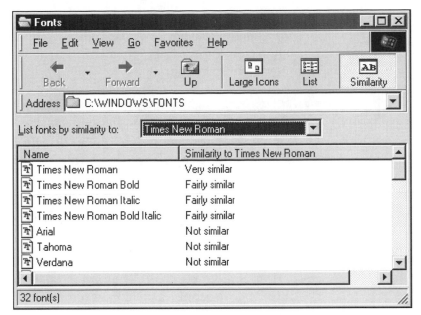

Figure 8-10 Compare how closely your other fonts resemble a selected font

2. Click the View tab and scroll to the bottom of the list of settings.

3. Select the Smooth Edges Of Screen Fonts check box and click OK.

 Tip: *You can also access the same Smooth Edges check box by right-clicking on your desktop, selecting Properties, and then clicking the Effects tab.*

Is there an easy way to view how a font looks besides opening each font individually?

Yes. Use the Character Map to quickly see how each of your installed fonts will look. Open the Character Map with these steps:

1. Click Start and choose Programs | Accessories | System Tools | Character Map.

2. Select the font family you want to look at from the Font drop-down list box. To see a close-up of a character, as shown in Figure 8-11, click the character and keep the mouse button depressed.

 Tip: *The Character Map is not installed as part of a Typical Windows 98 setup. You can install it from the Add/Remove Programs control panel by selecting the Windows Setup tab and choosing System Settings.*

 ### Is there a way to get more information about a font than what's available from its standard Properties dialog box?

Yes there is. Microsoft offers a free applet, TrueType Font Properties Shell Extension, that goes much more "under the hood" to describe font data. You can download this program from Microsoft's Web site, **http://www.microsoft.com/ typography/property/property.htm**. Download the self-extracting zip file, Ttftext.exe, from one of the listed

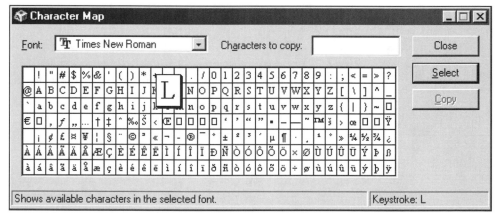

Figure 8-11 Quickly view different font families using the Character Map

locations to your desktop and double-click it. Follow the prompts and the next time you right-click a font in the Fonts control panel and choose Properties you will see this expanded set of properties:

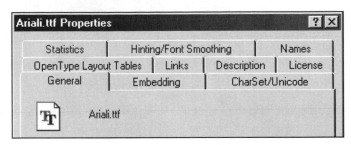

Chapter 9

Networking

Answer Topics!

Networking @ a Glance

Computer networking has become more the rule than the exception, and Windows 98 has responded to that by making networking an integral part of the operating system and not an add-on. The networking capabilities Windows 98 provides are significant. It is both a full and very competent client for Novell NetWare and Windows NT servers, and a complete peer-to-peer networking system among Windows 98, Windows 95, and Windows for Workgroups computers, with all the features needed for many organizations. In addition, Windows 98 supports networking with several other vendors' software including Novell NetWare and Banyan VINES. Not only can Windows 98 be a client in a client-server network and a full peer in a peer-to-peer network, it can do both at the same time. In all senses, Windows 98 is a networking operating system.

This chapter deals with the various considerations involved in setting up and using a computer on a network. Topics discussed here include the following:

- **Setting Up** covers various problems you might encounter when installing the network software and connecting to a server.

- **Using a Network** gives information about general features associated with being on a network, such as how to access a network drive, how to run an application from a network, how to load file and printer sharing, how to run various utilities on a network, and similar concerns.

- **Network Printing** addresses printer problems on a network.

- **Network Compatibility** gives information about several software products that are compatible with Windows 98.

- **Security Considerations** discusses the levels of security, protecting files, assigning passwords, and sharing folders on a network.

- **Administering and Monitoring Networks** covers administration problems and concerns, such as setting up the network and setting up individual accounts, and monitoring access and network activity.

- **Protocols** discusses what protocols can be used and how they can be used.

SETTING UP

 How do I change My Computer's name on the Network?

This is set in the Network Identification tab. You can set and change it with the following steps:

1. Click Start, choose Settings | Control Panel, and double-click Network.

2. Select the Identification tab.

3. Your computer name should be listed there, as you can see next:

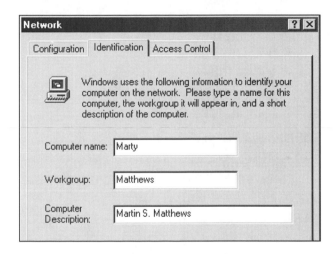

4. Make the change you want, click OK, and follow the prompts to reboot.

 How can I see and change settings like the FILE HANDLES variable in Net.cfg using Windows 98 and the Microsoft Client for NetWare?

In Windows 98, using Microsoft's 32-bit client software, file handles are set dynamically, so you do not have to have a specific setting as you would in Net.cfg. Windows 98 is doing this in the protected-mode redirector (NWREDIR).

Tips on Setting Up Windows 98 Networking

To utilize Windows 98 networking, you'll need the necessary networking hardware, which includes networking adapter cards in each computer on the network, cabling between computers, and, depending on the type of cabling, hubs or switches. Windows 98 makes the software setup easy by leading you through dialog boxes with lists of alternatives. If your network adapter is plug-and-play-compliant, setting it up is a snap. Here are some tips on setting up Windows 98 networking.

The most common network adapters are Ethernet cards that handle several types of cabling. Depending on your adapter and several physical considerations like the distances to be covered and the number of stations to be connected, you will need one of the following *types* of cabling:

- **10Base-T** twisted-pair cabling is the most common today and is the most flexible form of network cabling. It can handle up to 10 million bits per second (Mbps).

- **100Base-T** twisted-pair cabling that can handle up to 100 Mbps.

- **10Base-2** thin coaxial cable is common in small networks and is very cost-effective for them. It can handle up to 10 million bits per second.

- **10Base-5** thick or standard coaxial cable was the original networking standard. But it is both expensive and difficult to use, so it has been eclipsed by the other forms of cabling. It can handle up to 10 million bits per second.

- **Fiber optic** cabling is appearing for long-distance and high-speed networking, but is expensive and probably will not replace 10Base-T in the near future. It can handle either 10 or 100 Mbps.

- **Wireless** networking is beginning to be used where running a cable is very difficult. It too is expensive and may encounter problems with interference.

If you use 10Base-T or 100Base-T twisted-pair cabling you will need to specify the category grade of the cable. This specifies the quality of the cable where the higher the category, the better the grade. The minimum for 10Base-T is Category 3 and the minimum for

100Base-T is Category 5. If you are installing new cabling today you should probably not go below Category 5, even if you are only going to initially run 10Base-T, because you could upgrade the service without changing the cabling.

If you add networking after Windows 98 has been set up and without a plug-and-play adapter, you will need to set up the network manually. You can do this by opening the Start menu and selecting Settings | Control Panel | Add New Hardware. You will be guided through the network installation. If your networking hardware is running prior to installing Windows 98, Setup will often detect and properly set up Windows 98 to operate with your hardware. If you install a plug-and-play adapter after setting up Windows 98, it will automatically set up your network the next time you start up Windows 98.

How you set up Windows 98 networking depends on whether you want your computer to be a peer in a peer-to-peer network or a client in a client-server network. In peer-to-peer networking, generally used in smaller networks, all computers in the network share their resources equally. In this mode, all computers typically run Windows 98, Windows 95, or Windows for Workgroups, although other possibilities exist. Client-server networking, on the other hand, supports many computers, known as *clients,* accessing the resources of one or more designated server computers. The clients can be running Windows 98 or other client software, but for Windows 98 clients, the server must be running either Novell NetWare or Windows NT.

To set up or change the Windows 98 networking software configuration, open the Start menu and select Settings | Control Panel | Network. The Network dialog box will open, as shown in Figure 9-1. It allows you to install or change four types of networking software components:

- **Clients**, which allow you to access other computers in order to use their resources, are used for both peer-to-peer and client-server networking. Client For Microsoft Networks and the Client For NetWare Networks are the two most common choices.

- **Adapters**, which are the interfaces or drivers between your network adapter cards and Windows 98, are unique to your particular adapter card, and as with a printer, you must select a manufacturer and a model.

Generic NE1000-, NE2000-, and NE3200-compatible adapters are found under Novell/Anthem, and the Dial-Up Adapter is under Microsoft.

● **Protocols**, which are the communication languages used between computers, are determined by the type of networking you will be doing. In a Windows 98 peer-to-peer network or with a Windows NT client-server network, in most instances you should use Microsoft TCP/IP. With a NetWare client-server network, you should use Microsoft IPX/SPX or Novell IPX. With dial-up networking to the Internet, you should use Microsoft TCP/IP.

● **Services**, which allow you to share your resources with other computers or to provide other services such as file and printer sharing or directory services, are primarily needed to provide the server functions in a peer-to-peer network.

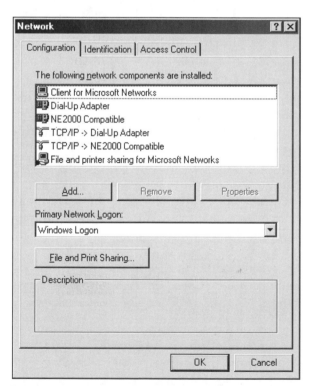

Figure 9-1 The Network dialog box allows you to select the software components you'll use in networking

Can I connect to a Novell server through Dial-Up Networking?

You need to install the Microsoft Client for NetWare Networks and the IPX/SPX-compatible protocol, which you need to bind to the Dial-Up Adapter. To install the client software, see the question later in this chapter about installing a NetWare client on a Windows 98 machine. The protocol is very likely already installed on your computer. Check this by opening your Network control panel and seeing if the following lines are in the list of network components:

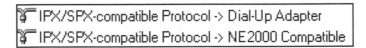

If the protocol software is not already installed on your computer, follow these steps to install it:

1. From the Network dialog box Configuration tab, select Add | Protocol | Add.

2. Select Microsoft from the list of Manufacturers, and click IPX/SPX-Compatible Protocol, as shown in Figure 9-2.

3. Click OK.

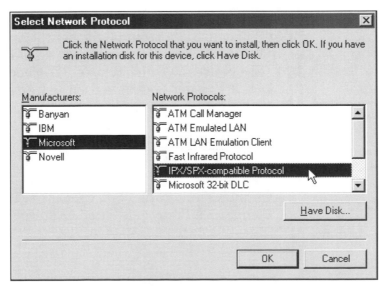

Figure 9-2   Selecting the IPX/SPX-Compatible Protocol

Next, make sure the protocol is bound to your Dial-Up Adapter. You can check this with the following set of steps:

1. Double-click your Dial-Up Adapter in the list of Network components on the Configuration tab of the Network dialog box.

2. Click the Bindings tab. Verify that the IPX/SPX-Compatible Protocol is checked. Click OK.

Finally, prepare the dial-up connection for use with a NetWare server using this last set of steps:

1. Open My Computer and the Dial-Up Networking folder, and then right-click the dial-up connection you want to use (if you don't have one, double-click Make New Connection and follow the instructions on the screen).

2. Click Properties in the context menu and then open the Server Types tab. In the Type Of Dial-Up Server list, click NRN: NetWare Connect Version 1.0 and 1.1, as you see in Figure 9-3. Click OK and close the Dial-Up Networking folder. If My Computer is still open in a separate folder, close it.

Why can't I connect to Novell servers?

One of the first steps is to verify that you have installed the IPX/SPX-compatible protocol and set the frame type to AUTO or to the specific frame type your server is using. (NetWare 3.11 servers use the frame type of Ethernet 802.3, and NetWare 3.12 and 4.0 servers use the frame type of Ethernet 802.2.) With the following steps you can check the protocol and frame type you are using:

1. Click Start, choose Settings | Control Panel, and double-click Network.

2. On the Configuration tab, check that IPX/SPX-Compatible Protocol is listed as one of the installed

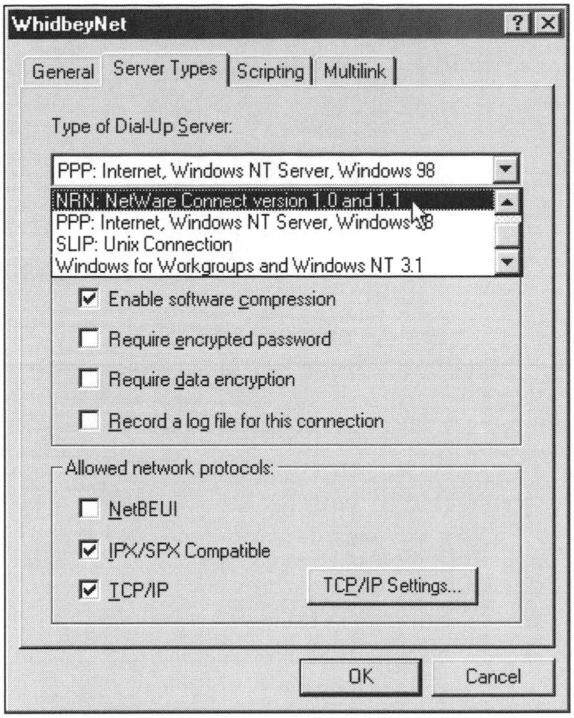

Figure 9-3 Selecting the correct server type allows you to dial into a NetWare server

network components. (If not, install it as described in the previous question.)

3. To verify that the frame settings are accurate, click the IPX/SPX-Compatible Protocol and click Properties.

4. Click the Advanced tab and then click Frame Type in the Property list. In the Value drop-down list select the type that is appropriate for you, as you can see in Figure 9-4.

If this does not solve your problem, use the Networking Troubleshooter in Windows 98 Help to step through possible network problems. To do this:

1. Click Start and choose Help.

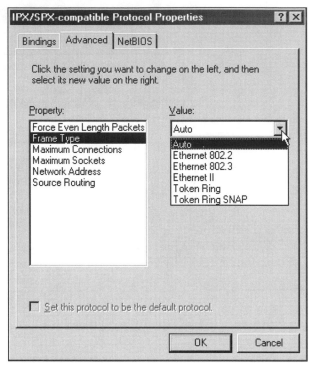

Figure 9-4   The default Auto frame type is typically the best choice

2. From the Contents tab, click Troubleshooting and then click Windows 98 Troubleshooters.

3. Click Networking. The Windows 98 Networking Troubleshooter will be displayed, as shown in Figure 9-5.

4. Step through the Help screens as you are prompted.

 **Can I connect two Windows 98 computers together, or do I need to buy a special peer-to-peer network program?**

Windows 98 has built-in networking capabilities. Provided you have the necessary network adapter cards and cables, linking two machines together is no problem. Just make sure both are using the same protocol, for example, TCP/IP.

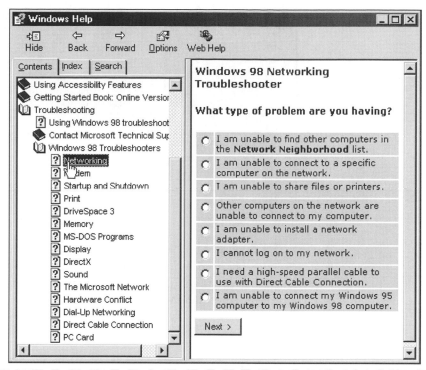

Figure 9-5 Windows Help provides a Networking Troubleshooter to help you identify problems

To verify that both computers are using the same protocol, follow these steps on both computers:

1. Click Start, choose Settings | Control Panel, and double-click Network.

2. On the Configuration tab, click the protocol and click Properties. Check that the settings in the Bindings tab on both computers are as shown in Figure 9-6.

How many users can I have connected to my shared drive?

The number of users connected to your shared drive is limited by the amount of memory, the speed and the throughput of the server, and the type and speed of the network you are using. Depending on your system, the shared drive should be able to handle as many as a dozen to several thousand users.

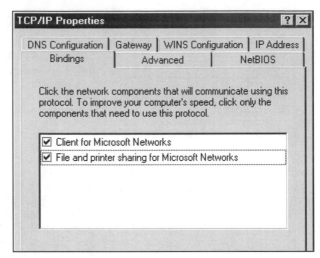

Figure 9-6 For peer-to-peer networking, all computers need to be using the same protocol and have a client as well as file and printer sharing for Microsoft Networks

How do I install a NetWare client on my Windows 98 machine?

First, you must determine whether to use Microsoft's 32-bit NetWare Client or one of Novell's clients. If your network is running either NetWare 3.*x* or 4.*x*, you can use the 32-bit Windows 98 Microsoft Client for NetWare. To do this:

1. Click Start, choose Settings | Control Panel, and double-click Network.

2. In the Configuration tab, select Add | Client | Add.

3. Select Microsoft and Client For NetWare Networks. This will give you full protected-mode support for NetWare, and you will not be using any conventional memory to load real-mode network drivers. Click OK.

However, if you need to use one of the Novell NetWare 16-bit real-mode clients (NetWare Workstation Shell 3.*x* or NETX), you have to load the Novell NetWare Workstation Shell 3.*x*. To do that:

1. Click Start, choose Settings | Control Panel, and double-click Network.

2. In the Configuration tab, select Add | Client | Add.

3. Select Novell and then Novell NetWare (Workstation Shell 3.*x* [NETX]). Click OK.

If you want to use NetWare Workstation Shell 4.*x* (Virtual Loadable Module or VLM), install the Novell NetWare (Workstation Shell 4.0 And Above [VLM]) client in step 3. To use the Novell 32-bit protected-mode client, choose Have Disk in step 3 and insert the Novell disks.

Where do I find Interlink in Windows 98?

The Interlink that shipped with MS-DOS 6.*x* is now called Direct Cable Connection. You can use it to connect between PCs via a parallel or serial cable and to share files between the two computers. The Direct Cable Connection is found on the Start menu by selecting Programs | Accessories | Communications | Direct Cable Connection. If you don't have this option on your Communications menu, you will have to install it first. You can do that with these steps:

1. Click Start, choose Settings | Control Panel, and double-click Add/Remove Programs.

2. Click the Windows Setup tab, select Communications, and then click Details for a list of the Communications components.

3. If there is no check mark next to it, click Direct Cable Connection to install it, as shown in Figure 9-7. Click OK twice. (If there is a check mark, it is already installed.)

Will I need new networking software to connect Windows 98 to my network server?

No. Windows 98 will continue to run existing real-mode networking components while enhancing the 32-bit protected-mode networking components first delivered with Windows for Workgroups.

Figure 9-7 Installing Direct Cable Connection

After installing Windows 98, I no longer can connect to my network. Why?

If your network is supported in Windows 98 with Windows 98 protected-mode drivers (primarily Microsoft and Novell networks), you may have a conflict between real- and protected-mode drivers. Make sure the appropriate client software is installed by opening the Network control panel. Then use Notepad to open your Autoexec.bat and Config.sys files, and remark out (put **rem** and a space at the left of the line) all real-mode network drivers (for a Microsoft or a Novell network with the Microsoft client you do not need any statements in your system files that load network drivers).

If the network you have is not supported in Windows 98 with Windows 98 protected-mode drivers, you have to load real-mode client drivers in your Autoexec.bat and/or Config.sys files. If it is an unsupported network, make sure to have the network fully installed and operating *before* starting Windows 98 Setup.

If you think that all of your networking software is correct, make sure that the resources are correctly assigned to your network adapter. Use the following steps to do that:

1. Click Start, choose Settings | Control Panel, and double-click System.

2. In the Device Manager tab, open Network adapters, select your adapter, and click Properties.

3. If you are *not* using a Plug-and-Play networking adapter, open the adapter's Properties dialog box, click the Resources tab, and check the Interrupt Request (IRQ) and Input/Output Range, as you can see in Figure 9-8. The settings you see should match what was set on your adapter card. (The ones in Figure 9-8 are probably *not* correct for you.)

4. Make the necessary changes to the IRQ and I/O address and click OK twice.

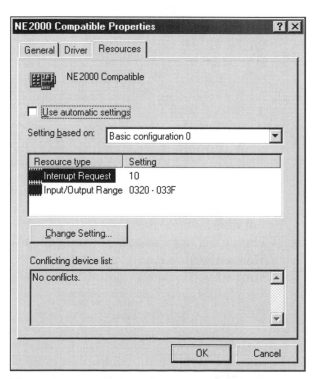

Figure 9-8 The resource settings in your network adapter's Properties dialog box must match those physically made on the card itself

I'm able to share files from my computer, so why am I not seen in my workgroup?

It may be that you are not identified with the workgroup that you think you are. To check or change your workgroup identification, use the following steps:

1. Click Start, choose Settings | Control Panel, and double-click Network.

2. Click the Identification tab and make sure the Computer Name, Workgroup, and Computer Description are correct.

3. Click OK and follow the prompts to reboot.

 I am trying to run an application from my Novell server, and I am receiving an error message: "Incorrect MS-DOS version." Why is this happening?

This occurs because either (or both) NetWare or the application were created before Windows 95 (MS-DOS version 7.0), and when it sees MS-DOS version 7.0 it mistakenly believes that it can't use that version of DOS. If you are using NetWare login scripts, you can have a script refer to a variable OSVersion to map a specific NetWare server according to the version of operating system the workstation is running. You will have to update the procedure to have MS-DOS version 7.0 recognized.

You might also have to modify the SETVER table to have the correct version reported to the program.

 What can I do if Setup does not recognize my network adapter?

If your network adapter was not identified or installed during Windows 98 Setup, you can, as a first step, run the Add New Hardware Wizard. To do this:

1. Click Start, choose Settings | Control Panel, and double-click Add New Hardware. To begin, click Next and then Next again.

2. A list of uninstalled plug-and-play devices is displayed if any exist. If your network adapter is on that list, click Yes and select the device in the list. Then click Next and Finish and follow instructions to complete the installation.

3. If your card was not found in step 3 but there were other plug-and-play devices, click No, and click Next. Then in any case click Yes to allow Windows to search for your new hardware and click Next. Click Next again to initiate the search. Chances are that the search will find the adapter card. Click Details to see the devices found. Select your network adapter and click Finish and follow instructions to complete the installation.

4. If the search does not find the card, click Cancel to get out of the Add New Hardware Wizard, and manually install it with the remaining steps.

5. From the Control Panel, double-click Network, and in the Configuration tab click Add | Adapter | Add.

6. Select the manufacturer and model of your card from the lists, and click OK. If you have a generic NE1000, NE2000, or NE3200 card choose Novell/Anthem as the manufacturer.

7. If the card is not listed, click Have Disk, insert the disk that came with your card, make sure the drive letter is correct, and click OK.

8. If you don't have a disk with an .INF file, you will have to quit and load the drivers through your Autoexec.bat file by following the instructions that came with the card. Having done that, open the Network control panel Configuration tab and select Add | Adapter | Add. This time, select the Existing ODI Driver from the Network Adapters list, as shown in Figure 9-9, and click OK.

Can I set up my PC to act as a server to answer calls through Dial-Up Networking?

Yes, but to enable Dial-Up Networking to act as a server, you may need to install the dial-up server. Follow these steps to install the dial-up server and then set it up:

1. Click Start, choose Settings | Control Panel, and double-click Add/Remove Programs.

2. Click the Windows Setup tab, click Communications, and then Details. Click Dial-Up Server to place a check mark in the box, and then click OK twice.

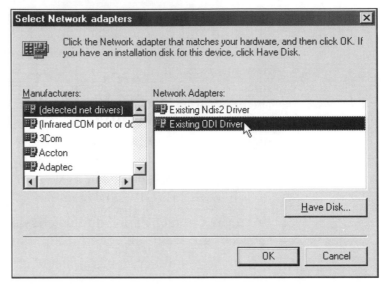

Figure 9-9 Use Existing ODI Driver as the network adapter when you load the driver for the adapter in your Autoexec.bat file

3. To set up the Dial-Up Server, double-click My Computer and then double-click Dial-Up Networking.

4. Open the Connections menu and click Dial-Up Server. The Dial-Up Server dialog box will open.

5. Click Allow Caller Access, as shown next, and click OK. Your computer can now serve as a dial-up server.

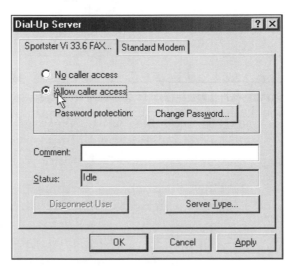

Tip: *You can see if someone is using your dial-up server in the Status box of the Dial-Up Server dialog box.*

I am using both Microsoft's Client for NetWare Networks and their Client for Windows Networks. How do I write logon scripts?

Logon scripts run when you log on to either a NetWare or Windows NT Server. If you have supervisor's or administrator's privileges on the servers, you can, in NetWare, type **syscon** and either create or edit logon scripts, or use User Manager on the NT Server.

USING A NETWORK

I often access a network drive. Can't I define that network drive as a drive on my computer?

Yes. This is called *mapping* a network drive. Follow these steps to map a network drive:

1. From Windows Explorer, click Map Drive on the toolbar (shown here; however, it is not displayed by default), or select it from the Tools menu.

2. In the Map Network Drive dialog box, click the Drive down arrow to find the drive to be mapped. Click it.

3. Using the format ***computer**drivename***, enter the path to be mapped to it.

4. Click OK.

Now the network drive will appear not only in the Windows Explorer and My Computer windows, but also in the File Open dialog boxes of all your applications, where you can open it and have immediate access to all the shared files. In Figure 9-10, drives E through H are mapped network drives.

Note: *Most applications written for Windows 95 and later have the ability to access Network Neighborhood and so mapping a network drive is not necessary for them.*

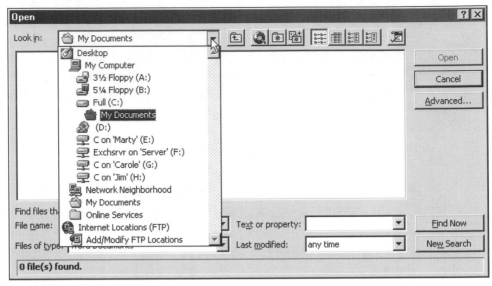

Figure 9-10 Once you have mapped a network drive to your computer, you can access the drive from within your applications

Do I have to have a disk or folder on my server mapped to a drive letter if I want to access this folder?

No. Windows 98 supports UNC (Universal Naming Convention), so you don't have to have a drive letter explicitly assigned to a network resource to use it. (You have to have appropriate rights to that resource, of course.) You can, for example, create a shortcut to a network folder right on your desktop. Let's say you want to have a shortcut to a folder named WinApps on drive C on the server named Rock. Then use the following steps:

1. Open Network Neighborhood, double-click the computer named Rock, double-click drive C, and then scroll the window so you can see the folder named WinApps.

2. Right-click WinApps and choose Create Shortcut. This will create a shortcut to the WinApps folder. You can drag it to your desktop, the Quick Launch toolbar, or into another folder in Windows Explorer or My Computer.

 Tip: *If you want to access a network drive or folder from within 16-bit or especially DOS applications, you will need to map the network resource to a drive letter on your machine.*

At work I have an icon on my desktop called Network Neighborhood, and at home I don't have this icon. Why?

The Network Neighborhood icon will only appear when you have a network installed. If you are on a standalone PC, you will not see the icon on your desktop.

When I have several users accessing one of my shared drives, how can I improve the performance so that my computer will give priority to shared files?

The following steps will give priority to shared files:

1. Click Start, choose Settings | Control Panel, and double-click System.

2. Select the Performance tab, and in Advanced Settings, click File System.

3. Select the Hard Disk tab, click the down arrow in the Typical Role Of This Computer box, and select Network Server as shown here:

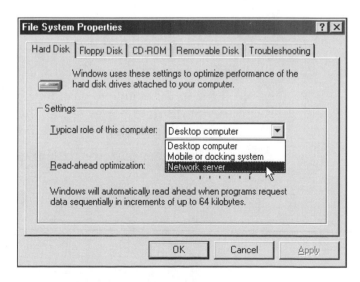

4. Respond to the prompts to reboot.

 I cannot load both file and printer sharing for NetWare Networks and file and printer sharing for Microsoft Networks at the same time. I need to work with both Novell and Microsoft Networks. What can I do about this?

Your Windows 98 machine can only act as one type of server—either the Novell or Microsoft Network server—at a time. You cannot do both simultaneously. You can have multiple clients loaded on the same machine, though. If you have file and printer sharing for Microsoft Networks loaded, you can also load Client for NetWare Networks and access your Novell servers.

 How can I locate a computer without going through Network Neighborhood or searching through My Computer or Windows Explorer when I know right where I want to go?

Rather than use one of the file management programs, use the Find command:

1. Click Start and choose Find | Computer.
2. Type in the computer name. You can use wildcards.
3. Click Find Now.

Another trick is to use the Run option. Use the following steps to locate a folder when you know where it is located:

1. Click Start and choose Run.
2. Type in the complete path in the form ***computername*\\ *drive**folder*.** For example, the Run command shown next will open the folder window you see in Figure 9-11.

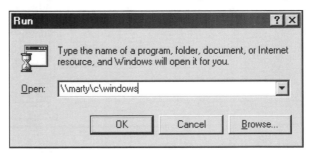

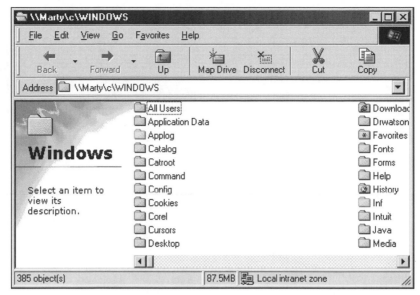

Figure 9-11 Using Run to find a remote drive and folder can give you fast access

You can also just use the computer name by itself. If you're looking for a computer, this is a lot faster than the other options.

 I am only connected to a network occasionally. How can I prevent Windows 98 from attempting to re-establish the connection if I am not on the net?

When you are restarting Windows 98 with a Novell network, click Cancel in the Network Password box. This will prevent Windows from re-establishing connections. If you are using a Microsoft network, you have a more elegant way of doing this with these steps:

1. Right-click Network Neighborhood and choose Properties.

2. Select Client For Microsoft Networks, click Properties, and select Quick Logon, as shown in Figure 9-12.

This will allow you to get into Windows without re-establishing connections. The connections will be established only when you need to utilize the network

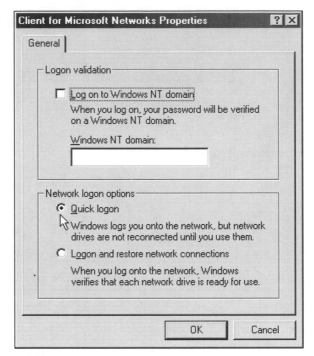

Figure 9-12 You can bypass the network logon until you want to use the network

resource, for example, to start a program that resides on the network.

 I used the Direct Cable Connection option to get my two computers to talk to each other. The Network Neighborhood icon is now a permanent part of my desktop. How can I remove the icon from my desktop without disconnecting the direct connect capabilities?

You can hide the Network Neighborhood icon using the System Policy Editor on the Windows 98 installation CD-ROM. Use the following steps to hide the Network Neighborhood:

1. Load your Windows 98 CD and close the Autorun screen.

2. Using Windows Explorer, locate the System Policy Editor in \Tools\Reskit\Netadmin\Poledit\ on the CD.

3. Run the Policy Editor by double-clicking Poledit.exe. When told it can't open a template file, click OK, and click Cancel in the Open Template File dialog box. Open the Options menu, choose Policy Template, and click Add in the Policy Template Options dialog box. Double-click Windows.adm, and click OK.

4. Open the File menu, choose Open Registry, and double-click Local User.

5. Open the folders as follows: Local User\Windows 98 System\Shell\Restrictions.

6. Under Shell Restrictions, click Hide Network Neighborhood so that it has a check mark.

7. Click OK and close the System Policy Editor.

 ### How can I run an application from a network drive?

You can map a network drive to a drive letter on your computer, open that drive in My Computer, locate the application, and run it. You can also create a shortcut to the application and put it on your desktop, on your Start menu, on the Quick Launch toolbar, or in a program group in the Programs menu.

 ### I am running Windows 98 and Novell NetWare on my Windows 98 workstation. How can I run NetWare system utilities Syscon, Pconsole, and Fconsole?

To run these utilities, you can go to the DOS prompt, change to the appropriate drive, and type the command. If you will be using these utilities a lot, you can create shortcuts to them. To do this:

1. Right-click the desktop.

2. Choose New and click Shortcut.

3. In the Create Shortcut dialog box, type the full path and the filename of the command and click Next. If you cannot remember what the path and filename are, you can click Browse to find them.

4. Enter the name for the shortcut and click Finish.

 Can I search for files on a network drive?

Yes. Use the following steps to search for files on
network drives:

1. Click Start and choose Find | Files Or Folders.

2. Type the filename you are searching for in the
    Named box.

3. Type the mapped drive letter and optionally a folder
    (*drive**folder*) or the UNC path (*computername*\\
    drive*folder*) in the Look In box.

4. Click Find Now.

 Tip: *You can also look for network files in Network
Neighborhood, Windows Explorer, or My Computer, and for
HTML files using Internet Explorer. See Chapter 6 for more
information on using Internet technology from your desktop.*

 Why can't I see other computers on my network?

There can be many reasons for this. In essence this is telling
you that you are not connected to the network. Here are some
things to check in a peer-to-peer network:

● Check the integrity of the cables connecting the
  computers in the network. This can be done by
  disconnecting two or three computers from the rest of the
  network and getting those computers to "talk" to each
  other, then slowly adding more computers until all the
  rest of the network is checked out and attached. For each
  group that you are checking, make sure the cables are
  properly connected on both ends, are not broken or loosely
  connected, and, if they are available, that there is activity
  in the adapter lights in the back of the networking card
  on the computer you are checking out.

● If you are using thin coax cable (also called thin Ethernet
  or 10Base-2), make sure you have a grounding resistor

properly connected on either end of the network. On *one* end the resistor should have a chain that is connected to the computer case, but the other end should not be connected to the case.

● If you are using RJ-45 twisted-pair "phone" cable (also called "copper pairs" or 10Base-T or UTP for unshielded twisted pairs), make sure the hub to which the computers are connected is itself properly connected, is plugged in, and is working. A quick way to do this is to switch hubs.

● Make sure all computers on the network are using the same protocol. To do this, click Start, choose Settings | Control Panel, and double-click Network. In the Configuration tab, select the network adapter in the list of network components, click Properties, and then in the Bindings tab, ensure that the adapter is bound to the same protocols, as you can see here:

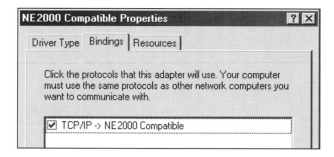

● Make sure the network adapter board is not in conflict with other hardware and that the settings in Windows 98 match those set on the board. To do this, click Start, choose Settings | Control Panel, and double-click System. In the System Properties dialog box, click the Device Manager tab, select your network adapter, and click Properties. Then select the Resources tab and compare the IRQ, I/O port address, and possibly the DMA channel with how the board is actually configured. Make sure you get a "No conflicts" message to show that the board does not conflict with other hardware. You can see this in Figure 9-8.

 How do you start Windows 98 when the network is not running? It will boot fine when the network is running.

When your computer is set up for client-server networking, it may not start up properly when it is not connected to a network or the network is not up and running. Windows may suggest starting in Safe mode. To restore the normal startup when you are not connected to the network, use the following steps:

1. Go ahead and start in Safe Mode.

2. Click Start, choose Settings | Control Panel, and double-click Network.

3. In the Configuration tab, change your Primary Network Logon from Client For Microsoft Networks (or Client For NetWare Networks) to Windows Logon, as shown in Figure 9-13.

4. Click OK to save your changes and reboot.

This will reboot your computer normally without forcing you to connect to the network. The Windows Logon option is useful not only when the network is not operating, but also when you have a portable computer that is connected to the network only some of the time.

NETWORK PRINTING

 I can't print to a network printer. How can I troubleshoot the problem?

There are several factors that have an impact on correctly networking printers. Check the following items:

● In the Network control panel of the computer with the printer, click File and Print Sharing. Make sure both of the check boxes are checked. If not, check them, click OK, and try your printer.

 ● Also on the computer with the printer, check to see that the printer is identified as being shared by clicking Start, choosing Settings | Printer, and seeing if the printer's icon has a hand beneath it, as shown on the left. If not,

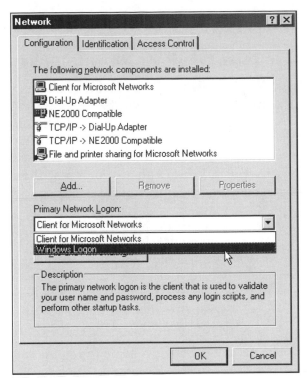

Figure 9-13 Changing to Windows Logon allows startup without a network

from the Printers folder, right-click the printer and choose Sharing from the context menu. Make sure that Shared As is selected and that the printer Share Name is the same as the one in your computer (see the next point).

- In the Printers folder on your computer, right-click the network printer and select Properties from the context menu. In the Details tab, check to see that the printer's name in the Print To The Following Port text box is the same as that found in the previous step.

- In the Printers folder on your computer, Properties dialog box, Details tab, click Capture Printer Port, and select a port other than the LPT1 that the local printer is probably using.

- When you access the printer, be sure to use the port address and not the shared name.

NETWORK COMPATIBILITY

 Can I use Windows 98 with Artisoft LANtastic?

Yes, you can use the 32-bit versions of LANtastic 7.0 and above with Windows 98. Be sure and have LANtastic installed and running *before* you run Windows 98 Setup. Windows 98 does not supply the LANtastic software—you must get the Windows 95/98 LANtastic *.INF files from Artisoft. When you do, you must then install them as client software by following these steps:

1. Click Start, choose Settings | Control Panel, and double-click Network.
2. From the Configuration tab, click Add.
3. Click Client and click Add again.
4. Insert the disk with your LANtastic *.INF files into a floppy drive and click Have Disk.
5. Follow the prompts to install the client software.

The LANtastic resources will only be accessible for you through the LANtastic utilities, which you can find by clicking Start, selecting Programs and then the LANtastic program group. You will not be able to access LANtastic through Network Neighborhood.

 Note: *Windows 98 does not support any 16-bit version of LANtastic or any 32-bit version before 7.0.*

 Can I use Windows 98 with a Banyan VINES network?

You can, provided you have VINES version 5.52(5) or later. The best way would be to have the Banyan VINES client installed and configured before upgrading to Windows 98. To make your Windows 98 PC work as a client on a Banyan VINES network, you have to have the following components installed in the Network control panel:

● Your network adapter should be set for a real-mode 16-bit NDIS driver (choose this by clicking your adapter in the Network dialog box, and then clicking Properties) if you are using an older VINES version.

● Your client software should be Banyan DOS/Windows 3.1 (choose this by clicking Add in the Network dialog box, choosing Client, and then clicking Add again).

● Your network protocol should be Banyan VINES Ethernet Protocol (choose this by clicking Add in the Network dialog box, choosing Protocol, and then clicking Add again).

Make sure your system files contain the following lines (assuming that Banyan VINES is your primary network, that your Banyan files are in the \Vines folder, and that Exp16.dos is your NDIS2 driver):

```
Autoexec.bat:
cd \Vines
ban
ndisban                 ; ndtokban if you are using token ring
redirall
arswait
z:login
c:
cd\
Config.sys:
device=c:\vines\proman.dos /i:c:\vines
device=c:\vines\exp16.dos
Protocol.ini:
[PROTOCOL MANAGER]
drivername=protman$
[VINES_XIF]
drivername=ndisban$     ; ndtokban$ if you are using token ring
bindings=MS$EE16
[MS$EE16]
drivername=EXP16$
interrupt=5
ioaddress=0x300
iochrdy=late
```

Banyan VINES servers will not appear in Network Neighborhood, because Banyan VINES servers do not support browsing. You can use Windows 98's Map Network Drive feature to locate and connect to the Banyan servers.

 Note: *You can correct a lot of issues with Banyan VINES by downloading the latest version of the Banyan VINES 32-bit client from **http://www.banyan.com**.*

Does Windows 98 come with support for DEC PATHWORKS?

No, although Windows 95 did, Windows 98 does not. You should use Microsoft's Client for Microsoft Networks and a DEC PATHWORKS protocol, or a 32-bit protected-mode driver supplied by DEC. Windows 98 will not work with any 16-bit version of DEC PATHWORKS.

I understand Windows 98 ships with NetWare client software from both Microsoft and Novell. What's the difference and how do I install my choice?

Windows 98 does include both the Microsoft Client for Novell Networks and the comparable software from Novell (Novell NetWare Workstation Shell for either 3.*x* or 4.*x* networks). The Microsoft version is 32-bit protected-mode software versus 16-bit real-mode software from Novell. The Windows 98 file system operates in 32-bit protected mode, so to use the Novell software, the processor is going to have to switch between real and protected mode, which will slow performance. The Microsoft software also supports long filenames and peer resource sharing, neither of which is supported by Novell 16-bit real-mode software. Another option is to use Novell's own 32-bit protected-mode software, which must be acquired separately.

You can choose and install a NetWare client using the following steps:

1. Click Start, choose Settings | Control Panel, and double-click Network.
2. In the Configuration tab, select Add | Client | Add.
3. Select Microsoft or Novell from the Manufacturers list, choose the network client you want, as shown in Figure 9-14, and then click OK. Or, if using software

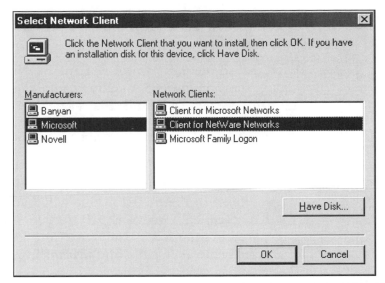

Figure 9-14 You can choose between Microsoft and Novell NetWare networking clients

from Novell, choose Novell and click Have Disk to install newer 32-bit protected-mode files.

How do I install Windows 98 on a computer that has networking support from a network vendor other than Microsoft or Novell?

First, before you install Windows 98, be sure that your network client software is correctly installed under MS-DOS, Windows 3.1, Windows for Workgroups, or Windows 95, and that the network is running when you start setup.

During setup, Windows 98 should detect a network adapter and install the Microsoft Client for Microsoft Networks by default. Notice that the Configuration tab in the Network control panel provides the same controls for adding and removing networking components after Windows 98 Setup is complete.

Tip: Install any non-Microsoft network before you install Windows 98, and then install networking support during Windows 98 Setup, not after the fact.

 ### Can a Windows 98 computer act as a Novell NetWare server?

If you install file and printer sharing for NetWare networks service, the Windows 98 machine can act as a NetWare file and print server. To install this service, do the following:

1. Right-click Network Neighborhood and click Properties.

2. On the Configuration tab, select Add | Service | Add.

3. Select File And Printer Sharing For NetWare Networks, as shown in Figure 9-15. This will load a virtual device driver (called Nwserver.vxd) that enables Windows 98 computers to process NetWare Core Protocol (NCP)-based requests for file and printer input/output.

 ### Can I use NetWare Directory Services (NDS) with Windows 98?

Yes, this is new with Windows 98. Use these steps to install NetWare Directory Services (NDS), which provides consolidated directory services for a Novell NetWare network:

1. Open the Start menu, choose Settings | Control Panel, and double-click Network.

2. In the Network control panel Configuration tab, click Add | Service | Add.

3. In the Select Network Service dialog box select Service For NetWare Directory Services.

SECURITY CONSIDERATIONS

 ### What is the difference between the levels of security—share level and user level?

Share-level access is password oriented. With it, a password can be attached to a computer, a printer, or a folder, and anybody on the network who knows the password can have access to the shared resource.

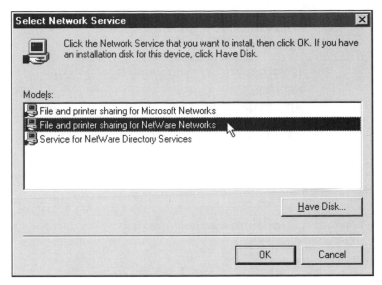

Figure 9-15 A Windows 98 workstation can share its files and printers over a NetWare network

User-level access is user oriented. With it, a security provider is specified, such as an NT domain or a NetWare server. This security provider supplies a list of users from which certain users can be specified for access to the shared resource as well as levels of access (read only, full access, or custom).

 Tip: *User-level security is available only when you are attached to a NetWare or Windows NT Server. In peer-to-peer networking you can only use share-level access.*

How do I grant access to others to use my computer's resources?

To allow others to use your computer's resources, do the following:

1. Open Windows Explorer and select the resource you want to share (disk, printer, folder, or CD-ROM drive).

2. Right-click it and choose Sharing.

3. Select the type of access you want to grant, and type the password if necessary, as shown in Figure 9-16.

 Warning: *If you share a disk drive, all of the folders on the drive are automatically shared, and if you share a folder, all of the subfolders and files within those folders are automatically shared.*

If you want others on remote computers to be able to administer your resources, follow these steps:

1. Click Start, choose Settings | Control Panel, and double-click Passwords.

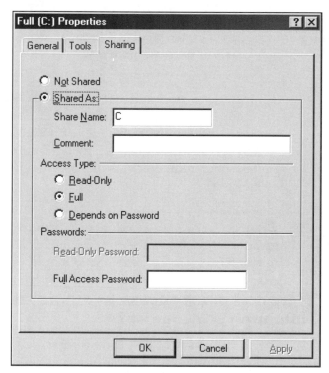

Figure 9-16   You can share a drive or folder for full use (read and write) or read-only

2. On the Remote Administration tab, click Enable Remote Administration Of This Server, like this:

3. If you are using password-level security, fill in the password, and then confirm it. If you are using user-level security, click Add, and select a person or group from the list on the left.

4. Click OK.

 I am logging into several network servers, and my passwords are different for each of them. In Windows 98, do I have to type all the different passwords as I log in?

No. When you log into Windows 98 and its various facilities for the first time after setup, you will be prompted for passwords. You will have an option to save the passwords for future use. If you choose to do this, Windows 98 will store the passwords in the *password cache*. Next time you start Windows 98, you will be prompted only for your primary password. The correct password will unlock the password cache, and you will be connected to all your servers without having to type additional passwords.

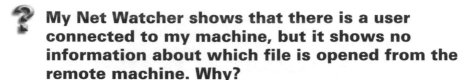 **My Net Watcher shows that there is a user connected to my machine, but it shows no information about which file is opened from the remote machine. Why?**

Some Windows applications do not keep files open. They are designed that way to save file handles. For example, applications like Notepad and WordPad open a file, load it into memory, and then close the file. When there is a need to write back to the file, the application will open it again.

I am not connected to a network on my computer at home; however, it always comes up with the "Enter network password" screen when I start Windows. Why does this happen?

You probably have a network logon selected as your primary logon. To eliminate this, follow these steps:

1. Click Start, choose Settings | Control Panel, and double-click Network.

2. In the Primary Network Logon drop-down list, choose Windows Logon, as shown here:

3. Restart Windows. You will no longer be prompted for a network password.

I had a RESTRICTIONS section in the Progman.ini file to impose certain restrictions for the users on my network. Do I have to re-create the restrictions, and how do I do that?

When you install Windows 98 on top of an existing Windows 3.*x* system, a program is automatically run. It converts the Windows 3.*x* program groups into Windows 98 folders. All data in the RESTRICTIONS section of the Progman.ini is migrated into the Policies section of the Registry.

If you installed Windows 98 into a different folder, you can convert the groups into folders by using the Grpconv.exe /m command. This will also migrate the restrictions.

How do I share a folder with another user?

Open Windows Explorer and find the folder to be shared. Then do the following:

1. Right-click the folder and click Sharing.

2. Choose Shared As and other options will become available, as you saw in Figure 9-16.

3. Fill in the Share Name and Comment text boxes, and specify the Access Type: Read-Only, Full (read and write), or Depends On Password. Select whether you want a Read-Only Password or Full Access Password. Then fill in the Password if needed.

4. Click OK.

ADMINISTERING AND MONITORING NETWORKS

I am a network administrator, and I am planning to install Windows 98 on my network. How do I do Administrative Setup? Is it setup /a, like in Windows 3.*x*?

No. In Windows 98, there are many tools for assisting an administrator in setting up Windows 98 throughout his or her network. Administrative Setup has been replaced with Microsoft Batch 98, which is a separate program called Batch.exe. It is installed with its own Setup program from the Windows 98 CD-ROM \Tools\Reskit\Batch\ folder. (Before running Batch 98 Setup, you *must have installed Windows 98* on the machine that will initially run Batch 98.) Once installed, you can open the Start menu and choose Programs | Microsoft Batch 98, which starts the Batch.exe program in the \Program Files\Microsoft Batch 98\ folder. Batch 98 is used to create a batch file that is used by Windows 98 Setup on other machines to supply the answers

to the questions raised during set up. This allows you to run Setup automatically on each client workstation.

Figure 9-17 shows Batch 98's primary dialog box and the areas for which you can gather answers. Start by clicking Gather Now to pick up the information in your Registry. You can then click on each of the five System Settings buttons to customize the settings you want. When you are done, click Save Settings To INF to save the settings to an .INF file in the folder that you identify (the default is the \Program Files\Microsoft Batch 98\ folder).

Once the batch file is created, you can set up each workstation by running Windows 98 Setup with the batch file as an argument (**setup msbatch.inf**). See Help in Batch 98 for further information.

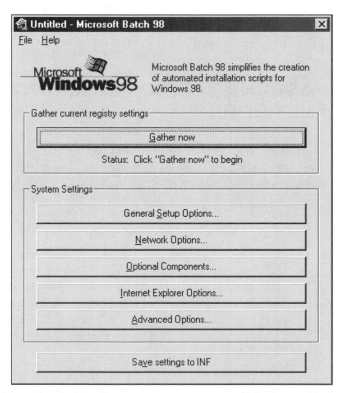

Figure 9-17   Batch 98 allows you to automate Windows 98 Setup

 ## How can I have different users log on to the same PC?

Not only can you have different users log on to the same computer, but each user can retain a unique configuration. Each user can have different access to the computer's resources, determined by the password used to log on to the computer. To enable this option:

1. Click Start, choose Settings | Control Panel, double-click Passwords, and click the User Profiles tab.

2. Select the option Users Can Customize Their Preferences And Desktop Settings, as shown in Figure 9-18.

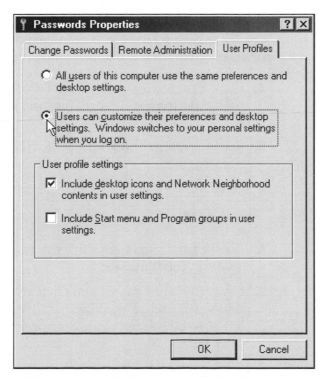

Figure 9-18 The Passwords Properties dialog box allows you to enable customized configurations for multiple users of one computer

Now when the computer is booted, Windows 98 will ask for a password and based on that password will load a different configuration. When users first log in they will be asked if they want the computer to retain their own settings. Each computer configuration will have its own desktop settings, hardware configurations, Start menu contents, and shortcuts. You can add and delete users and change their passwords by double-clicking Users in the Control Panel.

How can I monitor access to my resources on the peer-to-peer network?

You can monitor the use of your computer by others with Net Watcher. You have to have Client for Microsoft Networks installed, and the file and print sharing options for the network must be enabled. You also have to have Net Watcher installed. If you don't, use the following steps to do that:

1. Click Start, choose Settings | Control Panel, double-click Add/Remove Programs, and click the Windows Setup tab.

2. Select System Tools | Details and select Net Watcher from the list.

3. Click OK twice.

To start Net Watcher:

1. Click Start and choose Programs | Accessories | System Tools | Net Watcher.

2. Open the View menu and click By Connections. In the Net Watcher window, you'll see two panes. On the left are the names of all users currently connected to your PC.

3. Click any user and you will see the full list of resources they are using on the right, as seen in Figure 9-19.

You can view the network by user, by shared folders, or by shared files using either the View menu or the three buttons on the right on the toolbar.

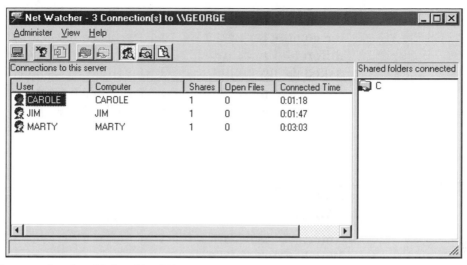

Figure 9-19 Using Net Watcher, you can monitor the users accessing your computer's resources

How can I monitor network activity through my Windows 98 PC?

Windows 98 gives you several useful network monitoring tools. One of them is Net Watcher, discussed in the previous question about monitoring access to resources on the peer-to-peer network. Another is the System Monitor. This application will allow you to monitor the amount of CPU resources used by local applications and by servicing remote requests of other users. If you don't have the System Monitor installed, do it now with these steps:

1. Click Start, choose Settings | Control Panel, and double-click Add/Remove Programs.

2. Click the Windows Setup tab, select System Tools | Details, and select System Monitor from the list.

3. Click OK twice.

To start and use the System Monitor:

1. Click Start and choose Programs | Accessories | System Tools | System Monitor. The System Monitor window will be displayed.

2. Add resources to be monitored by clicking the Add icon on the far left of the toolbar, or by selecting Add Item from the Edit menu. Pick the category and the specific measurement that you want to keep track of.

3. Select to view the data as a Line Chart, Bar Chart, or Numeric display by either clicking one of the icons on the toolbar, or selecting the display option from the View menu. One possible set of charts is shown in Figure 9-20.

 Tip: *At the same time you install System Monitor, consider installing System Resource Meter. Run it from Programs | Accessories | System Tools and an icon will appear next to the clock on the taskbar which provides a quick look at three system measurements.*

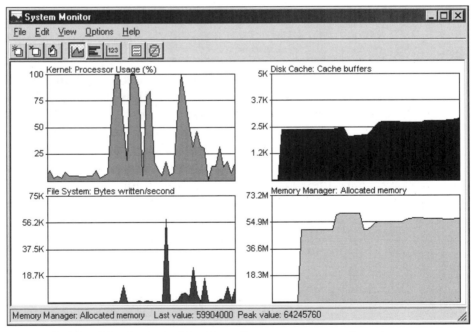

Figure 9-20 The System Monitor allows you to monitor the system resources used on your computer

 How do I set up individual accounts and restrict portions of the system to my users?

After installation, you can use the System Policy Editor to restrict a user's access to some or all of the features of Windows 98. To utilize the System Policy Editor, follow these steps:

1. On the Administrator's PC, copy the System Policy Editor folder from the Tools\Reskit\Netadmin \Poledit folder on the Windows 98 CD to a similarly named folder.

2. Open the new folder and double-click on Poledit.exe. Open the File menu and choose New Policy. The Default User and Default Computer icons will appear.

3. Double-click first Default User and then Default Computer, and edit the policy lists. This will establish a standard or default set of system policies, so that when you go to each machine, all you need to do is enter the exceptions.

4. Once you have created the default policies, open the Edit menu and choose Add User for each user, Add Computer for each computer, and Add Group for each group. For each one you create, make the policy changes for the exceptions.

5. When you are done with the policies, make sure the specific user, computer, and group policies are stored in the NetLogon directory of a Windows NT server, or in the Public directory of a NetWare server. With the policies in these directories, Windows 98 in the remote clients will automatically download the policies during network logon and update the local Registry with the policies.

6. In lieu of or in addition to establishing policies on the server, you can use the System Policy Editor's File | Connect command to connect to a remote computer and edit that computer's Registry files (User.dat and

System.dat). This will establish a set of policies for that one computer.

 Tip: *To set policies on remote computers, you must have administrative privileges for the remote computer, and in that case and when policies are downloaded at logon, the computer must be on a network with both user-level access and Remote Registry enabled.*

PROTOCOLS

 I'm using both TCP/IP- and IPX/SPX-compatible protocols on my networked computer in my office, as well as through dial-up networking at home. In the office I get the IPX/SPX-compatible login dialog box immediately after booting. At home this box does not appear because I don't connect at boot time. I would like to have one single action that produces the same NetWare access in both my office and my home. Can I invoke the login procedure by running a program?

There is a way to process the login script while in Windows. What you have to do is make sure that you attach to the server first. Use these steps to do this:

1. Go to Network Neighborhood and double-click the NetWare drive on the server you want to connect to. This will prompt you to log in. However, the system login script will not process.

2. After you attach to the network drive, open a DOS window and type the following:

   NWLSPROC/*SERVER*

   SERVER is your server name. For example, if the server is NWSERVER1, the command will be NWLSPROC/NWSERVER1. (Make sure to enter the server name in uppercase. If you enter it in lowercase, it will not work.) This will force the script to run. You can make a shortcut to this on your desktop for use whenever you want.

Can I use the IPX/SPX-compatible protocol to access a Windows NT server?

Yes, do the following:

1. Right-click Network Neighborhood and choose Properties.

2. Select the IPX/SPX-compatible protocol, click Properties, and click the NetBIOS tab.

3. Select I Want To Enable NetBIOS Over IPX/SPX, as seen here:

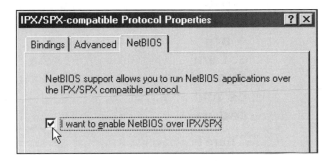

This will allow you to access Windows NT servers with IPX/SPX.

4. Click OK twice.

Which network protocol should I use with my network?

A *network protocol* is equivalent to a human language; it is the coding scheme used to communicate over a network. Different networks require different protocols. Here are the general rules of thumb:

● Use TCP/IP with Microsoft networks including Windows 98, Windows 95, and Windows NT networks.

- Use NetBEUI with Microsoft Windows for Workgroups and LAN Manager networks.
- Use IPX/SPX with all Novell networks.
- Use TCP/IP with dial-up networking to the Internet or when communicating on an intranet.

Chapter 10

Communications

Answer Topics!

Communications @ a Glance

While *networking* is connecting computers within a single facility or several closely located facilities, *communications* is connecting computers at remote facilities—anywhere in the world. Communications is primarily conducted over telephone lines connected to modems in the computers at either end. It consists of e-mail, faxes, bulletin boards, the Internet, information services such as CompuServe or Microsoft Network, and the simple transferring of files or information from one remote computer to another. Communications and networking do overlap. You can send e-mail via a network and use communications facilities (modems and phone lines) to do dial-up networking. Windows 98 provides a full complement of communications support, including handling your modem and providing the software for e-mail, transferring files, connecting to information services and the Internet, and doing dial-up networking. Chapters 6 and 9 more fully discuss the Internet and networking aspects of Windows 98 communications, including Internet mail. This chapter addresses the "other" communications support.

This chapter covers the following areas, which contain the most commonly asked questions about non-Internet communications:

 Setting Up a Modem deals with problems with modems that may arise during and after setup. Proper configuration is a priority subject.

 HyperTerminal addresses what this full-featured communications program is and how you can deal with several problems that can arise in setting it up properly.

 Phone Dialer covers questions about how you start this automatic dialing feature and use it in the most efficient manner.

- **Microsoft Exchange** answers several questions dealing with this messaging component that was brought into Windows 98 when you upgraded from a previous version of Windows.

- **Microsoft Fax** handles questions on configuring and then using this faxing feature, also carried over from previous Windows versions.

SETTING UP A MODEM

During setup, I let Windows pick my modem, and it didn't select the correct one. What can I do about this?

The modem automatically detected by Windows depends on the chip set and the type of modem. If you are having problems with the type of modem Windows has picked for you, you can manually choose your modem if it is on the list in Windows 98 (there are hundreds), install a modem driver from a disk that came with your modem, or select a generic modem driver that will allow you to go online. To manually install a modem, follow these steps:

1. Click Start, choose Settings | Control Panel, and then double-click Modems.

2. Click Remove to clear the currently installed modem from the system.

3. Click Add to start the Install New Modem Wizard.

4. Click Don't Detect My Modem; I Will Select It From A List and click Next.

5. From the list of Manufacturers, select the manufacturer, and then select your modem model from the Models list. If you don't see your modem, try the same manufacturer and speed if not the exact model. If you have a disk with your modem driver on it, click Have Disk, select the drive, click OK, select the modem, and click OK. If you don't see your manufacturer, select Standard Modem

Types, and from the Models list, select one with the bps modem speed equal to yours, as shown in Figure 10-1. Click Next.

6. Select the port to use with the modem. It is typically COM2 or COM4. Click Next and Windows will install the modem. You will be able to see it in the Modems Properties dialog box.

I cannot dial or connect with my modem. Why?

There could be several reasons for this. Here are some tips for troubleshooting your modem problems:

● Make sure the modem is set up properly. You should be using Windows 98 drivers, not Windows 3.*x*, which might be incompatible. Click Start, choose Settings | Control Panel, and double-click Modems to run the Install New Modem Wizard, which automatically detects the existing modem and loads the correct Windows 98 drivers.

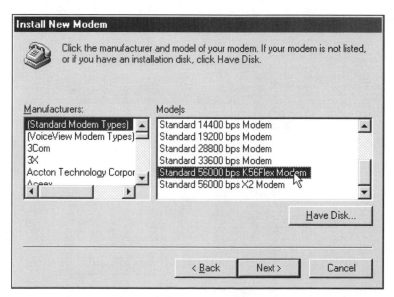

Figure 10-1 You can choose a modem that is different than the one Windows selects for you

● After the modem is installed, verify that your modem is correctly configured with these steps:

1. Click Start, choose Settings | Control Panel, and double-click Modems.

2. On the General tab, verify that the manufacturer and model for your modem are correct, as shown in Figure 10-2. If not, click Add and use the Install New Modem Wizard. If your modem is not detected, click Change and you will be presented with a list of modems. If your modem is not on the list, do you have a floppy disk or CD that came with your modem? If so, put it in its drive and click Have Disk, identify the correct drive, and click OK. When you find your modem, highlight it and click OK. If you cannot find your modem, try the Standard Modem Types and pick the speed of your modem. Make sure to remove any other modem listed as installed.

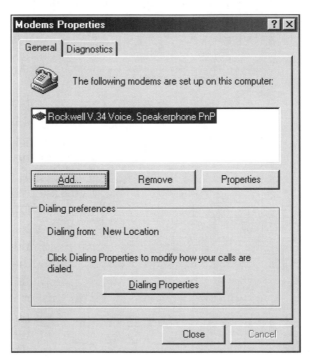

Figure 10-2 The General tab of the Modems Properties dialog box shows the modems that are installed

3. Make sure your modem is operating properly from the Modems Properties dialog box opened in step 1. Select the Diagnostics tab, choose the port on which your modem is installed, and click More Info. The answer to the commands should be "OK" or information about your modem. Click OK and Close to return to the Control Panel.

4. Verify that the modem is enabled. Open the System control panel. In the Device Manager tab, click Modem, select your modem, and click Properties. Make sure that the Device Status indicates "This device is working properly."

5. Verify the port while still in the modem's Properties dialog box opened in step 4 by clicking the Modem tab; also verify that the port listed is correct (for example, COM2). If not, select the correct port by clicking the Port down arrow and selecting the port you want. Then click OK to return to the Device Manager.

Note: *If you don't have available ports, you will not have a drop-down list to choose from. You will need to add a port using the Add New Hardware control panel.*

6. Verify the serial port I/O address and IRQ from the System Properties Device Manager as follows: Open Ports, choose the specific port for your modem, choose Properties, and then click the Resources tab. Check the Conflicting Device list on the bottom of the dialog box to see if the modem is using resources in conflict with other devices. If it is, select Change Settings (you may need to remove the check mark from Use Automatic Settings first), and then select a configuration that does not have resource conflicts. For example, if you have a serial mouse or other device on COM1, you cannot use a modem on COM3, because COM1 and COM3 ports use the same IRQ. The same IRQ addressing applies to COM2 and COM4. Click OK twice to return to the Control Panel.

7. Verify the port settings by double-clicking Modems in the Control Panel, selecting your modem, clicking

Properties, and clicking the Connection tab to check the current port settings, such as data bits, stop bits, and parity. Click Advanced to check Error Control and Flow Control. If you are using a Windows 3.*x* communications program, turn off these advanced features. Click OK.

8. Finally, click Port Settings to verify the universal asynchronous receiver-transmitter (UART) type. Data transmission problems may occur on an older 80486-based computer not equipped with a 16550 UART with a baud rate greater than 9600, or when multitasking during a file download. Try lowering the Transmit and Receiver buffers, click OK twice and then close to return to the Control Panel, and then close it.

If you are still unable to connect, use the Troubleshooter for modem problems in Windows Help. Use the following instructions to open the modem Troubleshooter:

1. Click Start and choose Help. On the Contents tab click Troubleshooting, then click Windows 98 Troubleshooters.

2. Choose Modem. The window shown in Figure 10-3 will open. Click the button for the type of problem you're having, and then scroll down and click Next at the bottom of the list to follow the problem-solving guide.

My modem connection fails! How can I find out what is going wrong?

One possibility is to look at the log file. Do the following to have a log generated:

1. Click Start, choose Settings | Control Panel, and then double-click Modems.

2. From the Modems Properties dialog box, select the modem you're having problems with, and click Properties.

3. In the modem's Properties dialog box, click the Connection tab and click Advanced.

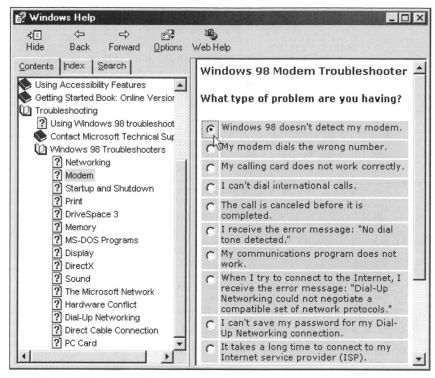

Figure 10-3 Windows Help can troubleshoot your modem problems

4. In the Advanced Connection Settings dialog box, click Append To Log. This will create a file called *your modem name*.log when you initiate the modem connection.

To view the log, click the View Log button. Notepad will open and display the log as you can see in Figure 10-4. Check and see if any action appears to have failed. You probably cannot tell what caused the failure from the log entry, but at least you might be able to tell which actions in the process were successful.

My system freezes when I try to set up my modem. What can I do about this?

Your problem may be one of conflicting port assignments or interrupt request lines (IRQs). Specifically, you may have either more than one serial device (for instance, your mouse

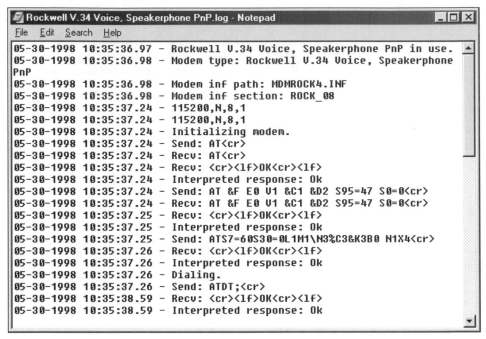

Figure 10-4 Your modem's log file displays what happened during a communications session

and your modem) assigned to the same port, or an interrupt request line used by two devices. Your serial ports are COM1 through COM4; your mouse is usually assigned to COM1 or COM3, and your modem, to COM2 or COM4. Interrupt requests are usually assigned so that COM1 and COM3 use interrupt request line 4 (IRQ 4), and COM2 and COM4 use interrupt request line 3 (IRQ 3).

Plug-and-play devices help you avoid this problem, but if you have older equipment that is "hard wired," you will have to search out the problem. To check the use of your ports and IRQs, use the following steps:

1. Click Start, choose Settings | Control Panel, and then double-click System.

2. Click the Device Manager tab. Here you can look at the IRQs assigned to your communications ports and see if there are any conflicts. You can do this in two ways: by looking at each port's properties, and by looking at all

the ports in the computer's properties. Do both of these to see the different information presented.

3. Double-click Ports to expand the list, select the Communications Port used for the modem (usually COM2 or COM4), and click Properties.

4. In the Communications Port Properties dialog box, click the Resources tab, as seen in Figure 10-5. You will see Interrupt Request followed by a setting, usually 03. Also, at the bottom of the dialog box, see that it says "No Conflicts." Close the Communications Port Properties dialog box.

5. From the Device Manager tab, click Computer in the list of devices. Then click Properties. In the View Resources tab, click Interrupt Request (IRQ). You'll see a list of ports and the interrupt requests assigned to them, like that shown in Figure 10-6. Here you can see that IRQ 3

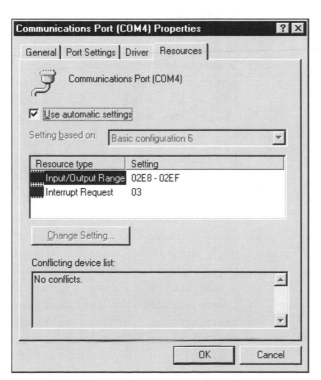

Figure 10-5   Verify your modem's IRQ in the Communications Port Properties dialog box

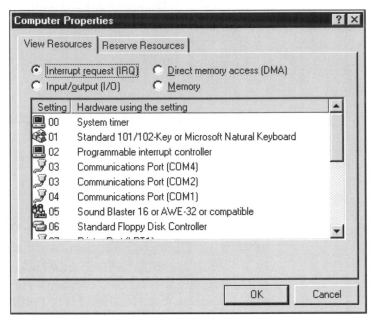

Figure 10-6 The Computer Properties dialog box will show you all your IRQ assignments in one list

is assigned to both COM2 and COM4, and IRQ 4 is assigned to COM1, all as expected. Close the Computer Properties and the System Properties dialog boxes. Next, check to see what is using the COM ports.

6. In the Control Panel, double-click Modems and click the Diagnostics tab, as shown in Figure 10-7. Here you can see the assigned usage of each COM port and make sure that your modem, mouse, and other serial devices are all assigned to nonconflicting ports.

7. Click your modem port (COM4 in Figure 10-7) and then click More Info. You will see a message telling you that the system is communicating with the modem. Your modem is being tested. The results are then displayed. If you see that the first several of the AT (attention) commands return OK, your modem is probably working. If some of the AT commands toward the end return ERROR, that simply means that your modem has not implemented that command.

8. If you do not see any response to the AT commands, then it is likely that your board is installed incorrectly and

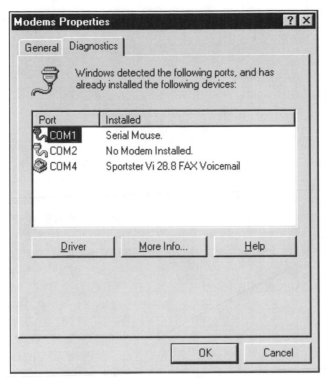

Figure 10-7 The Diagnostics tab of the Modems Properties dialog box will show you what is assigned to each port

that some setting on the board needs to change. You or a technician needs to open your computer and look at the board.

9. Click OK twice to return to the Control Panel.

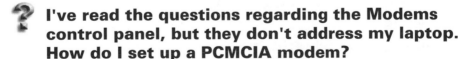
I've read the questions regarding the Modems control panel, but they don't address my laptop. How do I set up a PCMCIA modem?

To install a PCMCIA (Personal Computer Memory Card International Association) modem (or commonly called a *PC Card modem*), insert the card in the applicable port in your portable computer and restart Windows 98. During boot up, Windows 98 will recognize it as a new device and either install drivers of its own or prompt you for a manufacturer's disk. Follow the prompts to complete the installation.

Setting Up Windows 98 Communications

The modem hardware that you need for communications can be an adapter card in your computer or an external box that connects to your computer through a serial port. In either case a phone cable will plug into the modem and into a normal RJ-11 jack in the wall connecting you to your phone company and the worldwide telecommunications network beyond it. You can have a dedicated phone line for modem communications, or you may share a phone line between voice and data, or even among voice, data, and fax. With the majority of modems, you can use a phone line for only one type of communication at a time. If, for example, you try to place a voice call while the modem is transmitting data, the data transmission will be interrupted and you'll have to restart it.

Many modems today can handle faxes as well as data. This means that you can send information from your computer to a remote fax machine. For example, if you have a letter that you prepared on your word processor, you can send it to a fax machine across the world with the appropriate software.

If your modem or fax/modem is connected to or installed in your computer when you install Windows 98, in most cases Setup will detect your modem and properly set up Windows 98 to use it.

If you install a plug-and-play modem after installing Windows 98, your system will automatically be set up to use the modem. In other circumstances you will need to manually set up your modem. You can do this by clicking the Start button, choosing Settings | Control Panel, and then double-clicking Add New Hardware. You'll be guided through the modem installation.

With a modem installed, you can use the following Windows 98 communications tools without having to respecify your modem's characteristics:

● **Dial-Up Networking** connects you as a client to a remote network server and allows the use of all the normal networking resources including file access and transfer, printing, and e-mail. Dial-Up Networking, also called remote access service (RAS) or "razz," is the principal way that you connect to the Internet with Windows 98 using a modem. Chapter 9 covers Dial-Up Networking in detail.

● **HyperTerminal**, which is a full-featured communications package, connects you to a remote computer so that you may send or receive files, or access an information service or a bulletin board.

● **Phone Dialer** is used to dial the phone for you so you can talk to someone. You can either enter the number to be dialed or select it from a phone book that Windows 98 will maintain.

> *Note:* *Microsoft Exchange (and Microsoft Fax) are covered in this chapter for those users who have upgraded their Windows 95 installation with Windows 98. These capabilities carry over to Windows 98 and work, but are not included in Windows 98 itself. (Microsoft Exchange and Fax are available on the Windows 98 CD. See the section "Microsoft Fax" for installation instructions.) It's recommended to use Outlook Express for messaging as it contains several enhancements; however, Windows 98 doesn't provide a fax client, so unless you want to purchase a third-party faxing application such as WinFax, you might want to continue to use Microsoft Fax.*

● **Microsoft Exchange**, Windows 95's messaging center, allows you to send and receive e-mail and fax messages in one location. You also may access the mail facilities of information services such as CompuServe, Microsoft Network, or Internet mail.

HYPERTERMINAL

 Note: *HyperTerminal is not installed on your system if you used the Typical Windows 98 setup. To install HyperTerminal, insert your Windows 98 CD, click Start, choose Settings | Control Panel, and double-click Add/Remove Programs. Click the Windows Setup tab, double-click Communications, and select HyperTerminal. Click OK twice.*

HyperTerminal adds a number "1" to a number that I am trying to dial. The number is in an area code that is different from mine, but it is not a long-distance call for me. How can I bypass this "1" that is added?

By default, Windows 98 will add a leading "1" if the area code is different from the area code entered by the user as local. Use the following steps to bypass a number "1" when dialing.

Let us say you want to dial (333) 333-3333 from the (555) area code:

1. If you have already created a HyperTerminal connection for this number, double-click its icon in the folder displayed when you open HyperTerminal (Start | Programs | Accessories | Communications), and click Modify to change the Phone Number.

2. If no connection exists for it, start one by double-clicking Hypertrm.exe. Enter your name and choose an icon. Click OK.

3. In the Phone Number tab or dialog box (depending on whether you're modifying or creating a connection), enter your area code in the Area Code field, and enter the whole number to be called, including the area code, in the Phone Number field. For example, type **555** in the Area Code box, and then **(333) 333-3333** (including the actual area code) in the Phone Number box and click OK.

4. Select Dial. HyperTerminal will not add a 1, because it thinks that the call is local, and it will not dial 555 for the same reason. The number dialed will be (333) 333-3333!

How do I get HyperTerminal to answer an incoming call?

This was a major oversight in the original design of HyperTerminal that appeared in Windows 95, but was corrected in the Windows 98 version, as described in the next set of steps:

1. Click Start and choose Programs | Accessories | Communications | HyperTerminal.

2. Double-click Hypertrm.exe to create a new connection or double-click an existing connection icon. If you opened an existing connection, click Cancel in the Connect To dialog box. You need to enter the HyperTerminal window with a connection name appearing in its title bar, and New Connection won't work. If you already

have HyperTerminal running you can continue to use your current session.

3. In the HyperTerminal window, open the Call menu and click Wait For A Call. The status bar at the bottom of the window acknowledges your request with the message, "Waiting For Calls." When the incoming call is made, the status bar will first display "Connecting," followed by "Connected."

 4. Type a message to the sending party, if required, and when ready click Receive on the toolbar.

5. In the Receive File dialog box, browse to the folder where you want the received file stored and choose a protocol, as shown here:

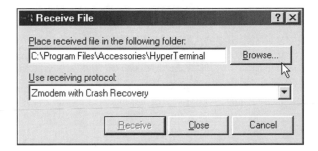

6. Click Receive when you think the sending party has just started sending the file. Timing is important and if you can communicate on a second phone line you may avoid several failed attempts. A status dialog box will monitor the arrival of the file and will close when the file is received.

 7. Click Disconnect from the toolbar after you have received all incoming files.

 ### I tried to connect to a bulletin board service, and it said to have my parity set to "odd." Where do I do that?

Parity allows the receiving computer to check on the integrity of the data being sent. There are several parity conventions: odd, even, mark, space, and none. To work, both computers

must be set to the same convention. The most common is None. To check and possibly change your parity setting, follow these steps:

1. Click Start and choose Programs | Accessories | Communications | HyperTerminal.

2. Right-click the connection that you want to change, and choose Properties.

3. Click the Connect To tab, and then click Configure.

4. In the modem's Properties dialog box, click the Connection tab.

5. You will see the Parity under Connection Preferences. Click the down arrow to be able to choose between Even, Odd, None, Mark, or Space, as shown in Figure 10-8. Make your choice and click OK twice.

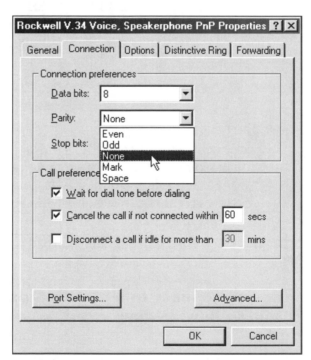

Figure 10-8   You can set the type of parity in the modem's Properties Connection tab

 ## How do I dial up a remote computer using HyperTerminal?

HyperTerminal is a full-featured communications program that can be used with a modem to connect two computers for the purpose of sending and receiving files or connecting to computer bulletin boards or other information services, including the Internet. To create a HyperTerminal connection, use these steps:

1. Click Start and choose Programs | Accessories | Communications | HyperTerminal.

2. Double-click Hypertrm, which will load the HyperTerminal program.

3. In the Connection Description dialog box, type the name of the connection you want to create, select an icon to associate with it, and click OK.

4. In the Connect To dialog box, specify the Country Code, Area Code, Phone Number, and modem for this connection, and click OK. If you haven't already installed a modem, you will be prompted for it now.

5. In the Connect dialog box, click Dialing Properties and look at the When Dialing From Here section, as shown in Figure 10-9. If you need to dial a prefix to get an outside line, to use a calling card, or if you want to turn off call waiting, this is the place to do it. Click OK when you have completed the entries you wish to make.

   If you clicked on Dialing Properties and then checked For Long Distance Calls, Use This Calling Card, you can choose a calling card from the drop-down list, or click Calling Card and you will see the Calling Card dialog box, which allows you to establish a new card; distinguish among calls made within the same area code, long-distance calls, and international calls; and save your personal identification number.

6. When the Connect dialog box reappears, click Dial, or click Cancel to avoid dialing the connection (you will

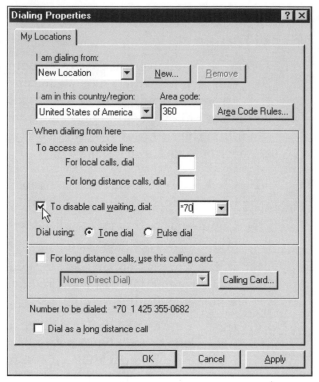

Figure 10-9 If you have call waiting, turn it off in the Dialing Properties dialog box

still have a chance to save the session). When the connection is made, the computer you are dialing will display its own terminal window similar to the one shown in Figure 10-10.

7. When you are finished with the connection, click Disconnect (hang up) on the toolbar, or open the Call menu and select Disconnect.

8. When you close the new HyperTerminal window after either dialing or canceling, it will prompt you to save your session definition. Click Yes and you will see an icon for the new connection in the Program Files\ Accessories\Communications\HyperTerminal folder.

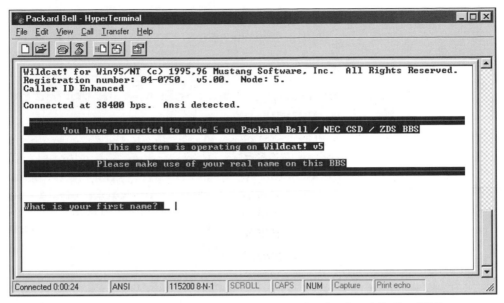

Figure 10-10 The HyperTerminal window for Packard Bell's BBS

When I use HyperTerminal I often get disconnected by an incoming call from "call waiting." How do I disable that?

You can disable call waiting by dialing a code (the code can be *70, 70#, 1170, or *80, depending on the area) before an outgoing call (on your phone you would dial the code and then 1, the area code, and the phone number). The best way to have the call-waiting code sent is to do it for all calls made from a given location through your modem. You do this through the Dialing Properties dialog box with the following steps:

1. Click Start, choose Settings | Control Panel, and double-click Modems.

2. Click Dialing Properties to open the dialog box as shown previously in Figure 10-9.

3. Click the To Disable Call Waiting, Dial check box.

4. Open the drop-down list on the right of the call-waiting line, and select the code that is correct for your area.

(This code is often listed in your phone book. If not, call your phone company.)

5. Click OK.

What file transfer protocols are supported by HyperTerminal?

HyperTerminal supports these file transfer protocols: Kermit, X-Modem, X-Modem-1K, Y-Modem, Y-Modem-G, Z-Modem, and Z-Modem with Crash Recovery. Both you and the other party with whom you are communicating need to use the same protocol. If you have a choice on which to use, start with Z-Modem with Crash Recovery and work backwards in the previous list until you find a protocol you both have that works with the phone services between you.

I am trying to type Attention (AT) commands in HyperTerminal, but I keep getting the New Connection dialog box. How can I bypass that box?

In addition to bypassing the New Connection dialog box, you must also set a switch that instructs HyperTerminal to bring up a terminal window before dialing the number. You can then enter your commands before dialing. To do this, follow these steps:

1. Click Start and choose Programs | Accessories | Communications | HyperTerminal. In the folder window, double-click Hypertrm.

2. In HyperTerminal, click Cancel in the Connection Description dialog box, leaving you in the New Connection window.

3. Open the File menu and choose Properties.

4. Click Configure and then click the Options tab.

5. Select the option Bring Up Terminal Window Before Dialing, as shown in Figure 10-11. This will allow you to type modem commands directly in a terminal window.

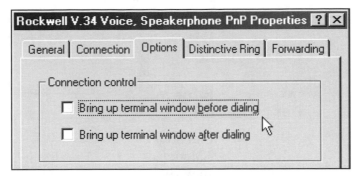

Figure 10-11 If you open a terminal window before dialing, you can set up your modem by typing commands to it

PHONE DIALER

How do I start the Phone Dialer?

Use the following steps to start the Phone Dialer:

1. Click Start and choose Programs | Accessories | Communications | Phone Dialer. A dialog box appears with a telephone pad and speed-dial buttons, as shown in Figure 10-12.

2. Type a phone number from your keyboard, choose one from the drop-down list, or use the Phone Dialer numeric keyboard, and click Dial; or click a Speed Dial button.

How do I create a speed-dial button to use in Phone Dialer?

To create a speed-dial button:

1. Click Start and choose Programs | Accessories | Communications | Phone Dialer.

2. In the Phone Dialer dialog box, click the speed-dial button (1 through 8) you want to set.

3. Type the Name that will appear on the button and the phone number to dial.

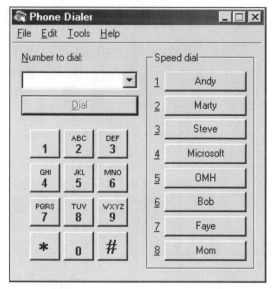

Figure 10-12 Phone Dialer dials your voice-line telephone calls for you

4. Click Save or Save And Dial to call the number right now. The name you typed now appears on the button.

5. When you want to speed dial the number, click the button and the number will be dialed.

 ### How do I change my speed-dial settings in Phone Dialer?

To quickly change one or more speed-dial numbers or names, follow these steps:

1. Click Start and choose Programs | Accessories | Communications | Phone Dialer.

2. When the Phone Dialer dialog box appears, open the Edit menu and choose Speed Dial.

3. Click the speed-dial button you wish to change.

4. Change or delete the information in the Name and the Number To Dial boxes.

5. When you are done editing, click Save.

MICROSOFT EXCHANGE

 I did a clean install of Windows 98 and lost the Inbox (Microsoft Exchange). Is there a way to get it back without reinstalling Windows 95?

Yes, there are both U.S. and international versions on your Windows 98 CD. Use these steps to install Microsoft Exchange:

1. Place your Windows 98 CD in its drive. Close the auto-open window when it appears.

2. With Windows Explorer, open the path D:\Tools\ Oldwin95\Message\Us (assuming D: is your CD-ROM drive). You should see the file Wms.exe for the Windows Messaging Service.

3. Double-click Wms.exe. When asked if you want to install Windows Messaging, click Yes. Again click Yes to accept

Where Does Microsoft Exchange Come From?

In Windows 95 the Microsoft Exchange client provided e-mail services for Internet mail, Microsoft Mail (including a post office), and several information services such as CompuServe. Its icon on the desktop said "Inbox." In Windows 98 the Microsoft Exchange client has been replaced by Outlook Express. If you install Windows 98 over Windows 95, you can leave Microsoft Exchange on your computer and use it under Windows 98. There is also a way to install Microsoft Exchange including a post office for LAN e-mail from the Windows 98 CD (see the first question).

Note: *In the OSR 2 version of Windows 95, Microsoft Exchange is called "Windows Messaging." Here we refer to it as Microsoft Exchange, which was the term used in the initial release of Windows 95.*

the license agreement. Windows Messaging and a Microsoft Mail post office will be installed. Click OK to acknowledge that Setup is complete.

4. If there isn't already a Microsoft Mail post office on your system you must set one up before you can complete setting up Windows Messaging. Do that by opening Start and choosing Settings | Control Panel and double-clicking Microsoft Mail Postoffice. Select Create A New Workgroup Postoffice and click Next. Identify the drive and folder to contain the post office, click Next, accept the directory for the post office, and again click Next. Enter the name of the administrator's mailbox and a password and click OK. Add additional users by again opening the Microsoft Mail Postoffice from the Control Panel and this time choosing Administer An Existing Workgroup Postoffice.

5. To use Windows Messaging, open Start and choose Programs | Windows Messaging. The Inbox Setup Wizard will open. Follow the instructions as they appear.

 In Microsoft Exchange the Outbox view on the column heading reads "From" and it should be "To." How can I change it back to "To"?

Follow these steps:

1. From the View menu, select Columns.

2. Select the From column on the right and click Remove. The "From" will be moved to the left.

3. Select the To field from the Available Columns list on the left and click Add. The "To" will be moved to the right.

4. Select the To column and click Move Up or Move Down until the column is where you want it placed. Figure 10-13 shows one possibility.

5. Click OK. The name of the column should be replaced.

 Tip: *If you want to return to the original view, click Reset.*

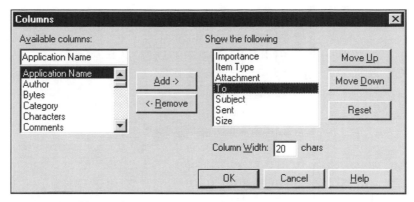

Figure 10-13 The columns in the views can be changed or resequenced

 How do I specify the address book I want to use in Microsoft Exchange?

Microsoft Exchange creates two address books when you install it: a Personal Address Book for all your personal messages and a Post Office Address list for your network, maintained by the post office administrator. You can select an address book from either the Tools menu in Microsoft Exchange or from the toolbar of a new electronic mail message. To select an address book:

1. Click Start and select Programs | Windows Messaging. (You can also click the Inbox icon on your desktop.)

2. Open the Tools menu and choose Address Book. The Address Book window is displayed as shown in Figure 10-14.

3. In the upper right of the Address Book dialog box, click the name of the address book you want to use in the Show Names From The list box. All the names from the address book you selected are listed.

Tip: *You can choose which address book appears first on the list (and is therefore your default) by opening the Tools menu in Exchange, choosing Options, and clicking the Addressing tab. Then open the Show This Address List First drop-down list and choose which you want. When you're done, click OK.*

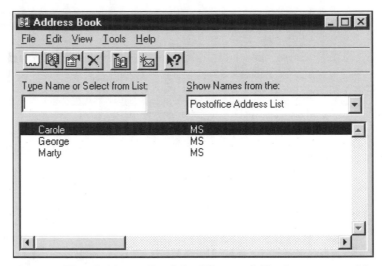

Figure 10-14 The Address Book in Microsoft Exchange provides a listing of e-mail aliases from your choice of address lists

How do I use Exchange's address book?

Once you open an address book as described in the previous question, here are some tips on how you can use it:

● To find a particular name in your address book, type the name or a sequence of letters beginning the name in the blank box on the left above the list. The name will be highlighted as you type. Press ENTER to open the entry.

● To add a name to your address book, choose New Entry from the File menu, or click New Entry on the left of the toolbar. Select the type of address you want to enter, and then fill in the information.

● To create a message to be sent to selected address(es), select the addressees by holding down CTRL while clicking them. Then either choose New Message from the File menu, or click New Message on the toolbar to create a new electronic mail message that is preaddressed to the selected people.

MICROSOFT FAX

I did a clean install of Windows 98 and lost Microsoft Fax. Is there a way to get it back without reinstalling Windows 95?

Yes, there are both U.S. and international versions on your Windows 98 CD. Use these steps to install Microsoft Fax:

1. Place your Windows 98 CD in its drive. Close the auto-open window when it appears.

2. With Windows Explorer, open the path D:\Tools\ Oldwin95\Message\Us (assuming D: is your CD-ROM drive). You should see the file Awfax.exe.

3. Double-click Awfax.exe. You will see a note that you must have Windows Messaging, Microsoft Exchange Client, or Microsoft Outlook 97. Given that you do have one of the listed programs (see the previous section for installing Microsoft Exchange client), click Yes. Microsoft Fax will be installed. Click Yes to restart your computer.

Faxing in Windows 98

In Windows 95 Microsoft Fax provided fax services. In Windows 98, Microsoft Fax has been removed. If you install Windows 98 over Windows 95, you can leave Microsoft Fax on your computer and use it under Windows 98. There is also a way to install Microsoft Fax from the Windows 98 CD (see the first question). Alternatively, you can purchase a separate faxing application.

4. After restarting, open Start and choose Programs │ Accessories │ Fax │ Compose New Fax. The Inbox Setup Wizard will open. Follow the instructions as they appear.

How do I configure Microsoft Fax?

Use the following steps to configure Microsoft Fax:

1. Click Start and choose Settings │ Control Panel and double-click Mail ("Mail" may also be "Mail and Fax").

2. If you have already installed it, you should see Microsoft Fax in the list of services. You can configure or reconfigure that service by selecting it and clicking Properties. The Microsoft Fax Properties dialog box will open, as you can see in Figure 10-15. This dialog box is described in step 5.

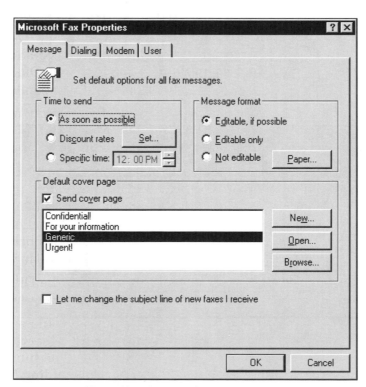

Figure 10-15   The Microsoft Fax Properties dialog box allows you to customize your fax settings

3. If you have not installed a fax service, click Show Profiles, choose a profile to which you want to add fax capabilities, and then click Properties. In the Services tab, click Add to open the Add Service To Profile dialog box shown here:

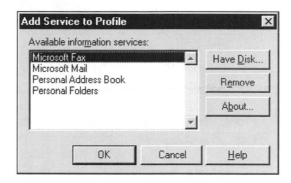

4. Click Microsoft Fax and then click OK. A message asks if you want to type your name, fax number, and fax modem now. Click Yes.

5. In the Microsoft Fax Properties dialog box, shown in Figure 10-15, click the Message, Dialing, Modem, and User tabs to verify and enter the following information:

   ● On the User tab, enter your fax number. Verify that the other information is valid. The information typed in the User tab automatically appears on the cover page.

   ● On the Modem tab, the modem information will already be entered if your modem has already been installed. If you have not installed a modem or want to choose a different modem, click Add in the modem folder and launch the Install New Modem Wizard.

   ● Check the information on the Dialing and Message tabs to see if it meets your requirements.

6. If you want to create a new profile with Fax in it click Add to do that under the list of services in the Mail control panel's Services tab. The Inbox Setup Wizard will open. Choose the services including Microsoft Fax that you want in the profile. Click Next, and follow the remaining instructions.

7. Click OK and Close to return to the Control Panel which you can also close.

8. To have Microsoft Fax available for sending and receiving, start or restart the Microsoft Exchange (Inbox) with the profile containing Microsoft Fax and your changes will take effect.

Tip: *Once you have set up Microsoft Fax, you can also change fax properties from Microsoft Exchange (Inbox). Select Tools | Microsoft Fax Tools and choose Options.*

How do I attach a predefined cover page to a fax message?

There are two ways to get predefined cover pages for your faxes. Microsoft Fax provides some predefined cover pages (Confidential, For Your Information, Generic, and Urgent) that are available to you. You can choose among these when you compose a fax from Microsoft Fax.

Another predefined cover page can be one that you have created in the Cover Page Editor and then saved. In this case, you can specify that filename or browse for it when you are asked if you want a cover page.

How do I create a custom cover page for my faxes?

Use these steps to create a custom cover page:

1. Click Start and choose Programs | Accessories | Fax | Cover Page Editor.

2. Click OK to bypass the Cover Page Editor Tips.

3. Follow these tips to create your fax cover page:

   ● From the Insert menu, click Recipient or Sender or Message. In each case a submenu with options will be displayed. When you click a field, an edit box with a placeholder for the field will be displayed, as shown

in Figure 10-16. Drag each placeholder where you want it on the cover page.

● If you want an object, such as a graphic for a logo, to be included, select Object from the Insert menu and then drag it where you want it.

● To include your own unique text, click Text on the Drawing toolbar. Your pointer will become a set of crosshairs. Drag it to form a rectangle that will contain the text. You can then type, highlight, and format your text with the font, size, and style you want.

● To align objects, select them by dragging a marquee around them, and then select Align Objects from the Layout menu.

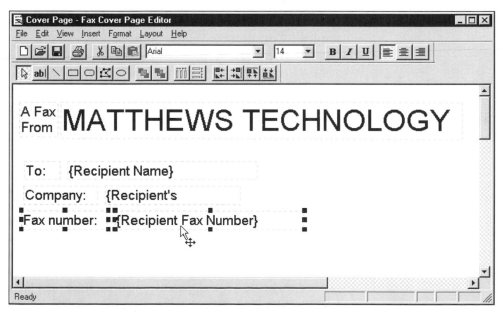

Figure 10-16 Fax Cover Page Editor allows you to create your own cover page

● When you are finished, save the cover page by selecting File | Save As and putting it in your Windows folder with the cover pages that came with Microsoft Fax.

 How do I create a shortcut to the fax printer?

You can place a shortcut to the fax printer on your desktop, drag a document to the shortcut icon, and have it automatically start the Compose New Fax Wizard without going through any menus. Follow the steps listed next to create a shortcut to a fax printer:

1. Click Start and choose Settings | Printers to display the currently installed printers.

2. Drag the Microsoft Fax printer icon to the desktop, and click Yes, you want to make a shortcut.

3. If you want to change the name, click the Microsoft Fax printer shortcut name and then click it again after a pause.

4. A selection box will surround the name, allowing you to change it. Press ENTER to finalize the name.

When you have a document you want to fax, simply drag it to the Fax icon on the desktop. The Compose New Fax Wizard will be loaded for you to address the document and send it.

 How do I send a fax from Microsoft Exchange?

Use the following instructions to send a fax from Microsoft Exchange:

1. Open Microsoft Exchange by double-clicking Inbox on your desktop. If the default profile does not include Microsoft Fax, select such a profile if you are given that option. (If you are not given an option and the default profile does not include Microsoft Fax, you will need to

open the Mail or Mail and Fax control panel, change the default profile, and restart Microsoft Exchange.)

2. From the Compose menu, choose New Fax to launch the Compose New Fax Wizard, shown next.

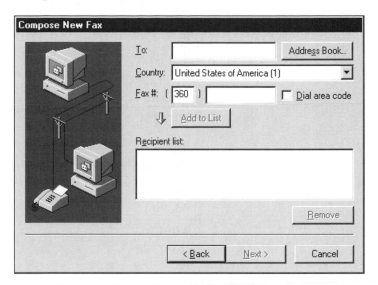

3. Click the Address Book to select a fax recipient, or type the name and fax number. Click Next.

4. If you want a cover page, make sure "Yes. Send this one." is selected. Click the type of cover page you want: Confidential, For Your Information, Generic, or Urgent. For additional options, click Options. Click Next when you are through.

5. In the Compose New Fax dialog box, type the subject, press TAB, and then type a message. If you want the fax note to be on the cover page, select that option. Click Next.

6. To include a file with your message, type the path to the file, or click Add File and follow the prompts. Click Next.

7. To finish the fax and send it, click Finish.

 Tip: *You can also send a fax from many applications by, in a sense, "printing" to the fax—you select Microsoft Fax as the printer you want to use, and the Compose New Fax Wizard will open and lead you through the process as described here.*

 ## How do I send a fax using Windows Explorer?

To use Windows Explorer to send a fax, do the following:

1. Right-click My Computer and click Explore.
2. Locate and right-click the document you wish to fax.
3. Select Send To from the context menu. A submenu will be displayed. Select Fax Recipient. This will launch the Compose New Fax Wizard, which will prompt you for information.

You can also drag the document to a shortcut of the Fax Printer on your desktop, if you have one.

 Tip: *You can also open Windows Explorer by pressing* SHIFT *and double-clicking My Computer on your desktop.*

 ## How do I receive a fax?

 To receive a fax the Microsoft Exchange (Inbox) must be loaded with a profile that includes Microsoft Fax. You can tell if this is the case if a fax machine icon is in the taskbar next to the clock. (If the fax icon does not appear, shut down Microsoft Exchange and restart it with the appropriate profile.) To prepare to receive a fax, double-click the fax icon in the taskbar to open the Microsoft Fax Status dialog box. When you hear the phone ring and know it is a fax coming in, click Answer Now to do that. Microsoft Fax will answer and receive the fax.

You can also have Microsoft Fax automatically receive a fax. In the Microsoft Fax Status dialog box, open the Options menu and click Modem Properties. The Fax Modem Properties dialog box will open as shown next. Here you can have Microsoft Fax automatically answer after so many rings.

Chapter 11

Multimedia

Answer Topics!

Multimedia @ a Glance

Multimedia is to computing as spice is to food—it may not fill you up, but it sure improves the taste. *Multimedia* is the addition of sound and video plus the use of CD-ROM and DVD (which doesn't have an exact meaning, but "digital video disk" seems to work well) technology in a computer environment. Windows 98 provides a substantial enhancement to the support for multimedia that has been available at the operating system level. Windows 98 includes built-in programs to record, edit, and play back digital audio, to play back digital video, to use the Internet for both collaborative audio/video meetings, and to enjoy streaming audio and video as it happens. Windows 98 also includes a substantial enhancement in the playback of full-motion video, has built-in support for many audio and video compression schemes, allows sharing disk drives over a network, and includes a new media control interface for controlling different types of media devices. Windows 98 is the first integrated local and online multimedia operating system.

To make full use of multimedia and, really, of Windows 98, you need a disk drive, a CD-ROM drive (8*x* and above) or DVD drive, an audio or sound board (preferably 16-bit), a pair of speakers, and an Internet connection. You also need to install the multimedia components that come with Windows 98. You can install them during setup or by using the Add/Remove Programs control panel. When installed, the programs are available by choosing Start | Programs | Accessories | Multimedia. Here are the most common multimedia applications that come with Windows 98:

 CD Player plays your CD audio disks. It allows you to play CD music or other files. You can start, stop, fast forward, rewind, and skip to the beginning or end. You can play a CD continuously or in random order, and select which tracks you want to play. You can also build and maintain a database of the selections on your CDs.

 DVD Player protects your investment in CDs by playing both your data and audio disks, and extends your multimedia horizon with the new DVD technology that contains full-length motion pictures with multiple sound tracks and several channels of dubbing, and allows up to 17GB of data on a single disk.

- **ActiveMovie Control** is the default Windows 98 video player for playing both downloaded audio and video from Internet Explorer and for viewing other multimedia files you have on your computer.

- **Media Player** is a general-purpose multimedia player that plays, like the ActiveMovie Control, all types of multimedia files: audio, video, and animation. It allows you to control the play of a clip, create a new clip by inserting one file into another, and edit an existing clip.

- **Sound Recorder** allows you to digitally capture sound from either a microphone or a CD. With it you can record, stop, go to the beginning or end of the recording, insert other files into it, and perform special tasks, such as increasing the volume for specific parts of the recording, adding an echo, or mixing two recordings so both are heard.

- **Volume Control** controls the volume and balance of your audio files by providing a slider for each function. Depending on your equipment, you will have a dialog box for volume and balance control of all multimedia, line-in, synthesizer, CD, wave, and microphone devices.

- **NetMeeting** provides an umbrella of tools for audio/videoconferencing, collaborative use of an application, "whiteboard" information exchange, and long distance telephoning using the Internet as the carrier.

- **NetShow Player** offers a means to view both real-time streaming audio and video over the Internet or across an intranet, and downloaded multimedia files.

- **RealPlayer** allows you to listen to audio over the Internet in a widely used format.

This chapter discusses the following topics:

- **Sound** covers such items as assigning sound to events, how to get sound from speakers even if you don't have a sound card, and adding a sound card to your computer.

- **Using CD-ROM and DVD** includes information about changing the configuration of your CD-ROM, how to play a music CD on your computer, how to correct problems that may occur with your CD-ROM after installing Windows 98, the effects of plug-and-play on your CD-ROM drivers, and shortcuts to use with the Windows 98 CD player.

- **Viewing Video** describes the ActiveMovie Control and the Media Player and covers how to use these features. This section also shows you how to find out if you have an MPEG driver installed.

- **Volume Control** gives information about volume problems that may occur and how to remedy them, and how to put Volume Control on the taskbar.

- **Sound Recorder** shows you how to use the recorder, and how to deal with problems when no Wave driver is installed.

- **Using Online Multimedia** covers the emerging audio and video technologies available over the Internet including Microsoft NetMeeting for conferencing and the NetShow Player for real-time viewing and listening.

SOUND

I have added an older sound card to my PC. What is the easiest way that I can set it up for use with Windows 98? The disk that came with the card is for Windows 3.*x*. Should I use it?

Don't use the disk with the card, because the driver provided was written for Win3.*x*. You should let Windows 98 do the setup for you. If your card is plug-and-play compliant (you will find that information in the card's label or user's guide), all you have to do is plug in the card and start Windows 98. If the card is not plug-and-play, do the following:

1. Click Start; choose Settings | Control Panel and double-click Add New Hardware.

2. In the Add New Hardware Wizard, click Next twice for Windows to try and locate plug-and-play devices, and then click Yes for the question "Do you want Windows to search for your new hardware?"

3. Click Next and after several seconds, Windows 98 will automatically detect the card and load the appropriate 32-bit driver. Follow the prompts on the screen.

4. If Windows 98 did not automatically detect the card, manually select the manufacturer and model by first selecting Sound, Video, and Game Controllers.

5. You will be shown a group of possible resource settings that you can print. Windows has considered the needs of the board and the available resources, and determined the best. If these settings do not match what is set on the board, you can either open the Device Manager in the System control panel and change the settings, or you can change the switches on the board. In either case, click Next and follow the instructions to complete the installation.

 ## How can I assign sound to program events?

Events, such as opening files, completing a job, or encountering an error, can have sounds assigned to them if you have a sound card. Use the following steps to do this:

1. Click Start; choose Settings | Control Panel and double-click Sounds. The Sounds Properties dialog box will open.

2. In the Events list, select the event you want to assign a sound to. (You can scan the list and see what events currently have sounds assigned to them, such as starting Windows. Events with sounds assigned are identified by a speaker icon, as shown in Figure 11-1.)

3. In the Name list, select the sound you want to hear when the event occurs. If you don't see the sound in the list, click Browse and locate the sound. Windows 98 has several sound schemes that come with it. More are available on the CD-ROM, although you might have to install them, because they are not installed by default.

4. You can create a scheme that is used with your own chosen sounds and save it by clicking Save As and naming the sound scheme.

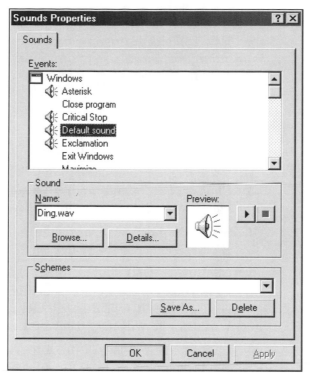

Figure 11-1 Assign a sound to an event by clicking the event and then selecting a sound

5. Click OK when you are finished.

Can I get sound from my PC speaker if I don't have a sound card?

Yes, if you have the PC speaker driver file Speaker.drv. You can obtain this from the Microsoft Web site. Start at **http://support.microsoft.com**; register if required, search for article Q138857, read the article, and then download the file Speak.exe. After you download the file (you should save it into an empty directory), double-click it to extract Speaker.drv and the other files. Read the text files by double-clicking them. When you are ready, use the following steps to install Speaker.drv.

 Tip: *You won't get very high-quality sound out of your PC speaker and, depending on your equipment, you may not get sound that you want to listen to. That's why Microsoft did not include it in Windows 98.*

1. Click Start; choose Settings | Control Panel and double-click Add New Hardware.

2. Click Next twice to start the Add New Hardware Wizard looking for plug-and-play devices.

3. Choose No to avoid having Windows 98 search for new hardware. Click Next.

4. Select Sound, Video, and Game Controllers from the Hardware Types list. Click Next.

5. Click Have Disk and then Browse to locate where you have your PC Speaker driver file. (The system looks for an .INF file. It will find the Oemsetup.inf file, which Windows 98 will use to set up the speaker driver.)

6. Choose OK and then Finish to install. When it is done, you'll be asked if you want to restart your computer to complete the installation. Click Yes.

To modify the settings for PC Speaker:

1. Click Start; choose Settings | Control Panel and double-click Multimedia.

2. Click the Audio tab. Under Playback, open the Preferred Device drop-down list box and you will see Sound Driver For PC-Speaker.

3. Click it to select it, and then click Advanced Properties to verify or change the settings. (If the Advanced Properties button is not available, the settings cannot be changed.)

4. Click OK. If you now go to the Sounds control panel, you should be able to click a sound and hear something.

USING CD-ROM AND DVD

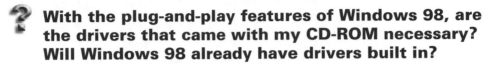 **With the plug-and-play features of Windows 98, are the drivers that came with my CD-ROM necessary? Will Windows 98 already have drivers built in?**

Windows 98 provides the drivers for the majority of CD-ROMs, so you probably don't need the drivers that come with your CD-ROM. You may need the drivers for use with the previous versions of MS-DOS if you are using a dual-boot system with an option of booting into a previous version of MS-DOS or Windows 98.

Note: With FAT32 you can no longer dual-boot with Windows 3.1/DOS.

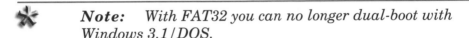 **I connected everything, but Windows 98 does not seem to recognize my CD-ROM drive. How do I install it?**

Make sure that your controller is recognized. Use the following steps to do this:

1. Right-click My Computer, choose Properties, and then click the Device Manager tab.

2. Locate the SCSI or IDE controller in the device tree. (If you do not immediately see it, it is probably hidden under the hard disk controller's device.)

3. Open the branch for your SCSI or IDE controller by clicking the plus (+) sign at the left. Click the controller and then click Properties.

4. On the General tab, verify that the Device Status message states, "This device is working properly," as shown in Figure 11-2, and that in the Device Usage section the check box for Exists In All Hardware Profiles is enabled. Click OK to return to the Device Manager.

If you have several devices connected to the controller, and any of the SCSI or IDE devices does not have a Windows

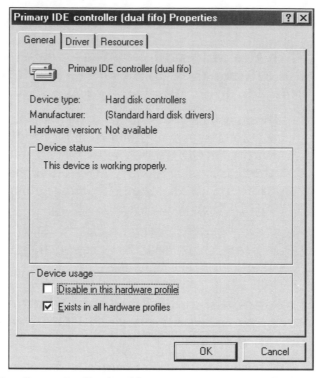

Figure 11-2 From the Device Manager, you can verify that Windows 98 thinks the device is operating correctly

98 driver, you can only use the devices connected to the controller with real-mode drivers.

 I have installed Windows 98 and now my CD-ROM no longer works. How can I get it to work?

The problem could be that Windows is using the real-mode drivers from your Config.sys file. See the discussion on this subject in Chapter 2. If your CD-ROM is a Sony, Mitsumi, Panasonic, Toshiba, or one of a number of others, Windows 98 will install the appropriate drivers. After removing the Config.sys statements, try running the Install New Hardware Wizard in the Control Panel and let the system autodetect the hardware.

If the system fails to detect the CD-ROM, you'll have to manually select the manufacturer and model.

 ## How can I optimize the performance and change the configuration of my CD-ROM drive?

You can optimize the performance of the CD-ROM drive by setting up a cache large enough to contain an entire multimedia stream. To do that, follow these steps:

1. Click Start; choose Settings | Control Panel and double-click System.

2. In the System Properties dialog box, click the Performance tab and click File System in the lower left.

3. Click the CD-ROM tab in the File System Properties dialog box, as shown in Figure 11-3.

4. Open the Optimize Access Pattern For drop-down list, and select the speed of the CD drive that you have.

5. Drag the Supplemental Cache Size slider to a setting according to the following guidelines:

Single speed	Set to Small
Double speed	Set to one-third across from the left
Triple speed	Set to two-thirds across from the left
Quad speed or higher	Set to Large

6. Click OK twice when you are finished.

7. Answer Yes to "Do you want to restart your computer now for changes to take effect?"

 ## Can I play a music CD on my PC?

You sure can. In fact, Windows 98 has an AutoPlay feature that begins playing the audio CD disk as soon as you insert the disk into the CD-ROM drive. (To prevent automatically playing the CD, hold down the SHIFT key when you insert it.) To permanently disable the AutoPlay feature so that it does not begin playing the CD automatically, follow these steps:

1. Double-click My Computer, open the View menu, and choose Folder Options.

2. Click the File Types tab.

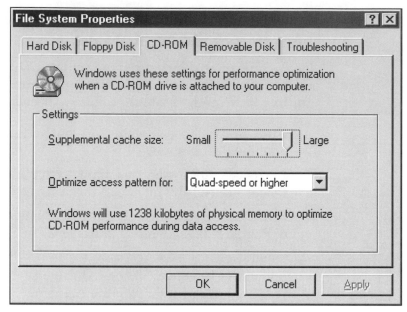

Figure 11-3 Optimize your CD-ROM from the File System Properties dialog box

3. Select AudioCD and then click Edit. The Edit File Type dialog box will be displayed, as shown in Figure 11-4.

4. Click Set Default to toggle AutoPlay off. If the Play command is in boldface, the CD will play when it is inserted; if "Play" is not bold, it will not.

5. Click OK when you're satisfied.

Are there any shortcuts or tricks that I can use with the Windows 98 CD player?

Yes. You can play or change songs using a variety of techniques. Try some of the following:

● Open Windows Explorer and click your CD-ROM drive with an audio CD in it. In the right panel you will see

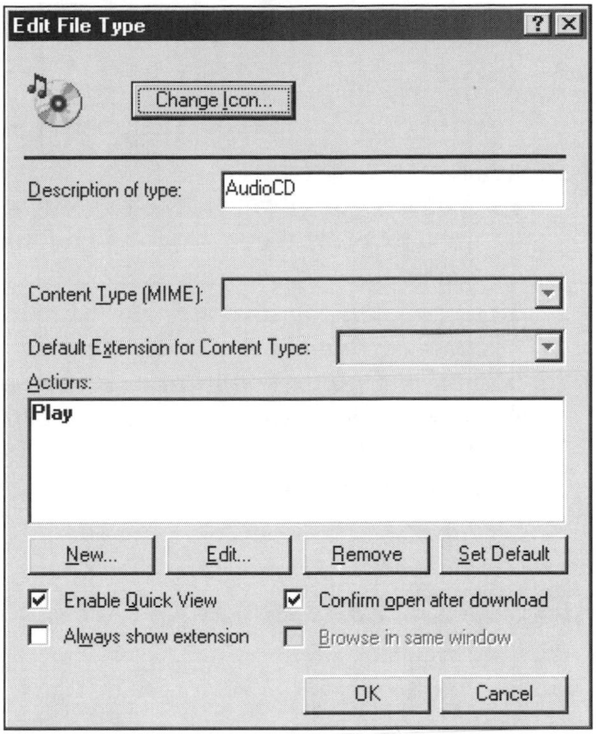

Figure 11-4   You can vary the default to automatically play a CD

Track01.cda, Track02.cda, and so on, as shown in Figure 11-5. If you right-click a track, you can play it automatically by choosing Play from the context menu. If you already are playing a track, it will change to the track you just selected.

- If you double-click a track displayed in Windows Explorer, it will play automatically.

- Try right-dragging a track onto your desktop and creating a shortcut. Rename the track's shortcut to the song's real name, as shown next. Whenever you have the CD in the drive, you can now double-click its icon on the desktop to play it.

● You can also drag tracks to your hard drive and put them in your Start menu, or create a folder with CD tracks in it.

 Tip: *When you drag a "copy" instead of a shortcut to your hard drive, you are not really copying the music file, only a pointer or link to it, similar to a shortcut. To get the music on your hard disk, you must record it, although you should note that the .WAV file sizes are quite large (a 48-second piece in 16-bit stereo is over 8MB).*

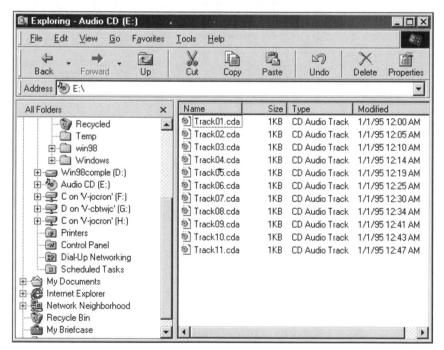

Figure 11-5 Viewing the tracks on a CD with Windows Explorer allows you to pick which one you want to play

 I've been hearing a lot about DVD lately. What is it?

DVD, or for lack of a standardized definition, digital video disk, is a new standard that uses a disk the same size as a CD, is backward-compatible to play CDs, but offers much greater capacity and quality of audio and video playback. For example, a single DVD disk can hold up to 17GB of data or play back over two hours of high-quality, full-screen video. As with its predecessor, the CD, DVD is available in purely read-only media (DVD-ROM), write-once media (DVD-R or DVD-WO), rewriting (DVD-RAM), and as video playback (DVD-Video or DVD-Movie). Of course, the more capabilities you receive will determine the price for the hardware, software, and media. If you are looking to replace or add a CD-ROM to your current system, or are buying a new computer, you should definitely consider acquiring a DVD-ROM instead—it's the next generation in onboard computer multimedia.

VIEWING VIDEO

 How can I find out if I have an MPEG driver installed on my system?

1. Click Start; select Programs | Accessories | Entertainment.

2. Click Media Player and then open the Device menu as shown here. If an MPEG device such as ActiveMovie is one of the devices listed, you have it. If not, you do not have MPEG installed.

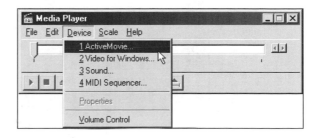

 Where can I find video files to use with ActiveMovie Control?

You can download any of the supported video formats from the Internet, but the most handy source is your Windows 98 CD. To open the ActiveMovie Control and view several video clips, follow these steps:

1. Click Start and choose Programs | Accessories | Entertainment | ActiveMovie Control.

2. In the Open dialog box, select your CD-ROM drive in the Look In drop-down list, open the Cdsample and Videos folders, and then double-click one of the sample files.

 3. Click the Run button to play the video, as shown in Figure 11-6.

After you start a video, the Run button turns into a Pause button, as shown to the left.

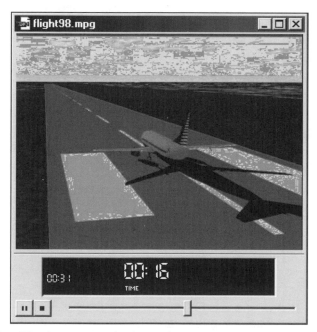

Figure 11-6 Playing a video clip in the ActiveMovie Control window

How do I enlarge the ActiveMovie Control window?

The ActiveMovie Control default window provides a very clean appearance that masks many of its capabilities. The gateway to its features is its context menu. To see how to change the size of the window, do the following:

1. Double-click a video file in My Computer or Windows Explorer to open the video in the ActiveMovie Control.

2. Right-click the viewing area and click Properties on the context menu, as shown next.

3. Click the Movie Size tab and select a size from the drop-down list.

4. Click OK.

 ### What is Media Player?

Media Player, much like ActiveMovie Control, is a multimedia application that allows you to play MIDI, video, and CD-Audio files. Unlike the Sound Recorder, this and ActiveMovie Control are playback-only devices. To access Media Player, you must have a sound card installed. If you have it installed, do the following:

1. Click Start; choose Programs | Accessories | Entertainment | Media Player. You will see the Media Player window open, as shown next.

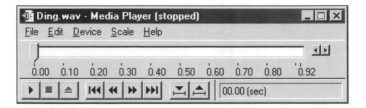

2. Play a file by clicking Device and choosing the type you will be using—for example, ActiveMovie, Video For Windows, Sound, MIDI, or CD Audio. The options you see will depend on the hardware you have installed.

3. Select the file for playback and click Open.

4. Click Play.

Tip: *Sound files usually have the extension .WAV; video files, .AVI; MIDI files, .MID; movie files, .MPEG; ActiveMovie files, .AU, .AIF, .AIFF, or .AIFC; and CD audio files, .CDA.*

VOLUME CONTROL

Why can't I get the Volume Control utility included with Windows 98 to work with my sound card?

Volume Control will only work if you install one of the sound drivers included with Windows 98 or a Windows 98-specific driver for your sound card. The Sound Blaster driver included with Windows 98 should work fine with Sound Blaster-compatible cards. To install that driver:

1. Click Start; choose Settings | Control Panel and double-click Add New Hardware.

2. The Add New Hardware Wizard will be displayed. Click Next twice to get it started. Choose No when it asks you if you want Windows to search for your new hardware. Then click Next.

3. From the list of Hardware Types, select Sound, Video, and Game Controllers. Click Next.

4. Choose Creative for the manufacturer and Sound Blaster Or Compatible as the model, as shown in Figure 11-7. Click Next.

5. You will be shown the default settings that will be used for the new device. You have the opportunity to print the settings, and it is a good idea to do so. Click Next.

6. Files will be copied at this point, so you may be required to insert the Windows 98 installation CD. Follow the onscreen instructions.

How do I open the Volume Control?

A Volume Control (or just Volume, according to your sound card) icon, a speaker, is placed by default on the taskbar next to the clock; it's very handy for controlling the volume and turning the sound on and off (for example, during phone calls). You can do this by double-clicking the Volume Control

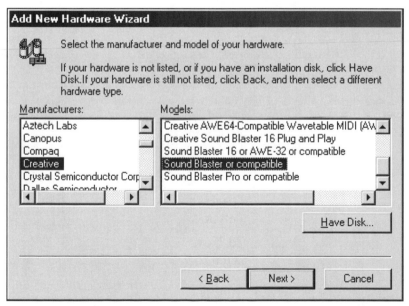

Figure 11-7 Select the sound device from the list of manufacturers and models

icon on the taskbar to open the Volume Control dialog box, shown in Figure 11-8 (your Volume Control dialog box may look different, depending on your sound card), or click the icon to open the Volume Control slider, as shown here:

Removing the Volume Control Icon from the Taskbar

1. Click Start; choose Settings | Control Panel and double-click Multimedia.

2. Click the Audio tab, and select the option Show Volume Control On The Taskbar to remove the check mark. Click OK.

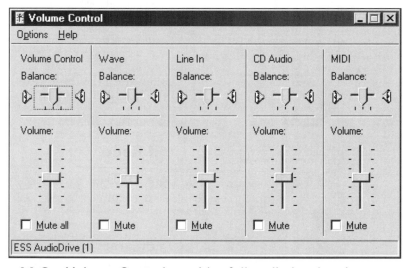

Figure 11-8   Volume Control provides full audio level and balance control

Tip: In the Audio tab, if the Show Volume Control On The Taskbar option is unavailable, make sure the Volume Control utility is installed. Do this by opening the Control Panel, double-clicking Add/Remove Programs, and selecting Windows Setup tab. Select Multimedia in the Components list, click Details, and check Volume Control in the Components list.

SOUND RECORDER

I tried to start Sound Recorder, but there is no Wave driver installed. What do I do?

The prerequisite is to have a sound card (or at least the Speaker.drv file described earlier). Then you can do one of the following:

- Install or reinstall the sound card using the Add New Hardware Wizard as described in several instances earlier in this chapter.

- If the sound card is Sound Blaster-compatible, use the Sound Blaster driver that ships with Windows. (To install that driver, see the question "Why can't I get the Volume Control utility included with Windows 98 to work with my sound card?".)

- If the correct driver for the type of sound card being used is not listed, try using Windows 3.1 drivers for the specific card.

How do I use the Sound Recorder?

If you have a microphone, DVD, or CD-ROM drive connected to your computer, you can record sound. Use the following steps to do this.

1. Click Start; choose Programs | Accessories | Entertainment | Sound Recorder. The Sound Recorder window will be displayed, as shown next.

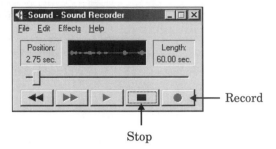

Record

Stop

1. Click the red Record button, on the right, to start recording.

2. Click the Stop button to end recording.

3. Open the File menu, choose Save As, and type a filename for this .WAV file.

USING ONLINE MULTIMEDIA

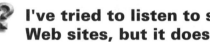 **I've tried to listen to some music samples on various Web sites, but it doesn't work. What does Windows 98 have that can help?**

The predominant audio format (file types of .RA, .RM, and .RAM) for most Internet sites is used by RealPlayer, made by RealNetworks. Windows 98 includes RealPlayer 4.0; however, as of the writing of this book, you can download an updated version (5.0) for free from **http://www.real.com**. To install RealPlayer 4.0, follow these steps:

1. Click Start; choose Settings | Control Panel and double-click Add/Remove Programs.

2. Click the Windows Setup tab, double-click the Internet Tools component, and select Real Audio Player 4.0. Click OK twice.

The first time you try listening to an audio clip you will have the opportunity to register and then the RealPlayer control will begin playing the clip, as you can see here:

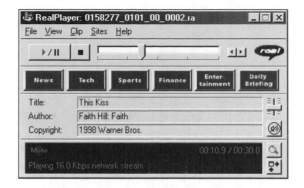

 I understand I can use NetMeeting to make Internet phone calls. What do I, as well as the person I'm calling, need to have to place a call?

As the saying goes, "If it was easy, everyone would be doing it"—which is why telephony over the Internet hasn't yet made it to primetime. There are several factors that come into play when using the Internet to make phone calls, such as the mechanics of setting up software, connecting to the Internet, and actually making the call. Then there are the variables of the quality of your equipment (microphone, sound card, and speakers) and the Internet itself, such as the speed of your connection (more Kbps is definitely better!), the traffic on the Internet, and the number of concurrent users on the supporting servers.

To call another person you both need to belong to a directory server that makes the necessary links between the Internet and standard phone lines, and each person needs to be using standards-based conferencing software such as NetMeeting, installed as part of a Windows 98 Typical setup. Microsoft supports several servers and allows you to choose from other popular servers from within NetMeeting. It is easiest if both parties belong to the same directory server, but it's not necessary. You can locate users on your directory server as shown in Figure 11-9, or you can locate people on other servers by using their IP (Internet protocol) address or computer name if on a LAN.

As with many Internet features, Internet telephony offers great promise, but is still a developing technology.

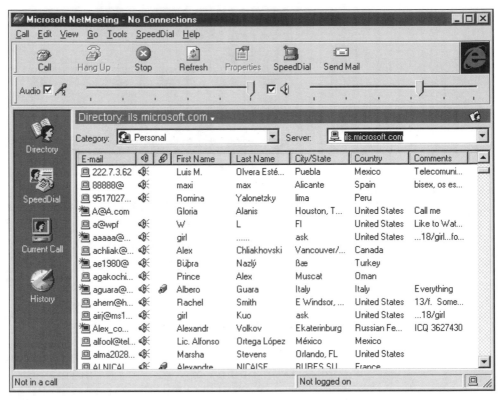

Figure 11-9 Locate other users on your directory server to place an Internet call

 How can I view real-time video over the Internet?

NetShow is Windows 98's method of viewing video as it's happening over the Internet. NetShow is available as a built-in Internet Explorer ActiveX control, which means it's available on demand when you try and view live or "streaming" video and audio. It's also available as a standalone application you can install and use to play .ASF (active streaming format) files. Although it is not part of the Typical setup, you can install the NetShow Player with these steps:

1. Click Start and choose Settings | Control Panel and double-click Add/Remove Programs.

2. Click the Windows Setup tab and double-click the Multimedia component.

3. Select Microsoft NetShow Player 2.0 and click OK twice.

You can open and play an .ASF file in the NetShow Player by double-clicking an .ASF file, as shown next, for an audio-only file. You can also open the NetShow Player by clicking Start | Programs | Internet Explorer | NetShow Player and locating an .ASF file using the File | Open (for files on your local computer or network) or File | Location (for Internet and intranet files) dialog boxes.

Chapter 12

Windows 98 DOS

Answer Topics!

Windows 98 DOS @ a Glance

Why does a Windows 98 book talk about DOS? There are two good reasons: First, because there are thousands of DOS programs out there, especially games, that people are not willing to quit using, and second, because DOS and its command language *are* a part of Windows 98. Why in this point-and-click world would someone want to type DOS commands? Because certain tasks are easier for longtime DOS users to perform with commands, and because some debugging tasks can only be performed at a DOS prompt. You therefore can look at DOS from two different, although related, standpoints: using DOS to run DOS programs and using its command language.

Here are the areas explored in this chapter:

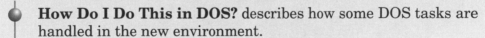

How Do I Do This in DOS? describes how some DOS tasks are handled in the new environment.

Improving Performance answers questions about response time, optimizing and customizing DOS, and otherwise improving the performance of DOS with Windows 98.

Running DOS Programs describes situations and troubleshoots problems that can arise when trying to run DOS programs, such as accessing specific drivers.

Managing Autoexec.bat and Config.sys Files covers how Windows 98 uses (or doesn't use) these DOS files and how they can be modified.

 Between DOS and Windows answers questions about how DOS and Windows 98 interact—to pass parameters or data, for example.

 Effects of Long Filenames covers how this feature in Windows 98 can raise questions in DOS.

HOW DO I DO THIS IN DOS?

 I have MS-DOS 3.3 on my system, and I cannot boot into the previous MS-DOS version. I edited Msdos.sys as suggested, added BOOTMULTI=1, and it still does not work. How can I solve this problem?

Unfortunately, you've just encountered a "no-solution" problem. To boot into the previous DOS version, you need DOS version 5.0 or greater.

 Note: *Windows 98 and Windows 95 OSR2 (OEM Service Release 2) cannot dual boot if they are running FAT32.*

 Can I change the way my MS-DOS window looks?

To change the DOS window, do the following:

1. Right-click Start and choose Open.
2. Double-click Programs and then right-click MS-DOS Prompt.
3. Choose Properties from the context menu.

   ● On the Font tab, you can select between font types of Bitmap Only, TrueType Only, or Both Font Types. You can also change the point size for the font on your DOS window. As you choose a Font Size, you can see how it will look by its effects on the Window Preview and the Font Preview, as shown in Figure 12-1.

   ● On the Screen tab, you can choose to run the program full screen or in a window, set an initial size or number of lines in the screen, and specify whether to display the toolbar.

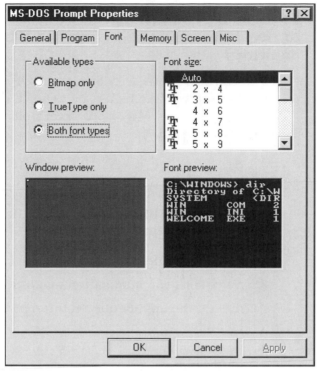

Figure 12-1 You can see how font changes will affect the DOS window

Has the DOS REPLACE command been removed from Windows 98?

Yes, it has been removed from the DOS in Windows 98. However, you can use the new version of Xcopy that comes with Windows 98 with the /y switch to overwrite existing files without prompting, or with the /-y switch to prompt before overwriting. This duplicates the functionality of REPLACE.

In MS-DOS mode, when I type CD \My Letters, I get an error message: "Too many parameters - Letters" to open a folder of that name. Why?

You just have to vary your command format. To switch to your new folder, type **CD \"My Letters"**. Enclosing the name of the folder in quotes makes MS-DOS read the name of the folder as one block of text.

Can I run a Windows program from the DOS prompt, or do I have to start it from the Windows 98 desktop?

You can start both Windows and DOS programs from the DOS command line using the new START command. For example, to start Microsoft Excel from the DOS command line, type this:

START *[drive letter]:\[full path]*\Excel.exe.

For example: **START C:\Excel\Excel.exe**.

You can add the following switches to the START command (for example, START/m):

● **/m** runs the application minimized in the background.

● **/max** runs the application maximized in the foreground.

● **/r** runs the application restored in the foreground (default).

● **/w** stands for wait; DOS will not return control to the user until another program exits.

 How can I specify a working folder for a DOS application?

A *working folder* is what the application uses as a default folder to store its output. You can specify a working folder in the program's properties stored with its shortcut. Use the following steps to access the properties for a DOS application and specify a working folder:

1. Click Start and select Programs | Windows Explorer.
2. Open the folder with your application, and then right-click the application.
3. Choose Properties and then click the Program tab. You can specify the working folder in the Working field, as shown in Figure 12-2. Click OK.

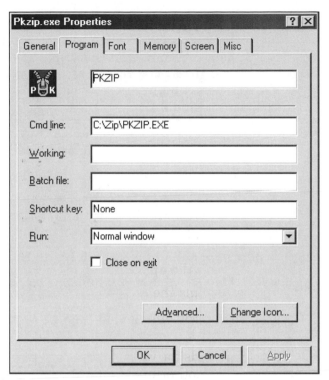

Figure 12-2 The Properties dialog box allows you to set a number of parameters for a DOS program

---

 Tip: *From the Properties dialog box you can establish a batch file that will run before starting a DOS program. Type in the name of the batch file in the Batch File text field.*

Can I always start Windows 98 in the DOS mode?

Yes. You can boot in DOS, and then start Windows 98 from DOS when you're ready for it. To do so, follow these steps:

1. Using Windows Explorer, open your root folder, right-click the file Msdos.sys, and choose Properties. (If you don't see the file, open the Explorer's View menu, click Folder Options, in the View tab click Show All Files, and click OK. Now try to right-click Msdos.sys.)

2. In the Msdos.sys Properties dialog box, if Read-Only and Hidden are checked in the bottom of the dialog box, click them to remove the check marks, and then click OK. This allows you to edit Msdos.sys and save your changes.

3. Right-click Msdos.sys and choose Copy. Right-click an empty area of the right pane of the Explorer window and choose Paste. This creates a copy of Msdos.sys that you can use if you make a mistake while editing it.

4. Right-click Msdos.sys again, choose Open With, and double-click Notepad in the list.

5. Locate the section entitled [Options], as seen in Figure 12-3.

6. Change the line BootGUI=1 to **BootGUI=0**.

7. Open the File menu and choose Save. Close Notepad and reboot.

8. The PC will now always start in DOS mode.

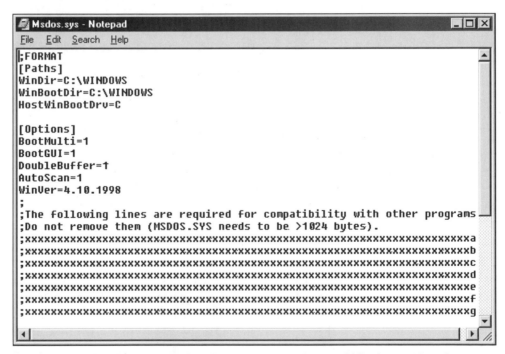

Figure 12-3 Msdos.sys is where you can change Windows 98 to boot into DOS mode

9. To go into Windows 98, at the command prompt type **WIN**.

10. When you're satisfied with the changes, you can reset the Hidden and Read-Only attributes of Msdos.sys to prevent overwriting, and delete the copy of Msdos.sys.

More About DOS and Windows 98

In most cases, Windows 98 will run DOS programs better and more easily than any prior version of DOS. This is true because Windows 98 takes less conventional memory (that below 640K) than prior versions of DOS, and because Windows 98 does a better job of providing memory and disk resources than was the case in the past. Windows 98 also gives you a number of ways to start DOS programs. Among these are

- Locating the program in Windows Explorer or My Computer and double-clicking it.

- Placing a shortcut to the program on the desktop where you can double-click it, or putting a shortcut on the Start menu where you can click it. (The Windows 98 shortcut replaces the .PIF files used in previous versions of Windows.)

- Placing a shortcut to the program in the Quick Launch toolbar where you can click it.

- Typing the path and filename for the program in the Start | Run dialog box.

- Opening a DOS window or booting into DOS, and typing the path and filename for the program.

While this last method describes the classical DOS approach to starting DOS programs, the first three methods are uniquely Windows, and the fourth is a combination of the two. The second, using shortcuts, works in Windows 95 or 98 and the third option is unique to Windows 98. As a matter of fact, shortcuts do more for DOS programs than for Windows programs. A shortcut for a DOS program allows you

to specify a number of settings about how you want the program to run, including whether you want the program to run

- in DOS mode.
- in a window.
- full screen.
- without detecting Windows. (If a DOS program tells you it can't run under Windows 98, try telling it to not detect Windows in its shortcut.)
- by shutting down Windows and starting DOS by itself.

A shortcut for a DOS program can be created in the same ways as with other programs: dragging a program's .EXE file to the desktop or Start menu, or choosing Create Shortcut from either the File menu or context menu. You can also create a shortcut to a DOS program by opening the Properties dialog box for the program. Since the program didn't come with properties, a shortcut is created for the program. It is the shortcut's properties that you will be looking at.

The DOS commands in Windows 98 are a mixture of some new commands and some old (and familiar) DOS commands. The old commands remaining in Windows 98, while retaining the same name and structure, have been rewritten to work in the 32-bit world and with long filenames. Windows 98 has also deleted some previous DOS commands. The best way to see if a command exists and see what parameters and switches are used with it is by typing the command followed by **/?** either in the Start | Run dialog box, or at the command prompt in a DOS window.

IMPROVING PERFORMANCE

 How can I speed up my MS-DOS application? It slows down to a crawl when it runs in the background.

You can adjust the speed of the application by doing the following:

1. Right-click Start, choose Open, and double-click Programs.

2. Right-click the MS-DOS Prompt icon.

3. Choose Properties, and then click the Misc tab, as shown in Figure 12-4.

4. Move the Idle Sensitivity slider to Low.

5. In the Background area, make sure that Always Suspend is not selected.

Will Windows 98 allow me to customize/optimize my DOS sessions for individual DOS applications as OS/2 does?

Yes, you can do that with the Properties dialog box for the DOS program. Here are the steps to follow:

1. Using Windows Explorer, find the program file (.EXE file) of the DOS program, and drag it to the desktop. That creates a shortcut to the DOS application.

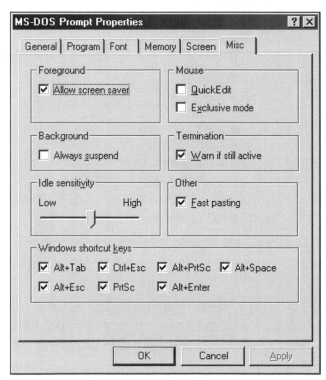

Figure 12-4 MS-DOS Prompt Properties can be modified for improved performance

2. Right-click the shortcut and choose Properties from the context menu. The program's Properties dialog box will be displayed. Here you can change and modify the settings for the application. The functions of each of the tabs are as follows:

● **General tab** displays the statistics and attributes about the program and allows you to set the attributes for Read-Only, Archive, Hidden, and System.

● **Program tab** displays the program name, path, working folder, batch file, shortcut key, and with which type of window (Normal, Minimized, or Maximized) it will begin. The Advanced button allows you to set whether the program can detect Windows and if you want the program to run in DOS-only mode, as shown in Figure 12-5.

● **Font tab** is used to set the type and size of fonts used in the DOS window.

● **Memory tab** controls the settings for Conventional Memory, Expanded Memory, Extended Memory, and MS-DOS Protected-Mode Memory. It is generally best to leave these settings on Auto.

● **Screen tab** controls whether the DOS program will run full size or in a window, what size it will be, whether a DOS toolbar is displayed, and whether to use Fast ROM Emulation or Dynamic Memory Allocation.

● **Misc tab** controls miscellaneous settings for foreground and background operations, using the mouse, terminating the program, shortcut keys, and more.

I am running Windows 98 as my operating system now. I would love to delete my old DOS to save some disk space. Do I still need it?

You only need your old DOS folder if you think you will need some of the commands in the previous DOS version. If you

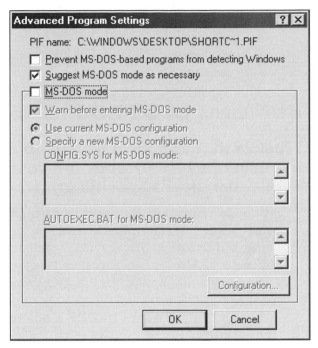

Figure 12-5 The Advanced Program Settings dialog box allows you to prevent a DOS program from seeing Windows

don't think you will ever be doing that, you can safely delete the DOS folder. The new versions of DOS files that some applications might need are now in the \Windows\Command folder and there are some additional DOS commands on the Windows 98 CD in the \Tools\Oldmsdos folder.

When typing the MEM /C command in an MS-DOS window to find out what free memory I have, I am told that I have zero kilobytes free memory in the upper memory area (UMA). How can this be? Isn't Windows 98 supposed to be better at allocating memory?

Windows 98 is, indeed, managing the memory very effectively. MEM /C reports zero kilobytes because after

loading all the real-mode drivers during startup, Windows 98 reserves all global upper memory blocks (UMBs) for Windows 98's own use or for expanded memory support.

RUNNING DOS PROGRAMS

 I realize that Windows 98 can do a lot for DOS applications in shortcuts, but what if my DOS application needs specific drivers?

You may find that you have certain DOS applications that still need to see specific drivers being loaded. Windows 98 can and will use a Config.sys file if the file exists in your root directory. Also, in the Advanced settings of the program's Properties dialog box, an MS-DOS mode can be specified, in which case, you can load specific drivers only when launching that program. To set MS-DOS mode to be loaded, follow these steps:

1. Open Windows Explorer and find your DOS program.
2. Right-click the DOS application's icon, and choose Properties from the context menu.
3. Click the Program tab and click Advanced.
4. Then select MS-DOS mode. Other options will then become available. If you select Specify A New MS-DOS Configuration, as shown in Figure 12-6, you can type in your desired configuration changes.
5. An easier way to change the configuration is to use a configuration checklist displayed when you click Configuration at the bottom of the Advanced Program Settings dialog box. Do that now and the Configuration Options dialog box in Figure 12-7 will open.
6. Click the options necessary for your program and then click OK.
7. Make any changes to the configuration that you need, and then click OK twice more.

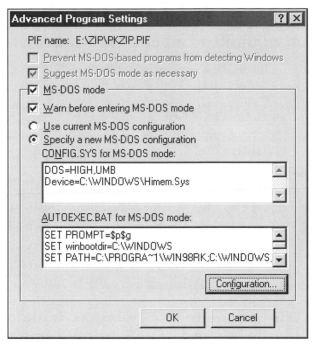

Figure 12-6   You can set a specific Config.sys and Autoexec.bat to run only when you run a specific DOS program

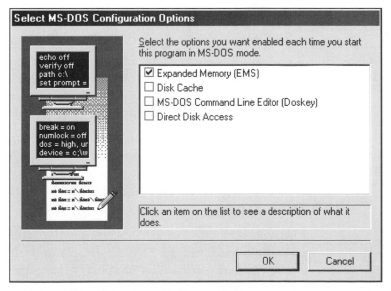

Figure 12-7   A Configuration Options dialog box gives you a checklist of possible options

 My DOS application will not load because Windows is running. How can I run this under Windows 98?

Some DOS-based programs are written not to load if they detect that Windows is running, so you must trick them a bit. Try this to run the program:

1. From Windows Explorer, right-click the program.

2. Choose Properties from the context menu.

3. Click the Program tab and then click Advanced.

4. Click Prevent MS-DOS-Based Programs From Detecting Windows, as you saw earlier in Figure 12-5, and click OK.

5. Click OK again. This will return a code to these applications that says Windows is not running.

 Why does the DOS window remain open with the text "Finished - application name" appearing on the title bar when it is finished?

The DOS window remains open so you can see any error messages that the DOS application may have displayed. You can change the program properties for the MS-DOS-based application so that it does close by following these steps:

1. From Windows Explorer, right-click the icon for the DOS application.

2. Choose Properties from the context menu and click the Program tab.

3. Select the Close On Exit option and click OK.

 What can I do with programs that won't run even in MS-DOS mode?

Many legacy DOS programs, especially those that needed a boot disk, will only run in MS-DOS mode under Windows 98. Sometimes, even when you specify that the program run in MS-DOS mode (see "Will Windows 98 allow me to customize/

optimize my DOS sessions for individual DOS applications as OS/2 does?" earlier in this chapter), the program will not run or will not run correctly. If you are using the current MS-DOS configuration for Config.sys and Autoexec.bat, beware that by default, Windows 98 gives you a "clean boot" configuration. Your DOS program may need specific device drivers and other settings not loaded by default in order to work. Finding and loading these drivers and settings manually can be quite a hassle. An easy way to do this is to copy the old Autoexec.bat and Config.sys files into the new ones that Windows 98 will use. Follow these steps to do this:

1. Find the appropriate boot disk the program used to work with.

2. Copy the Autoexec.bat and Config.sys files to your hard drive with identifying names (Darkfrce.aut and Darkfrce.cfg, for example).

3. From Windows 98, right-click the program shortcut icon and choose Properties. Click the Program tab and then Advanced. Select MS-DOS Mode and then click Specify A New MS-DOS Configuration.

4. While the Advanced Program Settings dialog box is open, click Start and select Programs | Accessories | Notepad.

5. Open the configuration files (Darkfrce.aut and Darkfrce.cfg in this case) one at a time.

6. Select all the contents of the file, press CTRL-C to copy them to the Clipboard, click the Advanced Program Settings dialog box, and press CTRL-V to paste the Clipboard contents into the Autoexec.bat and Config.sys text boxes, respectively.

7. Clean out any duplicate lines from the text boxes. Notice that some of the drivers from the old DOS folder should now be accessed from the Windows folder. Delete any of the default lines if necessary.

8. When you are finished, click OK twice.

 Note: *Windows 98 has an MS-DOS program troubleshooter that will lead you through the process of getting a DOS program to run. To start the troubleshooter, open the Start menu and choose Help. Click the Index tab, type **ms-dos** in the text box and click Display. In the Topics Found dialog box double-click MS-DOS Programs Troubleshooter.*

When I am running a program in MS-DOS mode, why can't I press ALT-TAB to go back to Windows?

When you are running a program in MS-DOS mode, the application has exclusive access to the system and all other applications are terminated, including Windows 98 Explorer, which is the Windows 98 shell. You are effectively shutting down Windows to run this application. Windows will restart when you exit.

MANAGING AUTOEXEC.BAT AND CONFIG.SYS FILES

Do I need Autoexec.bat or Config.sys in Windows 98?

Windows 98 doesn't need Autoexec.bat or Config.sys. In fact, it speeds up your computer if you don't have them and may even make your DOS programs run better because Windows 98 does a better job of managing memory than if you try to do it in those files. The reason they are there is twofold: First, for compatibility—some programs look at these files and their contents. Second, you may need a driver that has no Windows 98 equivalent, in which case you can load them in real mode with Config.sys and Autoexec.bat.

How do I add a "path" in Windows 98 similar to what existed in Autoexec.bat with PATH=?

Open the Start menu, choose Run, and type **Sysedit.exe**. Click OK. In the Autoexec.bat window add the path statement you need. Open the File menu, choose Save, and close Sysedit. Reboot your system and the path statement will be activated.

 ## If Windows 98 doesn't need Autoexec.bat or Config.sys, how does it load my necessary real-mode drivers, such as Himem.sys and Dblspace.bin?

In Windows 98, the functionality of Autoexec.bat and Config.sys is replaced by a new file, Io.sys. The drivers that are loaded by default through Io.sys are the following:

- Himem.sys
- Ifshlp.sys
- Setver.exe
- Dblspace.bin or Drvspace.bin (if found on the hard disk)

In addition to these drivers, the following values are set by default with Io.sys:

- DOS=high
- Files=60
- Lastdrive=z
- Buffers=30
- Stacks=9,256
- Shell=command.com /p
- Fcbs=4

Io.sys is not an editable file, but an entry in Config.sys will take precedence over the Io.sys settings. For example, Io.sys does not load Emm386, so if you have an application that loads data into the high memory area, you can load Emm386.exe in Config.sys.

 Tip: *Windows 98 does provide* expanded *memory support without your loading Emm386. See for yourself by removing the Emm386 statement and then looking at MEM /C in a DOS window.*

 Windows 98 removes several lines in my Autoexec.bat file that I need to run specific DOS applications. Does it mean that the commands are illegal? Why is that?

Setup remarks out lines starting with "Rem" that are no longer needed with Windows 98, although they are not illegal. After the setup is complete, you can use any text editor, such as Notepad, to edit Autoexec.bat and re-enable the lines. However, if you don't run these applications often, you might consider running them in MS-DOS mode with their own Autoexec.bat and Config.sys files and allowing Windows to run the way it set itself up.

BETWEEN DOS AND WINDOWS

 Can I cut and paste between MS-DOS applications and Windows applications, or between two MS-DOS applications?

Yes, you can if the applications are running in separate windows. To paste from a DOS window to a Windows application, do the following:

1. If the DOS program is running full screen, press ALT-ENTER to switch to window mode, click the MS-DOS icon on the left of the title bar, choose Properties, click the Screen tab, and select Display Toolbar (if not selected).

2. Click Mark on the toolbar, select the lines to be copied, and click Copy on the toolbar.

3. Press ALT-TAB to switch to the Windows application, open the Edit menu, and choose Paste.

To paste from a Windows application to a DOS window:

1. Select and copy the lines from the Windows application.

2. Switch to the DOS application.

3. Click Paste.

When I open a DOS window from Windows 98, I get an error message: "Parameter value not in allowed range." What did I do wrong?

Check to see if your MS-DOS Prompt settings are correct by looking at the properties. Make sure there are no additional settings that might confuse the system. To do this, follow these steps:

1. Click Start; choose Programs and double-click MS-DOS Prompt.

2. Then click Properties in the toolbar. (Or if you have a shortcut to MS-DOS Prompt on your desktop, right-click it and choose Properties.)

3. Check on the settings and verify that they are OK.

How can I pass parameters to my DOS application?

You can do this in three ways. First, you can start the program by typing its name and the parameters in the Start | Run dialog box. Second, if you want to have a permanent set of parameters passed to the application every time you start it, you can enter those parameters in the Cmd Line (command line) in the program's Properties dialog box Program tab. Finally, if you want to manually enter parameters when you run the program, you can add the **?** prompt to the end of the command line in the program's Properties dialog box Program tab, so that you will be asked to enter the parameters when the program starts. To add the prompt, follow these steps:

1. Using Windows Explorer, find your DOS program shortcut and right-click the icon. From the context menu, choose Properties, and then click the Program tab.

2. Add a **?** (question mark) to the end of the Cmd Line (command line), as shown here:

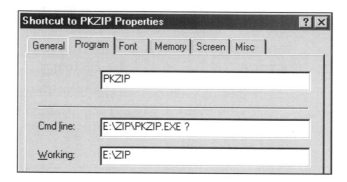

When you run the DOS program, you will be prompted to enter parameters in a little dialog box.

 I was looking through the \Windows\System folder and have come across a program called Mkcompat.exe. Is this how you make old DOS programs compatible with Windows 98? How do I use it?

Mkcompat.exe is used to make older Windows applications work with Windows 98. You use it by double-clicking it, opening the File menu, and specifying a program you want to work on. You then select the functions you want set, save your settings, and exit Mkcompat. Relatively few programs require the use of this program. The vast majority of both DOS and Windows programs work with Windows 98 without any help.

 Will Windows 98 run all my MS-DOS programs?

Windows 98 is designed to run MS-DOS programs. If you have problems with a specific MS-DOS program, try these steps in order (all of the settings are made in the program's Properties dialog box):

- Turn off the screen saver (on the Misc tab), and run Full-Screen (on the Screen tab).

- Prevent the program from detecting Windows (on the Program tab in the Advanced Program Settings section).

- Force the program to run in MS-DOS mode using the current configuration, which gives a program exclusive access to system resources but with the standard setup (on the Program tab in the Advanced Program Settings section).

- Force the program to run in MS-DOS mode using a custom configuration, which gives a program exclusive access to system resources and its own setup (on the Program tab in the Advanced Program Settings section under Configuration Options).

 Tip: *When you run a program in MS-DOS mode, it will shut down Windows 98 and load the program exclusively in an MS-DOS environment. When the program completes, it will automatically reload Windows.*

EFFECTS OF LONG FILENAMES

Why, when I am in a DOS window within Windows 98 or when I boot Windows 98 to a command line, is the ability to create long filenames limited to 127 characters?

The default command-line character limitation is 127 characters. In this default configuration, the DOS environment does not allow more than 127 characters to exist in a given command line. The command-line character limit can be increased to its maximum by placing the following line in the Config.sys file:

```
shell=c:\windows\ command.com /u:255
```

 When at a DOS prompt, I see many of my files have been renamed using a ~ character. Why is this?

While Windows 98 DOS does handle long filenames so that they are not lost or corrupted, it displays the 8.3 filename alias using a ~ (tilde). It takes the first six characters, adds the ~, and starts numbering consecutively, starting with 1. So, for example, if you have "Saturday's paper.doc" and "Saturday afternoon.doc," these will display as "Saturd~1.doc" and "Saturd~2.doc."

Chapter 13

The Registry and the Windows Scripting Host

Answer Topics!

The Registry and the Windows Scripting Host @ a Glance

There has been a lot of discussion of the largely successful attempt by Windows 98 to make personal computing easier to use with a more user-friendly interface. Another, but little discussed, success of Windows 98 was providing a powerful set of capabilities for customizing the way Windows looks and acts. Two sources of advanced customization capabilities are the Windows Scripting Host and the Windows 98 Registry, along with the tools that allow you to change the Registry: the Control Panel, the System Policy Editor, and the Registry Editor (also called Regedit). This chapter will cover advanced customization as follows:

 The Registry and Its Tools looks at questions on how to access the Registry, what the files related to the Registry are and how they are used, how to find settings in the Registry, and how to solve problems related to the Registry.

 Using the Windows Scripting Host covers how to write and run your own scripts to automate a number of tasks within Windows 98.

 Other Customization Areas includes a variety of questions that were not covered elsewhere in the book.

THE REGISTRY AND ITS TOOLS

> ***Warning:*** *The answers to some of the following questions suggest that you make changes to the Registry. Improper changes to your Registry can cause your system to perform erratically. You should therefore make the suggested changes very carefully and only after making a backup copy of your Registry files, System.dat and User.dat. See the question, "What is the easiest way to make a copy of my Windows 98 Registry?"*

How do I access the Registry settings?

You can access the Registry settings in four ways. These, in the order of their ease and safety (with the first being the easiest and the safest), are as follows:

- Using the **Control Panel** items allows you to change many of the settings in the Registry. The dialog boxes associated with the Control Panel give you a lot of information about what you are doing and are generally easy to use. To use the Control Panel, click Start | Settings | Control Panel, and then choose the area you want to access.

- **File type** associations (the associations between document types and the programs that can open them) are a major component in the Registry. To create an association for a file type (generally indicated by the three-letter file extension) that does not have one, simply double-click the file, and the Open With dialog box will appear. Here you can enter a description and identify the program you want used to open the file. If you want to change, delete, or add new file associations, open the View menu in either Windows Explorer or My Computer, choose Folder Options, and then click the File Types tab, which is shown in Figure 13-1.

- The **System Policy Editor**, which is hidden in the \Tools\Reskit\Netadmin\Poledit folder on your

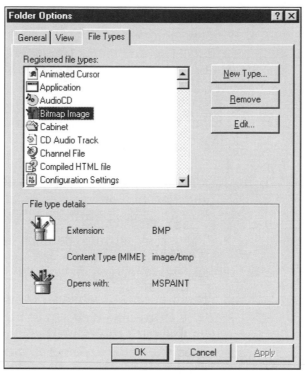

Figure 13-1 Change the Registry's file type associations from the Windows Explorer's View | Folder Options dialog box

Windows 98 CD-ROM, provides access to many areas of the Registry to allow the implementation of policies on the use of computers within an organization. The Policy Editor's settings, of course, can also be used to make desired Registry changes on a single machine. See the example in Chapter 4 ("How do I remove the Network Neighborhood icon on a PC that is not networked?"). To use the Policy Editor with your local Registry, insert your Windows 98 CD and use Windows Explorer to open the \Tools\Reskit\Netadmin\Poledit folder. Then double-click Poledit.exe, open the File menu, and choose Open Registry. See the question "Why am I missing my Network Neighborhood icon from the Windows 98 desktop?" later in this chapter for detailed steps on opening the Policy Editor.

● The **Registry Editor's** Regedit.exe program in your
Windows folder gives direct access to all of the Registry's
settings. The problem is that there is no information
about what your options are or what the effect of a change
will be. You simply select a setting and make a change, as
shown in Figure 13-2, hoping the change will give you the
desired results. You can access and use Regedit with the
following steps:

1. Click the Start button, choose Run, type **regedit**,
   and click OK. (If you will be using it a lot, create a
   shortcut to it on your desktop or under the Programs
   menu.) This will bring up the Registry Editor.

2. To display settings, double-click the folder and its
   subfolders for the key you want to access until you
   see the value you want to change on the right.

3. Right-click the value you want to change to bring up
   the context menu shown in Figure 13-2. Alternatively,
   double-click the value if you just want to modify it.
   This will bring up the Edit String dialog box
   shown here:

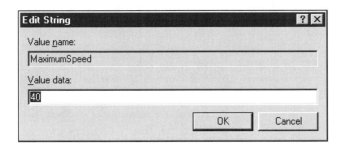

Warning: *Make sure you back up the Registry's User.dat
and System.dat files in your Windows folder* before *making
modifications to the Registry.*

What are the files System.dat, System.1st, and User.dat?

The System.dat file is your system Registry. This file stores
all information about your computer and software. The

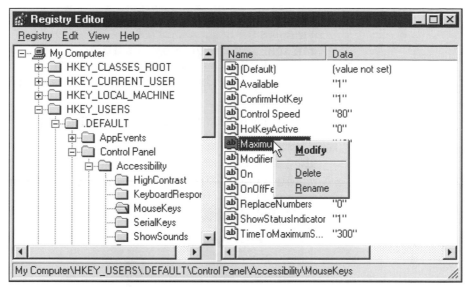

Figure 13-2   Regedit provides direct access to the Registry but little help
in changing it

System.1st file is a copy of System.dat from the first time
your computer booted successfully after the last installation
of Windows 98. Unlike the two primary Registry files
(System.dat and User.dat), which are in your Windows folder,
System.1st is in your root directory.

User.dat contains specific user information. A copy of
User.dat always exists locally. When User.dat is placed in the
user's logon folder on a server, a copy of that file is made on
the user's local computer when the user logs on.

System.dat and User.dat are hidden files and you will not
see them in the Windows folder in a Typical Windows 98
installation. To see these files in Windows Explorer you need
to open the View menu, choose Folder Options, click the View
tab, and click Show All Files followed by OK.

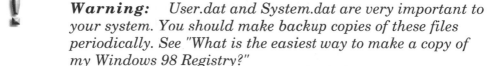

Warning: *User.dat and System.dat are very important to
your system. You should make backup copies of these files
periodically. See "What is the easiest way to make a copy of
my Windows 98 Registry?"*

 ### How can I find a specific setting in the Registry?

You can use Regedit to locate a setting:

1. Click the Start button, choose Run, type **regedit**, and click OK.

2. Open the Edit menu and choose Find.

3. Type a string to look for. For example, if you want to find the settings associated with a modem, open the Edit menu, choose Find, and type **modem**, like this:

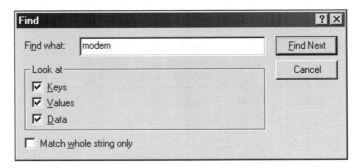

4. Click Find Next. To find another instance of the same string, press F3.

 ### How can I get rid of an application name in Add/Remove Programs that is still there even though I have removed the application?

You can accomplish this by making changes in the Registry. Use the following instructions:

1. Open the Start menu, choose Run, type **regedit**, and press ENTER.

2. Select HKEY_LOCAL_MACHINE and click on the plus sign to expand the tree in this order: \Software\ Microsoft\Windows\CurrentVersion\Uninstall. The Uninstall folder has all the 32-bit programs you've installed.

3. Select the one(s) that you want to remove and press DEL. Confirm that you do want to remove the application(s) from the list.

4. When you are done, close Regedit. If you then look at Add/Remove Programs, the program(s) will be gone from the list.

 What do the different keys in the Registry contain?

The Registry keys are described next:

● **HKEY_CLASSES_ROOT** contains information similar to that in Reg.dat in Windows 3.*x*—information about file associations and OLE parameters. All the file association information is here, as are drag-and-drop rules. Windows 98 has added information on shortcuts and some information on the user interface.

● **HKEY_CURRENT_USER** contains user-specific information that is generated when the user logs on and is based on information for that user in HKEY_USERS.

● **HKEY_LOCAL_MACHINE** contains information about the computer being referenced. It includes the drivers loaded on the system, what kind of devices are installed, and the current configuration of installed applications. This is machine-specific, not user-specific, information.

● **HKEY_USERS** contains information about all users of the PC, plus a description of a default (generic) user. The information stored here concerns applications configuration, desktop settings, and sound schemes, among other things.

● **HKEY_CURRENT_CONFIG** contains information about the current configuration of the workstation. This is used when you create different configurations for the same workstation—for example, laptop versus docked configuration.

● **HKEY_DYN_DATA** contains dynamic status information for system devices used in plug-and-play. The device

information includes its current status and any detected problems.

Is there a way I can make a change to the Registry take effect without rebooting?

Yes, but you need to reload the Registry. You can do this by pressing CTRL-ALT-DEL to bring up the Windows 98 Close Program window. Select Explorer and click on End Task. When Windows asks if you want to shut down, select No. Then you have to wait a couple of seconds, and at the next dialog box click End Task. This will refresh the Registry.

What is the easiest way to make a copy of my Windows 98 Registry?

Your Registry is made up of two files, System.dat and User.dat, in your C:\Windows folder. You can copy them in the same way you would copy any other files. Open Windows Explorer, open the Windows folder, find and select the files, right-click one of them, and choose Copy from the context menu. Then select the disk and folder where you want the copies, right-click any blank area in the right pane of the Windows Explorer, and choose Paste. Copies of the two files will appear in the folder you choose, as shown here:

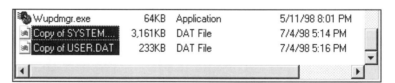

 Note: *Windows 98 automatically makes a backup of your Registry files, System.dat and User.dat, when you start Windows, but unlike Windows 95 the backup is not named System.da0 and User.da0. The backup file is a compressed file named Rbxxx.cab in the \Windows\Sysbackup hidden folder.*

You can manually create one of the Rb*xxx*.cab files by opening the Start menu, choosing Run, typing **scanregw.exe**, and clicking OK. The Registry will be

scanned for errors, you will be told that the Registry was already backed up today (the last time you started Windows), and you will be asked if you want to back it up again. Click Yes.

If you can't find the two Registry files, open the Start menu, choose Find | Files Or Folders, type **system.dat user.dat**, and click on Find Now. The result should look like Figure 13-3. Once you have found the two files, you can copy them as described earlier right from the Find dialog box.

Warning: *The files displayed in the Find dialog box are not copies but the original files. If you move or delete these files, you are moving or deleting the original files.*

Why am I missing my Network Neighborhood icon from the Windows 98 desktop?

The Hide Network Neighborhood option may be enabled in your system policy. You can edit your system policy with the System Policy Editor (Poledit.exe), which is on your Windows 98 CD in the \Tools\Reskit\Netadmin\Poledit folder. Use the

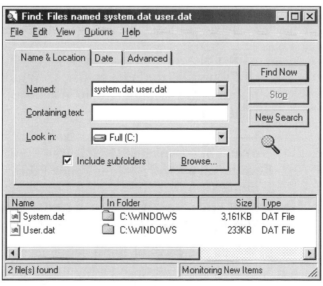

Figure 13-3 Finding the Registry files

following instructions to turn the Network Neighborhood back on:

1. Load your Windows 98 CD. With the Windows Explorer, locate and start the System Policy Editor (\Tools\Reskit\Netadmin\Poledit\Poledit.exe).

2. If you get an error message that says "Unable to open template file..." click OK and click Cancel in the Open Template File dialog box that appears. Open the Options menu, choose Policy Template, click Add, double-click on Windows.adm, and click OK.

3. Open the File menu and select Open Registry. Two icons will appear, Local User and Local Computer, as you can see here:

4. Double-click on Local User to open the Local User Properties dialog box. Click \Windows 98 System\ Shell\Restrictions to open their components, as shown in Figure 13-4.

5. Click the Hide Network Neighborhood check box to clear it, and then click OK to close the Properties dialog box and close the System Policy Editor.

How do I recover if I ever corrupt or have a problem with the Windows 98 Registry?

If you do not have either a set of good System.dat and User.dat files (or System.da0 and User.da0 files that you have created, since Windows no longer does it), you will get a DOS error message that tells you of the problem and recommends that you run Scanreg at the DOS prompt. Also

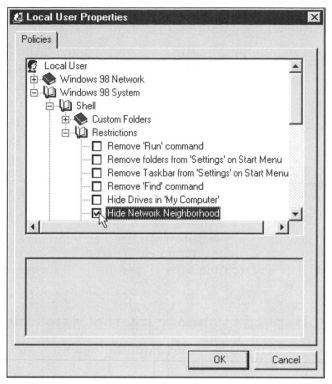

Figure 13-4 Making changes in the system policy

the Command Prompt Only choice is selected. Press ENTER and at the DOS prompt type **scanreg /restore**. Windows will display the Registry backups that are available with their date of backup and whether they have been used to start Windows or not. (If they have been used to start Windows, then they are proven to be good.) These internal Registry backups are named Rb*xxx*.cab and are in the \Windows\ Sysbackup hidden folder (if you have Show All Files turned on in the Folder Options dialog box's View tab you will see it).

When you select one of the backup files and press ENTER, Windows will automatically rebuild your Registry based on the selected backup. After the backup has been restored, you will be asked to restart your computer. Again press ENTER. Your system should be restored to its original state with all settings restored.

If you have a backup copy of the Registry files named System.da0 and User.da0, Windows will start without stopping at the DOS prompt using the .DA0 files. In Windows you will be told there is a Registry problem and it will suggest that you restart your computer to fix the problem. When you click OK, Scanreg will be automatically run with the latest backup (Rb*xxx*cab file) and your Registry and system will be restored as it was in the DOS method.

Windows 98 stores the recent history of Run commands somewhere. Where can I find it?

The recent contents of the Run Open drop-down list are in the Registry under HKEY_CURRENT_USER\Software\ Microsoft\Windows\CurrentVersion\Explorer\RunMRU. The contents are listed under Data opposite the names a, b, c, and so on.

How can I change my registered owner name?

This is maintained in the Registry, and you can change it there, as follows:

1. Open the Start menu, choose Run, type **regedit**, and press ENTER.

2. Select HKEY_LOCAL_MACHINE and click the plus sign to expand the tree in this order: \Software\ Microsoft\Windows\CurrentVersion. Then click the CurrentVersion folder.

3. In the right pane locate the "RegisteredOwner" entry and double-click it.

4. In the Value Data box of the Edit String dialog box, change the name and click OK.

You can repeat the procedure for the "Registered-Organization" entry.

Can I remove the shortcut arrows in shortcut icons on the desktop?

Yes. From the Start menu choose Run, type **regedit**, and press ENTER. When the Registry Editor opens, click on the

Edit menu, choose Find, type **IsShortCut**, and click Find Next. The Registry will be searched and the first instance of IsShortCut will be found, like this:

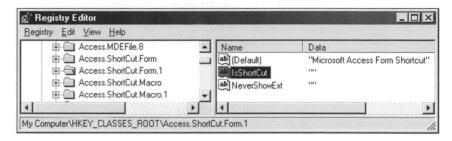

By pressing DEL and answering Yes, you really want to delete the value, you can remove the shortcut designation and arrow from this item. You can continue finding additional instances of IsShortCut by pressing F3. When you have removed all instances of IsShortCut, you'll get a message that you are finished searching the Registry. Close Regedit, select the desktop, and press F5 to refresh it. There will be no more shortcut arrows.

USING THE WINDOWS SCRIPTING HOST

 ### What is the Windows Scripting Host (WSH)?

The Windows Scripting Host (WSH) allows you to automate tasks using scripts written in Visual Basic Scripting Edition (VBScript) or JavaScript (JScript). These scripts are executed on the desktop or from a command prompt and allow you to perform tasks such as logging on to your computer, configuring networking features, launching applications with particular settings, modifying the Registry, and mapping disk drives and printers. WSH provides two programs or "engines" for running scripts. One, Wscript.exe, allows you to simply double-click a script and run it in the Windows environment. The other, Cscript.exe, allows you to run scripts from the command prompt (either a DOS command prompt or from the Run command in Windows).

For example, with a script and WSH you can create a new Word document, ask the user some questions about it, grab required supporting data from other sources, and then

present the user with a document that's almost ready for printing. In other words, you could automate many common office tasks. Consider the simple process of using a form letter. You start the letter using a template; the template might provide boilerplate text, but you still have to customize it. You open a database manager and copy the name and address from it. You then add some information from a spreadsheet, perhaps some accounting information. All three of these tasks can be automated using a script. In fact, writing such a form letter could come down to starting the script, providing the name of the person you want to send the letter to, and typing a little custom text.

How does WSH differ from scripting in Internet Explorer?

The WSH provides a superset of the objects and methods that are available in Internet Explorer. The scripts you have written for Internet Explorer should run directly in WSH. Of course, you'll want to write data to the display instead of a browser screen, so you'll need to make changes to the script to make it work properly, but the business logic of your browser scripts can move directly to the WSH environment.

The easiest way to look at the WSH environment is as a supercharged browser. The addition of objects means that you gain a lot of access to the machine itself, but the basic principles are the same as in a browser. You'll still encounter the same language limitations in WSH that you found in the browser environment. Adding objects won't suddenly allow VBScript to provide additional looping mechanisms or more data types. Likewise, JavaScript won't suddenly develop any more C++-like features simply because you improve its access to the hardware through the use of objects.

How do I Install WSH?

Installing WSH is about as easy as installing any other part of Windows 98. It is not a part of the Typical install, so if you didn't custom install it when you ran Setup, you will need to separately install it now. Do this by opening the Control Panel, choosing Add/Remove Programs, and clicking the Windows Setup tab. Within the Accessories component

you'll find the Windows Scripting Host option, as shown in Figure 13-5. Check this option, and then click OK twice to close the Accessories folder and the Add/Remove Programs control panel. Windows 98 will display several messages as it gets the Windows Scripting Host installed for you.

 ## What are some sample scripts I can use?

 On your hard disk you have a number of sample scripts that you can try out and use as examples while you are writing your own scripts. The sample scripts placed on your hard disk are in the \Windows\Samples\WSH folder, as you can see in Figure 13-6. The yellow icons are scripts written in JavaScript and the blue are written in VBScript, with an almost equal number of each. All of these scripts give you examples you can use to understand how scripts are written in both languages, see the differences between them, and give you a starting place for your scripts.

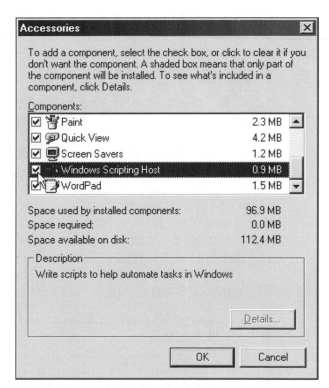

Figure 13-5 Installing the Windows Scripting Host

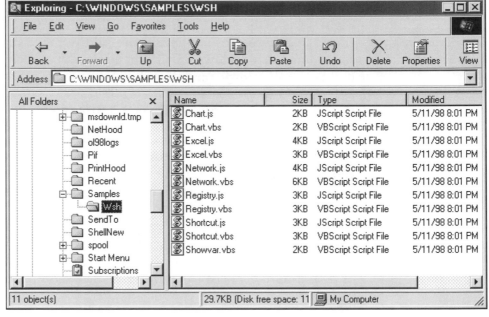

Figure 13-6 Sample scripts included in Windows 98

 Note: *Microsoft gives you the royalty-free right to use, modify, reproduce, and distribute the sample scripts in any way that you choose provided you agree that Microsoft has no warranty, obligations, or liability for the files.*

The function of each of the sample scripts is described in Table 13-1. You can start the scripts by simply clicking them and seeing what they do. They all begin by putting up a message telling you what they will do and allowing you to cancel out. You can also look at the underlying code by right-clicking a script and choosing Edit. Notepad will open and display the code, as shown in Figure 13-7.

If WSH runs .JS and .VBS files, what are .WSH files?

WSH files are like shortcuts for DOS files. They provide settings that are used to run a particular script file and are used to start a script file, although you can also directly start the script file. Using .WSH files, you can start a single script with several different options. WSH files are created

Sample Script	Description
Chart.js or .vbs	Loads Excel, creates a chart, and then rotates the chart
Excel.js or .vbs	Loads Excel and creates a spreadsheet containing the properties of WSH
Network.js or .vbs	Demonstrates how the WSH Network object returns network properties
Registry.js or .vbs	Creates, sets the value of, and deletes Registry keys
Shortcut.js or .vbs	Creates a shortcut to Notepad and places it on the desktop
Showvar.vbs	Lists all of the environment variables on your computer

Table 13-1   Sample Scripts Included with Windows 98

automatically when the properties for a particular script file are set. You can do that by right-clicking a script file in the Windows Explorer, choosing Properties, changing the settings that need changing, and clicking OK. The .WSH file is created in the same directory as the script file with the same name and the .WSH extension. To start the script with

```
// Windows Script Host Sample Script
//
// -----------------------------------------------------------------
//              Copyright (C) 1996-1997 Microsoft Corporation
//
// You have a royalty-free right to use, modify, reproduce and distribute
// the Sample Application Files (and/or any modified version) in any way
// you find useful, provided that you agree that Microsoft has no warranty,
// obligations or liability for any Sample Application Files.
// -----------------------------------------------------------------

// This sample demonstrates how to access Microsoft Excel using the Windows Scripting Host.

var vbOKCancel = 1;
var vbInformation = 64;
var vbCancel = 2;

var L_Welcome_MsgBox_Message_Text    = "This script demonstrates how to access Excel using
var L_Welcome_MsgBox_Title_Text      = "Windows Scripting Host Sample";
Welcome();

///////////////////////////////////////////////////////////////////////////////
//
// Excel Sample
//

var objXL;

objXL = WScript.CreateObject("Excel.Application");
objXL.Workbooks.Add;
objXL.Cells(1,1).Value = 5;
objXL.Cells(1,2).Value = 10;
objXL.Cells(1,3).Value = 15
```

Figure 13-7   Code behind the Chart.js sample script

the .WSH settings, double-click the .WSH file or use it at the command prompt.

What are the differences between Cscript.exe and Wscript.exe?

The major difference between the two scripting applications is that the command-line version (Cscript.exe) operates at the DOS prompt and runs the script in a DOS window, while the Windows version (Wscript.exe) operates within Windows itself. WScript is the default application. Among the reasons for this default is that WScript provides access to the host configuration dialog box that you can use with WSH.

You can use the //C command-line switch to make CScript or //W to make WScript your default application. The choice of the default scripting application is important. Besides starting scripts at the command line or with a shortcut file, you can also double-click them from within Windows Explorer. Double-clicking starts the default scripting application. If you want to change the default scripting engine for an individual script, right-click the script to open the context menu shown next. There is both an Open and an Open With MS-DOS Prompt option in the script file context menu. The Open option starts the script with Wscript.exe and Open With MS-DOS Prompt starts the script using Cscript.exe.

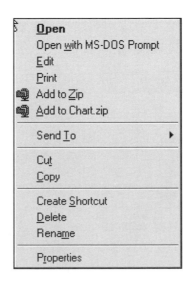

Is there a way I can control how all my scripts are run?

Yes, you can make global setting changes to WSH itself through the dialog box that opens when you double-click Wscript.exe in the Windows folder or type **wscript** in the Run command. For Cscript.exe you can make global changes by adding command-line switches after Cscript.exe. The command-line switches that are documented are explained in Table 13-2.

What is the difference between using VBScript and JavaScript?

The quick answer is that it is a matter of personal taste. Both VBScript and JavaScript provide a strong language base from which to write scripts, so either is a good choice.

JavaScript is most like the programming languages C and C++; however, JavaScript is simple enough for just about anyone to learn, unlike C++. JavaScript is a unique language that you can use in either the browser or WSH environment, and which can handle a wide variety of WSH scripting needs. JavaScript, which was developed by Netscape, provides many C-like features, but has very little in common with the Java language.

VBScript is actually a special version of Visual Basic for Applications (VBA), which in turn is a subset of the full Visual Basic product. In fact, Microsoft's full name for this particular product is Visual Basic Scripting Edition. The following list defines some of the benefits of using VBScript.

- If you already know how to use Visual Basic, then VBScript is simply a few steps away.

- Developers will realize several benefits from using VBScript. If you're a browser developer, Microsoft is licensing the source implementation for VBScript free of charge (at least as of this writing).

- VBScript is designed to work with Java applets and ActiveX objects. You can use this language to interface with ActiveX controls you create.

- VBScript is a true subset of the other languages in the Visual Basic family, therefore any applications you write

Switch	Name	Description
//?	Help	Allows you to display all of the currently documented command line switches.
//B	Batch Mode	Suppresses all non-command line console user interface requests from script. Use this mode when you don't want the user to interact with the script.
//Entrypoint:*SubName*	Call Subroutine	Calls a specific subroutine once core code path is complete. You may include more than one script (subroutine) within a script file. WSH displays the following error message if the subroutine you request doesn't exist: Input Error: There's no subroutine named "*subname*".
//H:Cscript	Command Line	Makes Cscript.exe the default application for running scripts. (WScript is normally the default application.)
//H:Wscript	Windows	Makes Wscript.exe the default application for running scripts.
//I	Interactive	Allows full interaction with the user. Any pop-up dialog boxes will wait for user input before the script continues.
//Logo and //Nologo	Logo	Prevents WSH from displaying the following logo message: Microsoft® Windows Scripting Host Version 5.0 for Windows (build #) Copyright (C) Microsoft Corporation 1996. All rights reserved.
//S	Save Options	Allows you to save current command line options for a user. WSH will save the following options: //B, //I, //Logo, //Nologo, and //T:n.
//T:*nn*	Time Out	Limits the maximum time the script can run to *nn* seconds. Normally there isn't any timeout value. You would use this switch in situations where a script might end up in a continuous loop or unable to get the requested information for other reasons. For example, you might use this switch when requesting information on a network drive.

Table 13-2 WSH Command Line Switches

with it will also run in those environments. Theoretically, this means you could write code for an HTML page and move it to your application programming environment or WSH as well.

 How can I find out more about WSH?

On your Windows 98 CD there is an excellent Help file, Wshadmin.hlp in the \Tools\Reskit\Scripting folder. You can use it directly from the CD by double-clicking it, or you can drag it to your hard disk and use it from there. Also, Microsoft has a Web site set up to help you with WSH at **http://www. microsoft.com/management/scrpthost.htm**. From the Web site you can also download a Microsoft Word version of what you see on the site.

OTHER CUSTOMIZATION AREAS

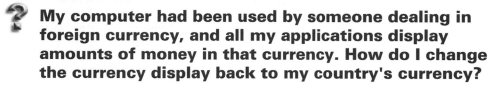 **My computer had been used by someone dealing in foreign currency, and all my applications display amounts of money in that currency. How do I change the currency display back to my country's currency?**

This is controlled in the Regional Settings. Open the Start menu, choose Settings | Control Panel and double-click Regional Settings. In the Regional Settings tab select your country and answer Yes to let the system restart your computer. After restarting, reopen the Regional Settings dialog box and open the Currency tab. Your currency should be displayed. If it isn't, you need to reload Windows 98 from the CD, source files, or floppy disk.

How do I enable daylight saving time so my system automatically adjusts the time twice a year?

This is done in the Date/Time control panel. Either double-click the time on the right of the taskbar or open the Start menu, choose Settings | Control Panel and double-click Date/Time. In the Time Zone tab put a check in Automatically Adjust Clock For Daylight Saving Changes, as you can see in Figure 13-8. Click OK.

I deleted the Briefcase icon from my desktop; how do I get the Briefcase back?

Right-click the desktop, choose New from the context menu, and then click Briefcase.

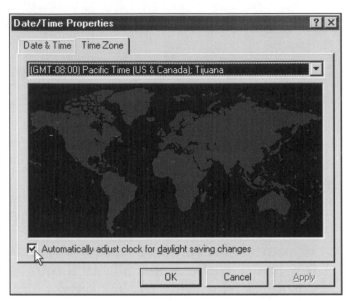

Figure 13-8 You can have Windows automatically adjust for daylight saving time

The active window I am using is outside what the monitor displays, and I can only see the lower half of it. I can see neither the toolbars nor the menus. How can I get the window back in the middle of the screen?

Hold down ALT, press SPACEBAR, and then while continuing to hold down ALT, press the M key. This activates the Move feature. Now use the arrow keys or the mouse to move the window back toward the center of the screen. Once you have the window where you want it, click or press ENTER.

I just got a new computer with Windows 98 already installed. When I'm away from my computer for a period of time and come back to use it, there is an annoying delay. What causes this startup delay and can I change it?

Windows 98 has a power-management feature that in newer computers can tell the disk drive to power down (*spin down*)

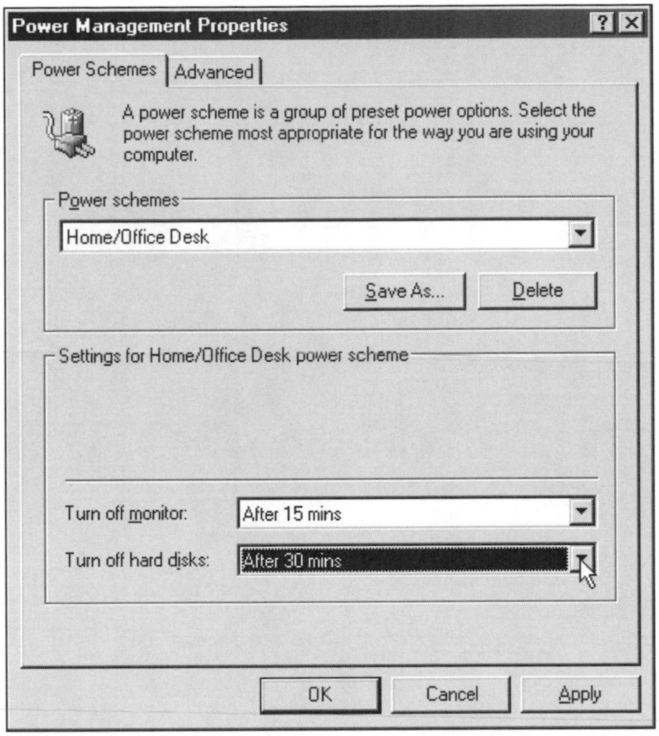

Figure 13-9 You can set how long your system is idle before shutting down your monitor and disks

if it has not been used for a period of time as an energy conservation measure. You can turn this feature on and off, and you can control the length of time the machine must be inactive before the disk is shut down. You can do this through the Power Management control panel (Start menu | Settings | Control Panel | Power Management). In the Power Schemes tab select the scheme that is correct for your computer and your drive will be turned off after the length of idle time set. You can then additionally adjust the Turn Off time, if you wish, from Never to several hours, as shown in Figure 13-9.

Appendix A

Installation Components

The following table shows you which components are installed in the various types of installations for the retail version of the Windows 98 CD.

 Note: *When upgrading a Windows 95 installation, Windows 98 detects your installed component information and upgrades accordingly. You are only given a choice of components to be installed on a clean installation. You can add or remove components after installation from the Add/Remove Programs control panel, Windows Setup tab.*

	Available on			
Component	**Compact**	**Portable**	**Typical**	**Size (MB)**
Accessibility				
Accessibility Options	Yes	Yes	Yes	0.5
Accessibility Tools	No	No	No	2.3
Accessories				
Briefcase	No	Yes	No	Negligible
Calculator	No	Yes	Yes	0.2
Desktop Wallpaper	No	No	No	0.6
Document Templates	No	No	Yes	0.2
Games	No	No	No	0.6
Imaging	No	No	Yes	4.0
Mouse Pointers	No	No	No	Negligible
Paint	No	No	Yes	1.0
Quick View	No	No	No	4.2
Screen Savers	No	No	Yes[1]	1.2[1]
Windows Scripting Host	No	Yes	Yes	0.9
WordPad	No	Yes	Yes	1.9
Communications				
Dial-Up Networking	Yes	Yes	Yes	0.8
Dial-Up Server	No	No	No	0.1
Direct Cable Connection	No	Yes	No	0.4

| | Available on | | | |
Component	Compact	Portable	Typical	Size (MB)
HyperTerminal	No	Yes	No	0.6
Microsoft Chat 2.1	No	No	No	4.5
Microsoft NetMeeting	No	No	Yes	4.2
Phone Dialer	No	Yes	Yes	0.1
Virtual Private Networking	No	Yes	No	0.1
Desktop Themes[2]	No	No	No	0.5-2.3 each
Internet Tools				
Microsoft FrontPage Express	No	Yes	Yes	4.1
Microsoft VRML 2.0 Viewer	No	No	No	3.2
Microsoft Wallet	No	No	No	0.9
Personal Web Server	No	Yes	Yes	0.1
Real Audio Player 4.0	No	No	No	2.3
Web-Based Enterprise Mgmt.	No	No	No	3.2
Web Publishing Wizard	No	No	No	1.0
Microsoft Outlook Express	No	Yes	Yes	3.8
Multilanguage Support[3]	No	No	No	2.9-3.1 each
Multimedia				
Audio Compression[4]	Yes	Yes	Yes	0.2
CD/DVDPlayer[5]	Yes	Yes	Yes	0.2
Macromedia Shockwave Director	No	No	Yes	0.5
Macromedia Shockwave Flash	No	No	Yes	0.2
Media Player	No	Yes	Yes	0.2
Microsoft NetShow Player 2.0	No	No	No	3.9
Multimedia Sound Schemes	No	No	No	5.8
Sample Sounds	No	No	No	0.5
Sound Recorder[4]	Yes	Yes	Yes	0.2
Video Compression	No	Yes	Yes	0.5
Volume Control[4]	No	Yes	Yes	0.2

Component	Available on			Size (MB)
	Compact	Portable	Typical	
Online Services[6]	Yes	Yes	Yes	0.1-0.4
System Tools				
Backup	No	No	No	4.2
Character Map	No	No	No	0.1
Clipboard Viewer	No	No	No	0.1
Disk Compression Tools	Yes	Yes	No	2.0
Drive Converter (FAT32)	No	Yes	Yes	0.4
Group Policies	No	No	No	0.1
Net Watcher	No	No	No	0.2
System Monitor	No	No	No	0.2
System Resource Meter	No	No	No	0.1
WinPopup[7]	Yes	Yes	Yes	0.1
WebTV for Windows				
WaveTop Data Broadcasting	No	No	No	10.3
WebTV for Windows	No	No	No	23.8

[1] Flying Windows and OpenGL are the only screen savers installed. Others are available on the CD.

[2] There are 16 desktop themes available and a supporting applet that is required for some themes.

[3] Language support is provided for Baltic, Central European, Cyrillic, Greek, and Turkish.

[4] Audio Compression, Sound Recorder, and Volume Control are only installed if a sound card is detected.

[5] CDPlayer or DVDPlayer are only installed if a DVD or CD-ROM drive is detected.

[6] You can sign up for Internet access with the following online services: America Online, AT&T WorldNet Service, CompuServe, Prodigy Internet, and The Microsoft Network.

[7] WinPopup is only installed if networking is detected.

Index

Note: *Page numbers in italics refer to illustrations or charts.*

To **speak to the support experts** who handle more than one million technical issues every month, call **Stream's** Microsoft® Windows 98 ® answer line. Trained specialists will answer your Microsoft Windows 98 questions including setup, built-in networking, printing, multi-media, Microsoft Exchange Mail client and Wizards.

Have all your questions been answered?

1-800-298-8215 $34.95 per problem. (Charge to a major credit card.)

1-900-555-2009 $34.95 per problem. (Charge to your phone bill.)

Visit our web site at www.stream.com.